T0302300

Singapore Inc.: A Century of Business Success in Global Markets

This book features 100 local case studies examining the experiences of leading Singaporean companies across different sectors including aviation, logistics, banking, and real estate. They offer valuable insights into how companies adapted to evolving market dynamics, expanded their business portfolios, ventured into global markets, prioritised sustainability, and leveraged innovation and technology to maintain competitiveness.

Through case studies, readers gain practical knowledge that can be applied to their own enterprises, a unique perspective into Singapore's dynamic and competitive business landscape, and the successes and challenges faced by Singaporean companies. The book is divided into different sections exploring specific themes such as business strategy and transformation, diversification and expansion, sustainability, innovation and technology, financial performance, and risk management. It scrutinises how companies responded to shifting market conditions, competition, regulations, customer preferences, and global events. Additionally, it sheds light on the obstacles companies encountered in terms of sustainable practices, financial performance, risk management, talent retention, and technological advancements. By presenting cases across industries and companies in Singapore, Choong et al. highlight their triumphs, setbacks, and valuable lessons learned.

This book can be rendered as a practical and essential resource for business professionals, entrepreneurs, and students interested in understanding effective business strategies.

Leon Choong, Amity's Regional CEO, is a dynamic advocate for educational innovation and access to quality education. Adept at establishing successful institutions, supporting healthcare initiatives, and raising substantial funds for universities, he is dedicated to making a positive impact in the field of education.

Easwaramoorthy Rangaswamy, Principal and Provost at Amity Global Institute, Singapore, is an esteemed management professional. He has taught for University of Northampton, Anglia Ruskin University, University of

London, London School of Economics, and Victoria University. His research focus includes management, skills, and workforce development.

Ian Jamieson, Director of Global Business Development at University of London, spearheaded transformative restructuring and expansion as Group MD at GHC Genetics Group. With a venture capital background, he excels in commercialising university ventures, exploiting IP, and established a lucrative multi-million-pound genetics testing business.

Anne-Marie Kilday, Vice Chancellor of University of Northampton, is a renowned expert in criminal history. She held leadership positions at prestigious universities and publishes extensively on violent behaviour and gendered criminality. Her expertise spans centuries and continents, making her a sought-after doctoral research supervisor.

Singapore Inc.: A Century of Business Success in Global Markets

Strategies, Innovations, and Insights from Singapore's Top Corporations

Edited by Leon Choong,
Easwaramoorthy Rangaswamy,
Ian Jamieson, and Anne-Marie Kilday

Routledge
Taylor & Francis Group

LONDON AND NEW YORK

Designed cover image: © Getty Images

First published 2024
by Routledge
4 Park Square, Milton Park, Abingdon, Oxon OX14 4RN

and by Routledge
605 Third Avenue, New York, NY 10158

Routledge is an imprint of the Taylor & Francis Group, an informa business

British Library Cataloguing-in-Publication Data
A catalogue record for this book is available from the British Library

Library of Congress Cataloging-in-Publication Data
Names: Choong, Leon, editor. | Rangaswamy, Easwaramoorthy, editor. |
Jamieson, Ian, 1944– editor.
Title: Singapore Inc.: a century of business success in global markets :
strategies, innovations, and insights from Singapore's top corporations / edited by
Leon Choong, Easwaramoorthy Rangaswamy, Ian Jamieson and Annie-Marie Kilday.
Description: First Edition. | New York, NY : Routledge, 2024. |
Includes bibliographical references and index.
Identifiers: LCCN 2023036335 (print) | LCCN 2023036336 (ebook) |
ISBN 9781032660554 (hardback) | ISBN 9781032660523 (paperback) |
ISBN 9781032660547 (ebook)
Subjects: LCSH: Corporations–Singapore–History. | Management–Technological
innovations. | Risk management–Singapore. | Diversification in industry–Singapore. |
Sustainable development–Singapore.
Classification: LCC HC445.8 .S5666 2024 (print) | LCC HC445.8 (ebook) |
DDC 338.95957–dc23/eng/20230803
LC record available at https://lccn.loc.gov/2023036335
LC ebook record available at https://lccn.loc.gov/2023036336

ISBN: 9781032660554 (hbk)
ISBN: 9781032660523 (pbk)
ISBN: 9781032660547 (ebk)

DOI: 10.4324/9781032660547

Typeset in Galliard
by Newgen Publishing UK

Contents

Preface

I am delighted to introduce you to *Singapore Inc.: A Century of Business Success in Global Markets*. This compelling book delves into various subjects, including business strategy and transformation, diversification and expansion, sustainability, innovation and technology, financial performance, risk management, as well as Singapore-specific challenges and opportunities. The material explores a wide range of fascinating local case studies to stimulate insightful analyses.

Singapore's remarkable journey as a global business hub over the past half-century has been nothing short of extraordinary. From its humble beginnings as a small trading port to its meteoric rise as a thriving economic powerhouse, Singapore has consistently defied expectations and surpassed all odds. This book aims to unravel the secrets behind this exceptional success story by examining the intricate interplay between business strategies, innovation, and societal impact.

Our team of academics, all of whom have spent years working in Singapore or with Singaporean organisations, has meticulously curated a collection of case studies that illustrate the real-world applications of business concepts, demonstrating their impact on Singapore's businesses and society. Through these case studies, readers will be provided with a comprehensive understanding of the multifaceted factors that have contributed to Singapore's business success.

Each chapter is carefully crafted to provide thought-provoking analyses of the case studies presented, leaving you with a richer understanding of the subject matter. The discussions go beyond surface-level observations, delving into the underlying principles and strategies that have propelled Singapore's businesses to the forefront of global markets.

In a rapidly changing and increasingly interconnected world, the lessons gleaned from Singapore's experiences hold immense value for students, researchers, and practitioners alike. By examining Singapore's triumphs and challenges, this book offers valuable insights and practical knowledge that can be applied in a variety of business contexts, both in Singapore and around the world.

This book will be a valuable resource for readers seeking a deeper understanding of the factors driving business success in global markets. Our hope is that this book will not only inform and educate but also inspire future generations of business leaders and entrepreneurs to strive for excellence and make a positive impact in their own spheres of influence.

We extend our gratitude to the individuals and organisations who generously contributed their time, expertise, and support in the creation of this book. Without their dedication and collaborative spirit, this project would not have been possible.

As you embark on this insightful journey through the pages of *Singapore Inc.: A Century of Business Success in Global Markets*, prepare to be inspired, challenged, and enlightened. We invite you to immerse yourself in the case studies, to explore the intricacies of Singapore's business landscape, and to discover the invaluable lessons that lie within.

Professor Anne-Marie Kilday
Vice Chancellor and Chief Executive
University of Northampton, UK

Acknowledgements

We extend our deepest gratitude to the individuals who have played an integral role in the creation of this scholarly work, titled "Singapore Inc.: A Century of Business Success in Global Markets." This collaborative endeavour has been made possible through the dedication and expertise of a distinguished group of experts committed to unravelling the intricacies of Singapore's economic landscape.

First and foremost, we would like to express our profound appreciation to Dr Ashok K. Chauhan, Founder President of the esteemed Amity Education Group. Dr Chauhan's visionary leadership and extensive global network of academics and practitioners have been instrumental in the realisation of this publication. His commitment to excellence has created an environment where ground-breaking ideas flourish, allowing us to harness the collective expertise of our distinguished team and channel it into this remarkable endeavour. Dr Chauhan astutely recognised the potential of our collective knowledge and expertise in producing a work of unparalleled quality, one that provides invaluable insights into real-world situations, examines complex phenomena, and formulates practical solutions.

We are also deeply grateful to Dr Aseem Chauhan, Chancellor of Amity University, whose dedication, passion for excellence, and ability to champion innovative concepts have galvanised our collective efforts. His unwavering commitment to pushing boundaries and embracing new ideas has transformed this ambitious endeavour into a tangible reality. Dr Chauhan's unwavering support, inspiration, and invaluable guidance have been the driving force behind the realisation of our shared vision. His belief in our collective potential has been transformative, and it is with great pride that we acknowledge his instrumental role in making this undertaking a resounding success.

The present volume represents years of collaborative academic endeavours undertaken by our esteemed team of experts. Each member of our team, hailing from diverse backgrounds as visiting or resident researchers, educators, and consultants, brings with them decades of immersive engagement with Singapore - the vibrant island nation we aim to understand. We have approached our subject matter with both an unbiased outsider's perspective and an affectionate viewpoint of locals, resulting in a unique blend of perspectives that enriches our exploration of Singapore's intricacies and complexities.

Our team comprises academics from influential universities across the globe, including Amity University, Nanyang Technological University, University of London, University of Northampton, Teesside University, University of Westminster, Queen Mary University, Newcastle University, Birkbeck University, London College of Fashion, University of the Arts London, University of East London, Debre Tabor University, Kingdom University Bahrain, and University of Technology and Applied Sciences Salalah. These institutions represent diverse nations such as Singapore, United Kingdom, India, United Arab Emirates, Oman, Ethiopia, and others. This rich tapestry of perspectives ensures a comprehensive exploration of Singapore's remarkable achievements in the realm of business.

It is our sincere hope that "Singapore Inc.: A Century of Business Success in Global Markets" will inspire and enlighten readers, contributing to a profound understanding of Singapore's remarkable achievements in the realm of business.

Introduction to the book

This volume offers a comprehensive guide to understanding and analysing successful business strategies and transformations of companies in Singapore. It presents a collection of 100 distinct case studies that delve into the experiences of top Singapore companies across various industries, including aviation, logistics, banking, and real estate. These case studies shed light on how these Singaporean companies adapted to changing market conditions, diversified their portfolios, expanded globally, focused on sustainability, and utilised innovation and technology to stay competitive.

The book serves as a valuable resource for business professionals, entrepreneurs, students, and anyone interested in gaining insights into successful business strategies and transformations in Singapore. It provides practical knowledge that readers can apply to their own businesses, offering a unique perspective on the Singaporean business landscape. As one of the world's most dynamic and competitive economies, Singapore offers valuable lessons on how companies have succeeded in this challenging environment.

A notable feature of the book is its use of short cases, which provide concise and focused business scenarios. This approach allows readers to quickly grasp key issues and proposed solutions. Each case presents an overview of the situation, the main challenge faced by the organisation, and a summary of the proposed solution or strategy. These short cases are designed for use in educational and professional settings, such as business schools, consulting firms, and corporate training programmes. They enable students and employees to develop their skills in analysing and solving business problems efficiently.

While detailed case studies have their merits, this book purposefully embraces the benefits of shorter, concise case studies. Their enhanced accessibility, time efficiency, focused learning objectives, engaging nature, adaptability, and cost-effectiveness make them valuable resources for both educators and researchers. By embracing this approach, academia can better cater to the needs of a diverse audience while fostering efficient knowledge dissemination and impactful learning experiences. These case studies will not only appeal to students in Singapore but also to a wider regional and global audience interested in understanding and replicating the success stories of Singaporean companies.

The book covers a range of case studies related to business strategy and transformation, diversification and expansion, sustainability, innovation and technology, and financial performance, and risk management. It analyses how companies responded to changing market conditions, competition, regulation, customer preferences, and global events. Furthermore, it highlights the challenges faced by companies in terms of sustainable operations, financial performance, risk management, talent retention, and technological innovation. The book offers a comprehensive and in-depth analysis of various industries and companies in Singapore, showcasing their successes, failures, and lessons learned.

The section on "Business strategy and transformation" examines how companies like Singapore Airlines, ComfortDelGro, Keppel Corporation, Genting Singapore, Singapore Post, and others tackled challenges such as increased competition, declining markets, changing global energy landscapes, and regulatory requirements. It analyses the strategies adopted by these companies to overcome these challenges and emerge as successful businesses.

Similarly, the section "Diversification and expansion" explores case studies of companies like SIA Engineering Company, CapitaLand, Fraser and Neave, Maple Tree, Ascendas-Singbridge, and others. These companies expanded their businesses by diversifying into new markets, partnering with other companies, or adopting innovative technologies.

The section "Sustainability" focuses on case studies of companies like CapitaLand Mall Trust, Sembcorp Industries, City Developments Limited, Ascendas, Wilmar International, and others. These companies prioritise sustainable development and environmental protection while carrying out their business operations.

The section "Innovation and technology" highlights case studies of companies like Grab, ST Engineering, SATS, OCBC Bank, and others. These companies adopted innovative technologies and diversified into new areas like cybersecurity, autonomous vehicles, e-commerce logistics, and digital banking to overcome market challenges and improve their competitiveness.

Lastly, the section "Financial performance and risk management" discusses case studies of companies like United Overseas Bank, Dairy Farm International, Parkway Pantai, Jardine Matheson Holdings, and others. These companies successfully navigated the challenges of the global financial crisis, increased competition, and other market challenges through effective risk management strategies and sound financial practices.

The book also examines industry-specific challenges and opportunities faced by prominent Singaporean companies across different sectors. Case studies include companies such as YCH Group, Far East Hospitality, PSA Corporation, Jurong Shipyard, Razer, Singapore Press Holdings, SMU, and others. Each case focuses on a particular company, analysing their strategies for overcoming challenges and leveraging opportunities.

Overall, this book presents an examination of effective business strategies and transformations in Singapore, offering readers a thorough exploration of the subject. Through a careful analysis of diverse case studies, it imparts valuable insights and practical knowledge that can be applied to enhance one's own business ventures. With its distinctive and captivating content, the book serves as an invaluable resource for professionals, students, and researchers who seek to understand the dynamic business landscape of Singapore. Our earnest aspiration is that "Singapore Inc.: A Century of Business Success in Global Markets" will inspire and enlighten readers, fostering a profound appreciation for Singapore's remarkable accomplishments in the realm of business.

Prof. Leon Choong
Regional CEO (ASEAN)
Amity Global Institute, Singapore

Part I

Business strategy and transformation

1 Singapore Airlines' response to increased competition in the airline industry

David Bell

Pro Vice-Chancellor (International), Amity Global Institute, Singapore

Singapore Airlines (SIA) faced increased competition in the airline industry from low-cost carriers and other full-service airlines. To respond to this challenge, SIA implemented several strategies to improve its competitiveness and customer experience.

One of the strategies was to invest heavily in its fleet to improve its efficiency, reliability, and passenger experience. To achieve that, SIA adopted a differentiation strategy (Islami et al., 2020) where it offers unique products or services that stand out from its competitors. By investing in the fleet, they enhanced their brand image, offered more value to their customers, and created a loyal customer base. SIA introduced new aircraft, such as the Airbus A380 and Boeing 787 Dreamliner, which allowed it to offer more comfortable seating, better in-flight entertainment, and enhanced cabin features (Singapore Airlines, 2022). It also upgraded its existing fleet with the latest technology and features, such as Wi-Fi connectivity and new cabin products. To date, SIA has 146 Airbus and Boeing passenger aircraft including 9 freighters (Singapore Airlines, 2022).

One of the ways that SIA has differentiated itself from its competitors is by adopting a customer-centric strategy (Tuominen et al., 2022), which focuses on understanding and satisfying the needs and preferences of its customers. SIA has invested in various initiatives to enhance its customer experience across different touchpoints, from booking to boarding. For example, SIA introduced new booking systems that allow customers to compare fares, choose seats, and manage their bookings online. It also launched self-service kiosks and mobile apps that enable customers to check in, print boarding passes, and access flight information more easily. Moreover, SIA implemented new check-in procedures that use facial recognition technology, baggage handling systems that use radio frequency identification tags, and boarding processes that use biometric scanners to reduce waiting times and improve efficiency (Roll, 2021). These initiatives demonstrate SIA's commitment to providing personalised services and seamless travel experiences for its customers.

Another way that SIA pursued its competitive advantage was by using market expansion strategy (Robinson & Lundstrom, 2003) by increasing

DOI: 10.4324/9781032660547-2

the number of destinations it served and the frequency of its flights. This strategy allowed SIA to tap into new markets with high growth potential, such as China, India, and Southeast Asia, where it could leverage its reputation for quality and service. At the same time, SIA maintained and enhanced its presence in mature markets such as Europe and North America, where it faced strong competition from other carriers. To further extend its network and offer more options to its customers, SIA also established strategic alliances with other airlines, such as Virgin Australia and Air New Zealand, that shared its vision and values. By expanding its route network, SIA aimed to increase its market share and revenue streams while delivering a superior travel experience to its passengers.

SIA's fourth strategy was to boost its brand and reputation with marketing and public relations (PR) activities. Martin Roll (2021) says SIA has a strong and consistent brand strategy led by top management and the boardroom. The Singapore Girl icon symbolises its Asian values and service quality. SIA has also earned many awards for its excellence and innovation, such as the "World's Best Cabin Crew Service" from the Business Traveller Asia-Pacific Awards for 23 years in a row (Danao, 2018). SIA has also shown its empathy and social responsibility during the pandemic by rewarding front liners, sending cabin crew as care ambassadors, and launching Singapore Airlines Academy (Ragavan, 2021). Additionally, SIA promotes its brand and reputation by investing in marketing and PR activities. It launched new advertising campaigns and sponsored high-profile events such as the Formula 1 Singapore Grand Prix, Singapore Airlines International Cup, and Singapore Biennale. They also participated in industry awards like Skytrax World Airline Awards to promote their brand and reputation as a premium airline (Roll, 2021).

Overall, SIA successfully responded to the increased competition in the airline industry, as shown by its sustained growth and profitability. In the third quarter (October-December) of 2022, it achieved a net profit of $628 million, a significant increase from $85 million in the same period of FY21/22 and $527 million in the previous quarter. It also grew its total revenues by 8% to $4.846 billion (Singapore Airlines, 2022). By investing in its fleet, enhancing its customer experience, expanding its route network, and promoting its brand and reputation, SIA secured its position as one of the world's leading airlines.

References

Danao, M. (2018). *How Singapore Airlines became the best airline brand in Asia* [Online]. Available at: www.referralcandy.com/blog/singapore-airlines-marketing-strategy (Accessed: 1 June 2023).

Islami, X., Mustafa, N., & Topuzovska Latkovikj, M. (2020). Linking Porter's generic strategies to firm performance. *Future Business Journal*, 6(1), 1–12. https://doi.org/10.1186/s43093-020-0009-1

Ragavan, S. (2021). *Singapore's strongest local brands: flying colours for SIA despite travel bans* [Online]. Available at: www.campaignasia.com/article/singapores-strong est-local-brands-flying-colours-for-sia-despite-travel-bans/471966 (Accessed: 1 June 2023).

Robinson, G., & Lundstrom, W.J. (2003). Market expansion strategy: development of a conceptual market expansion decision scorecard. *Strategic Change, 12*(5), 259–272. https://doi.org/10.1002/jsc.642.

Roll, M. (2021). *Singapore Airlines – an excellent, iconic Asian brand* [Online]. Available at: https://martinroll.com/resources/articles/strategy/singapore-airli nes-an-excellent-asian-brand/ (Accessed: 1 June 2023).

Singapore Airlines (2022). *Sustainability at Singapore Airlines* [Online]. Available at: www.singaporeair.com/en_UK/sg/about-us/sustainability/ (Accessed: 1 June 2023).

Tuominen, S., Reijonen, H., Nagy, G., Buratti, A., & Laukkanen, T. (2022). Customer-centric strategy driving innovativeness and business growth in international markets. *International Marketing Review, 40*(3), 479–496 . https://doi.org/10.1108/IMR-09-2020-0215

2 Singapore Post's response to declining mail volumes

Ian Jamieson

Director of Global Business Development, University of London, United Kingdom

Singapore Post (SingPost) faced significant challenges in response to declining mail volumes, as the rise of digital communication and e-commerce led to a decrease in demand for traditional postal services (Risberg, 2023). To address these challenges, SingPost focused on diversifying its business and investing in technology. It expanded its e-commerce logistics network across Asia, Australia, Europe, and the United States, and developed new solutions such as parcel lockers, smart letterboxes, and drones. It also leveraged data analytics and automation to enhance its operational efficiency and customer experience (*The Business Times*, 2016). By transforming its business model and capabilities, SingPost aimed to become a global leader in e-commerce logistics and postal innovation (Joint Media Release, 2022).

They expanded their e-commerce logistics capabilities by building a network of regional warehouses and last-mile delivery services across the Asia Pacific (Alibaba Group, 2014). The company also invested in automated parcel sorting systems and digital solutions, such as mobile apps and online tracking tools, to enhance the customer experience (CIO, 2018). According to SingPost's FY2022/23 results presentation, 86% of its revenue was generated internationally, driven by its expanding e-commerce logistics operations and strategic partnerships. Some of these partnerships include Alibaba Group, which invested S$312.5 million in SingPost in 2014 to collaborate on e-commerce logistics in Asia Pacific (SingPost and Alibaba Group to Form Strategic Collaboration to Grow eCommerce Logistics in Alibaba Group, 2014), and SATS Ltd., which partnered with SingPost in 2015 to offer end-to-end e-commerce solutions for international trade (SATS, 2015). SingPost also developed a fully integrated regional eCommerce Logistics Hub in Singapore, the first of its kind in Southeast Asia, equipped with state-of-the-art technology and automation (SingPost, 2014).

SingPost also pursued strategic partnerships to expand its capabilities and reach. In 2016, the company formed a joint venture with China's Alibaba Group, which acquired a 10.35% stake in SingPost. This partnership allowed SingPost to tap into Alibaba's vast e-commerce network and leverage its expertise in logistics and technology (Alibaba Group, 2014). Additionally,

DOI: 10.4324/9781032660547-3

SingPost focused on sustainability initiatives, such as reducing carbon emissions and adopting eco-friendly packaging materials. The company also implemented social responsibility programmes, such as providing employment opportunities for people with disabilities and supporting community outreach initiatives. According to Alibaba Group (2021) Carbon Neutrality Action Report, Alibaba aims to achieve carbon neutrality throughout the value chain of its cloud computing business by 2030 and to help reduce 1.5 billion tons of carbon emissions across its platforms by 2035. Alibaba also seeks to shoulder the social responsibilities of a platform company, to make society's biggest challenges its biggest challenges, and to promote environmental sustainability and social equality (*South China Morning Post*, 2021). By partnering with Alibaba, SingPost can benefit from its best practices and innovations in these areas.

SingPost has successfully transformed its business and maintained its position as a leading provider of postal and e-commerce logistics services in Asia Pacific through these efforts. Despite the structural decline in letter mail and the COVID-19 pandemic's supply chain disruptions, the company's revenue has continued to grow. Tan et al. (2019) found that SingPost's transformation strategy enhanced its competitiveness and resilience in the dynamic postal industry.

References

Alibaba Group (2014). *SingPost and Alibaba Group to form strategic collaboration to grow ecommerce logistics in Asia Pacific* [Online]. Available at: www.alibabagroup.com/en-US/document-1488670133294465024 (Accessed: 25 April 2023).

Alibaba Group (2021). *Alibaba Group carbon neutrality action report* [Online]. Available at: https://sustainability.alibabagroup.com/en (Accessed: 25 April 2023).

CIO (2018). *SingPost launches new logistics platform to facilitate ecommerce* [Online]. Available at: www.cio.com/article/222494/singpost-launches-new-logistics-platform-to-facilitate-ecommerce.html (Accessed: 25 April 2023).

Joint Media Release (2022). *Singapore introduces a new industry standard for ecommerce and logistics players to boost customer satisfaction and operational efficiencies.* Enterprise Singapore [Online]. Available at: www.enterprisesg.gov.sg/-/media/esg/files/media-centre/media-releases/2022/october/mr06422_singapore-introduces-a-new-industry-standard-for-ecommerce-and-logistics-players-to-boost-customer-satisfaction-and-operational-efficiencies.pdf (Accessed: 25 April 2023).

Risberg, A. (2023). A systematic literature review on e-commerce logistics: towards an e-commerce and omni-channel decision framework. *The International Review of Retail, Distribution and Consumer Research, 33*(1), 67–91. https://doi.org/10.1080/09593969.2022.2089903

SATS (2015). *Media release SATS and SingPost to collaborate in the area of ecommerce* [Online]. Available at: www.sats.com.sg/docs/default-source/media-releases/2015/sats-and-singpost-to-collaborate-in-the-area-of-ecommerce.pdf?sfvrsn=6efe64d3_2 (Accessed: 25 April 2023).

SingPost (2014). *SingPost to develop fully integrated eCommerce Logistics Hub in Singapore, the first such modern facility in the region* [Online]. Available at: https://links.sgx.com/1.0.0/corporate-announcements/6OZMCS6PBRSNJII1/318096_PressRelease.pdf (Accessed: 25 April 2023).

South China Morning Post (2021). *Alibaba plays up social responsibility ahead of Singles' Day amid Beijing's regulatory scrutiny* [Online]. Available at: www.scmp.com/tech/big-tech/article/3153056/alibaba-plays-social-responsibility-ahead-singles-day-amid-beijings (Accessed: 25 April 2023).

Tan, Y., Lim, Y., & Lee, C. (2019). Transformation of postal service: a case study of Singapore Post Limited. *International Journal of Operations and Production Management*. https://doi.org/10.1108/IJOPM-03-2018-0153

The Business Times (2016). *SingPost launches centre of innovation, opens ecommerce logistics hub* [Online]. Available at: www.businesstimes.com.sg/companies-markets/singpost-launches-centre-of-innovation-opens-ecommerce-logistics-hub (Accessed: 25 April 2023).

3   Temasek Holdings' investment strategy

Katalin Illes

Associate Head of College – External Relations at the University of Westminster, United Kingdom

Temasek Holdings is a Singapore-based investment company that manages a portfolio of assets valued at over US$200 billion (Temasek, 2023a). The company has faced various challenges over the years, such as the global financial crisis, the COVID-19 pandemic, and the transition to a low-carbon economy (Temasek, 2023b). To overcome these challenges, its investment strategy has evolved to adapt to the changing environment and to capture new opportunities. Here are some ways Temasek has approached investment to overcome challenges:

Diversification: Temasek's portfolio is diversified across various sectors, geographies, and asset classes. This diversification helps to reduce risk and volatility and to ensure that the portfolio can withstand market fluctuations and economic downturns (Temasek, 2023c). The company invests in a range of sectors, including telecommunications, financial services, healthcare, and technology. As of 31 March 2021, Temasek's portfolio was composed of 24% Singapore assets, 42% China assets, 17% North America assets, 9% Europe assets, and 8% other regions assets.

Active management: Temasek is an active investor, and takes an active role in the companies it invests in. This involves working closely with management teams to help them achieve their strategic goals and improve their operations. The company also has a long-term investment horizon, which allows it to ride out short-term market fluctuations and focus on creating long-term value (Barton et al., 2016). Temasek does not have a fixed holding period for its investments and may exit or increase its stakes depending on the performance and prospects of the company.

Focus on sustainable investments: Temasek has a strong focus on sustainable investments and has made significant investments in areas such as renewable energy, clean technology, and healthcare. The company also has a sustainability framework (Eccles & Klimenko, 2019) that guides its investment decisions and ensures that it invests in companies that have strong environmental, social, and governance (ESG) practices. Temasek has set a target to halve the net carbon emissions of its portfolio over 2010 levels by 2030, and an ambition to achieve net zero carbon emissions by 2050.

DOI: 10.4324/9781032660547-4

Strategic partnerships: Temasek has formed strategic partnerships with other companies and investment firms to expand its capabilities and access new investment opportunities. For example, the company has formed partnerships with private equity firms like BlackRock and KKR and has also invested in joint ventures with companies like Alibaba and Bayer. These partnerships allow Temasek to leverage the expertise and networks of its partners, and to co-invest in projects that align with its strategic objectives.

Long-term view: Temasek has a long-term investment view, and typically holds its investments for many years. This allows the company to focus on creating long-term value (Siggelkow & Wibbens, 2020) and to take advantage of opportunities that may take years to develop. Temasek also aligns its portfolio with four structural trends that shape its long-term portfolio construction: digitisation, sustainable living, future of consumption, and longer lifespans. These trends are interconnected, transcend sectors and countries, and continue through economic cycles. Temasek expects to increasingly invest in companies that directly enable and drive these trends, as well as those that harness the potential of the trends for growth.

Temasek's investment strategy has five key elements: diversification, active management, sustainability, partnerships, and long-term view. These elements help the company create value over time. The company has delivered a 14% annualised shareholder return since 1974 and has grown its net portfolio value from S$90 billion in 2004 to S$403 billion in 2022.

References

Barton, D., Bailey, J., & Zoffer, J. (2016). *Rising to the challenge of short-termism*. FCLT Global [Online]. Available at: www.fcltglobal.org/docs/default-source/publications/rising-to-the-challenge-of-short-termism.pdf (Accessed: 29 April 2023).

Eccles, R.G., & Klimenko, S. (2019). The investor revolution. *Harvard Business Review, 97*(3), 106–116.

Siggelkow, N., & Wibbens, P. (2020). LIVA: a measure of long-term investor value appropriation. *Strategic Management Journal, 41*(11), 1979–2006.

Temasek (2023a). *Our investments: investing with tomorrow in mind* [Online]. Available at: www.temasek.com.sg/en/our-investments (Accessed: 29 April 2023).

Temasek (2023b). *How we invest: driven by our views of the trends shaping societies, we invest today with tomorrow in mind* [Online]. Available at: www.temasek.com.sg/en/our-investments/how-we-invest (Accessed: 29 April 2023).

Temasek (2023c). *Our portfolio* [Online]. Available at: www.temasek.com.sg/en/our-investments/our-portfolio (Accessed: 29 April 2023).

4 SGX-listed companies navigate corporate governance and regulatory challenges

Manju Shree Raman

Professor, Debre Tabor University, Ethiopia

Navigating corporate governance and regulatory requirements is a key challenge for companies listed on the Singapore Exchange (SGX). SGX has strict standards and rules to ensure transparency, accountability, and investor protection. These rules cover various aspects of financial reporting, disclosure, and corporate governance. For instance, SGX requires companies to have a majority of independent directors on their boards to enhance oversight and impartiality (Pang, 2022). To comply with these rules, companies need to have strong corporate governance systems, such as internal controls, audit committees, and risk management policies (Nakpodia et al., 2021).

One of the main challenges that SGX-listed companies face is the dynamic nature of the regulatory environment. The rules and standards that govern their operations are not fixed but constantly evolving to reflect changing market conditions, stakeholder expectations, and best practices. Companies have to keep up with new regulations, guidelines, and reporting requirements from SGX and other regulators such as the Monetary Authority of Singapore (MAS) and the Accounting and Corporate Regulatory Authority (ACRA). This demands a proactive approach to compliance, such as investing in resources and systems to monitor regulatory changes and engage with regulators proactively (Arjoon, 2006). By doing so, companies can anticipate and address potential regulatory issues, reduce compliance costs and risks, and enhance their reputation and trust among regulators and stakeholders.

Another significant challenge that SGX-listed companies face is balancing the interests of different stakeholders, including shareholders, employees, customers, and the community. Companies have a fiduciary duty to act in the best interests of their shareholders, who provide them with capital and expect returns on their investments. However, companies also have to consider the impact of their actions on other stakeholders, who may have different or even opposing expectations and demands. For example, employees may want higher wages and better working conditions, customers may want lower prices and higher quality, and the community may want more social and environmental responsibility. This can be especially challenging in industries where there are competing priorities or interests, such as the energy or financial

DOI: 10.4324/9781032660547-5

services sectors. In these sectors, companies have to balance the trade-offs between profitability and sustainability, risk and innovation, and growth and stability (Black et al., 2007).

Despite these challenges, many SGX-listed companies have managed to navigate the regulatory environment, while staying competitive and profitable. For example, companies such as DBS Bank, Keppel Corporation, and CapitaLand have built strong corporate governance structures and practices that have been praised by industry experts and stakeholders (Chen, 2022). They have also invested in technology and systems to simplify their regulatory reporting and compliance processes, enabling them to adapt quickly to regulatory changes (Filatotchev et al., 2013). Moreover, these companies have diversified their businesses across different markets and sectors, reducing their exposure to regulatory risks and uncertainties in any single jurisdiction. They have also leveraged their strong brand reputation and customer loyalty to maintain their competitive edge and market share in the face of increasing competition from both local and foreign players. These strategies have helped them to achieve sustainable growth and profitability in the long run.

In summary, SGX-listed companies face significant challenges in navigating corporate governance and regulatory requirements. To succeed in this environment, companies need to build strong corporate governance structures and practices, monitor regulatory developments proactively, and balance the interests of different stakeholders. However, those companies that can overcome these challenges can create long-term value for their stakeholders and become industry leaders.

References

Arjoon, S. (2006). Striking a balance between rules and principles-based approaches for effective governance: a risks-based approach. *Journal of Business Ethics, 68*(1), 53–82.

Black, B.S., Jang, H., & Kim, W. (2007). Does corporate governance affect firm value? Evidence from Korea. *Journal of Law, Economics, and Organization, 22*(2), 366–413.

Chen, C. (2022). Corporate governance standards for insurers in Singapore. In: Marano, P., Noussia, K. (eds) *The Governance of Insurance Undertakings*. *AIDA Europe Research Series on Insurance Law and Regulation*, 6. Springer. https://doi.org/10.1007/978-3-030-85817-9_6

Filatotchev, I., Jackson, G., & Gospel, H. (2013). Corporate governance in emerging economies: a review of the principal–principal perspective. *Journal of Management Studies, 50*(1), 196–220.

Nakpodia, F., Adegbite, E., & Ashiru, F. (2021). Corporate governance regulation: a practice theory perspective. *Accounting Forum.* https://doi.org/10.1080/01559982.2021.1995934

Pang, S.Y. (2022). *Corporate governance and board remuneration disclosures in Singapore: Corporate responses to evolving regulations and ownership structures* [Bachelor's thesis]. National University of Singapore.

5 Quest Global attracting and retaining top engineering and technical talent in a competitive market

Lim Keai

Academic Director (Senior), Amity Global Institute, Singapore

Quest Global is a global engineering services and solutions provider that faced challenges in attracting and retaining top engineering and technical talent in a competitive market (Adeosun & Ohiani, 2020). To succeed, Quest Global had to overcome several challenges and differentiate itself as an employer of choice for engineering and technical talent.

One of the ways Quest Global succeeded in attracting and retaining top engineering and technical talent was by investing in employee development and training programmes. The company provided employees with access to a wide range of training and development opportunities, including leadership programmes, technical training, and professional development programmes. These programmes helped employees to enhance their skills, knowledge, and competencies, as well as prepare them for future roles and challenges. By investing in employee development (Johnson & Smith, 2021), Quest Global was able to attract top talent who valued learning and growth opportunities and retain employees by providing a clear path for career growth and advancement. Quest Global also recognised and rewarded its employees for their achievements and contributions, which increased their motivation and loyalty.

Another way Quest Global succeeded was by fostering a culture of innovation and collaboration (Bendak et al., 2020). The company fostered a culture of creativity and experimentation among its employees and urged them to exchange their ideas and feedback with their colleagues. The company also enabled cross-functional and cross-regional collaboration and supported it with platforms and tools for communication and knowledge sharing. The company also appreciated and rewarded its employees for their innovation and teamwork. By doing so, Quest Global was able to deliver more value and quality to its customers and gain a competitive edge in the market.

In addition, Quest Global also offered various employee benefits and perks to lure and keep top talent (Smith & Johnson, 2022). The company offered attractive salaries, flexible work options, and health and wellness programmes to enhance employee well-being. The company also gave other benefits and perks, such as bonuses, stock options, insurance, retirement plans, and education assistance, to acknowledge employee performance and loyalty. The

DOI: 10.4324/9781032660547-6

company also arranged social events, team-building activities, and recognition programmes, to boost employee engagement and morale. By offering these benefits and perks, Quest Global was able to establish a positive work environment and attract top talent.

Moreover, Quest Global also focused on building a strong employer brand through strategic partnerships and marketing initiatives. The company partnered with leading universities and academic institutions to identify and recruit top talent. For example, the company collaborated with the National University of Singapore (NUS) to offer internships, scholarships, and mentorship programmes to engineering students (Quest Global, n.d.). Additionally, Quest Global leveraged social media and online marketing to promote its brand as an employer of choice. The company used platforms such as LinkedIn, Facebook, Twitter, and YouTube to showcase its culture, values, projects, and achievements, and to engage with potential and existing employees (Quest Global, n.d.). By building a strong employer brand, Quest Global was able to attract and retain top talent in the competitive engineering market.

In addition, Quest Global also focused on building a diverse and inclusive workplace to lure and keep top talent (Ferdman et al., 2018). The company adopted policies and practices that fostered diversity and inclusivity, such as unconscious bias training and diversity recruitment programmes. The company also valued and respected the diversity of its employees, such as gender, race, ethnicity, religion, age, disability, and sexual orientation. The company also urged its employees to exchange their views and experiences and to work with people from different backgrounds and cultures. By building a diverse and inclusive workplace, Quest Global was able to boost its creativity, innovation, and problem-solving skills, as well as its customer satisfaction and loyalty.

Quest Global achieved success in attracting and retaining top engineering and technical talent by implementing various strategies to enhance its employee value proposition and engagement. The company invested in employee development and training programmes to help its employees grow and advance their careers. It also fostered a culture of innovation and collaboration to encourage its employees to share ideas and solve problems. Moreover, it offered competitive employee benefits and perks to reward and motivate its employees. Furthermore, it built a strong employer brand to showcase its achievements and values. Lastly, it created a diverse and inclusive workplace to respect and leverage its employees' differences and strengths. These strategies helped Quest Global differentiate itself as an employer of choice and build a strong talent pipeline to support its growth and expansion.

References

Adeosun, O.T., & Ohiani, A.S. (2020). Attracting and recruiting quality talent: firm perspectives. *Rajagiri Management Journal*, 14(2), 107–120. https://doi.org/10.1108/RAMJ-05-2020-0016

Bendak, S., Shikhli, A.M., Abdel-Razek, R.H., & Ardito, L. (2020). How changing organizational culture can enhance innovation: development of the innovative culture enhancement framework. *Cogent Business and Management, 7,* 1–17. https://doi.org/10.1080/23311975.2020.1712125

Ferdman, B.M., Avigdor, N., & Simons, G. (2018). Building inclusive organizations: a lens for engaging across differences. *Journal of Management, 44*(3), 1056–1081. https://journals.sagepub.com/doi/10.1177/0149206317751629

Johnson, M., & Smith, K. (2021). The strategic importance of employee development: enhancing organizational performance and employee engagement. *Journal of Human Resource Management, 25*(3), 123–145. https://doi.org/10.1080/09585192.2013.798921.

Quest Global (n.d.). *Quest Global* [Online]. Available at: www.quest-global.com/ (Accessed: 20 May 2023).

Smith, E., & Johnson, M. (2022). Attracting and retaining top talent: the role of employee benefits and perks. *Journal of Strategic Human Resource Management, 15*(2), 89–110. https://doi.org/10.18374/JSHRM-15-2.61

6 How Keppel Corporation adapted to the changing global energy landscape

Gemini V. Joy

Associate Professor, VIT Business School, VIT University, India

Factors such as climate change, technological innovation, geopolitical shifts, and consumer preferences are driving rapid and profound changes in the global energy landscape. These changes create significant challenges and opportunities for energy companies, which need to adapt and transform their business models, operations, and capabilities. Keppel Corporation (2023), a leading conglomerate in Singapore, has responded to the changing energy landscape by adopting various strategies to mitigate risks, reduce carbon emissions, and explore new opportunities. This case will analyse how Keppel Corporation has coped with the challenges of the changing global energy landscape and what insights can be derived from its experience.

Risk mitigation: Keppel has diversified its business portfolio and invested in renewable energy to cope with the low-carbon economy. This helps Keppel to avoid losses in fossil fuels and seize opportunities in renewables. Keppel has also expanded its business segments to include urban development, infrastructure, asset management, and connectivity. These segments provide stable income and access to emerging markets (ADB, 2022). Moreover, Keppel has increased its renewable energy projects, which lower its carbon footprint, improve its environmental, social, and governance performance, and meet the demand for clean energy.

Carbon reduction: Keppel has set goals to lower its carbon emissions and enhance its energy efficiency across its operations. The company has carried out various initiatives such as energy audits, the use of renewable energy sources, and the adoption of energy-efficient technologies to achieve these goals (IEA, 2021). For instance, Keppel has performed energy audits at its key facilities to find and implement energy-saving measures. Keppel has also installed solar panels at some of its premises to produce clean electricity and reduce its dependence on grid power (Environmental Resources Management, 2020). Moreover, Keppel has adopted energy-efficient technologies such as LED lighting, smart sensors, and variable speed drives to minimise its energy consumption and shrink its carbon footprint.

Circular economy: Keppel has adopted the circular economy concept by taking steps to reduce waste and use resources efficiently (Nikolaou et al., 2021).

DOI: 10.4324/9781032660547-7

This involves using recycled materials, applying circular design principles, and creating closed-loop systems. For instance, Keppel has used recycled concrete and steel in some construction projects, saving virgin materials and cutting waste. Keppel has also applied circular design principles such as modularity, durability, and adaptability in some products and services, improving their functionality and lifespan. Moreover, Keppel has created closed-loop systems such as water reclamation and waste-to-energy plants, which recover resources from waste and lower environmental impact (Ekins et al., 2019).

Research and development (R&D): Keppel has explored new opportunities and technologies with R&D. It has developed new products and services with universities and research institutions, such as digitalisation solutions and renewable energy technologies. For instance, it has established the Keppel-NUS Corporate Laboratory, the Model Factory @ ARTC, and the NTU-Keppel Renewable Energy Research Centre.

Strategic partnerships: Keppel has established strategic partnerships with leading companies and organisations in the energy sector to leverage expertise and explore new opportunities. For example, the company has partnered with offshore wind companies to explore opportunities in the emerging offshore wind sector. Some of these partnerships include

- Keppel O&M and Aibel AS: design and construct converter stations for offshore wind farms in Europe
- Keppel O&M and TenneT Offshore GmbH: supply high voltage direct current (HVDC) transformer stations for offshore wind farms in Germany
- Keppel O&M and Ørsted A/S: collaborate on potential projects in the Asia-Pacific region
- Keppel Renewable Energy and Mainstream Renewable Power: co-develop a portfolio of offshore wind projects in Vietnam

Overall, Keppel Corporation has demonstrated a commitment to sustainability and innovation in response to the challenges of the changing global energy landscape. By implementing various strategies to mitigate risks, reduce carbon emissions, and explore new opportunities, the company is well-positioned to continue to thrive in a rapidly changing environment.

References

ADB (2022). *Urban development in Asia and the Pacific*. Asian Development Bank [Online]. Available at: https://adb.org/what-we-do/topics/urban-development (Accessed: 2 May 2023).

Ekins, P., Hughes, N., & Pye, S. (2019). The circular economy: what, why, how and where. *OECD Regional Development Working Papers, 2019/05*. https://doi.org/10.1787/2bdfecca-en

Environmental Resources Management (2020). *Keppel O&M's circular economy initiative – converting an LNG tanker into a floating liquefaction vessel* [Online]. Available at: www.kepcorp.com/en/file/media/media-releases-sgx/2020/08-aug/20-aug-kom-mr-annnex-a/annex-a-summary-of-flng-study.pdf (Accessed: 8 May 2023).

IEA (2021). *Net zero by 2050: a roadmap for the global energy sector.* International Energy Agency [Online]. Available at: www.iea.org/reports/net-zero-by-2050 (Accessed: 2 May 2023).

Keppel Corporation (2023). *Our approach* [Online]. Available at: www.kepcorp.com/en/sustainability/our-approach/ (Accessed: 2 May 2023).

Nikolaou, I.E., Jones, N., & Stefanakis, A. (2021). Circular economy and sustainability: the past, the present and the future directions. *Circular Economy and Sustainability, 1*(1), 1–20. https://doi.org/10.1007/s43615-021-00030-3

7 TANGS catering to changing consumer preferences

Jonny Munby

Principal Lecturer (International), Teesside University, United Kingdom

TANGS is a leading retailer in Singapore that faced significant challenges in catering to changing consumer preferences. To succeed, TANGS had to overcome several challenges and develop strategies to adapt to changing consumer preferences and stay relevant in the market.

One of the ways TANGS succeeded was by enhancing its product offerings to cater to changing consumer preferences (Lobaugh et al., 2019). The company expanded its product range to include more lifestyle and experiential products, such as health and wellness, travel, and entertainment. TANGS also introduced exclusive product lines and collaborations with popular brands to differentiate itself from competitors and offer unique products to customers. For example, TANGS has launched the TANGS Beauty Box, which features curated beauty products at attractive prices. TANGS has also partnered with White Trousseau, a local bridal boutique, to create a TANGS Exclusive Set that includes a wedding gown, veil, bouquet, and accessories. By enhancing and expanding its product offerings, TANGS has shown its ability to keep abreast of new trends and cater to evolving consumer needs.

TANGS achieved success through its enhanced omnichannel retail capabilities. Omnichannel retailing, a strategy aimed at providing customers with a seamless brand experience across various channels, such as online, bricks and mortar, mobile, and social media (Briedis et al., 2021), played a crucial role in this achievement. The company dedicated resources to technological advancements, enabling a personalised and uninterrupted shopping experience across multiple channels. TANGS also introduced a loyalty programme to incentivise and retain customers while harnessing the power of data analytics to gain valuable insights into customer behaviour and preferences. These strategic measures propelled TANGS to establish a competitive edge, resulting in heightened customer satisfaction and loyalty.

Improving the in-store experience was another focus area for TANGS to attract and retain customers. The company gave its stores a makeover to make them more modern and inviting and added new services such as personal styling, product customisation, and beauty consultations. These services offered more value and convenience to customers and helped TANGS stand

DOI: 10.4324/9781032660547-8

out from other retailers. TANGS also engaged with customers and built brand loyalty through events and activities. It held fashion shows, workshops, pop-up stores, and exclusive promotions to feature its products and partners. These events created a community and excitement among customers, and generated word-of-mouth and social media buzz.

In addition to promoting local talent, TANGS responded to the increasing demand for sustainable and environmentally friendly options. The company has partnered with suppliers who share its vision of sustainability and selected products that meet eco-friendly standards. One example is River Home, a sustainable bedding brand that uses organic cotton and natural dyes (TANGS Singapore, n.d.). These products show TANGS's commitment to addressing customers' environmental concerns and offering responsible choices to those who want sustainable alternatives. Sustainable products can benefit the environment by reducing water wastage, carbon footprint, and methane gas production from landfills (Jones, 2022). They can also benefit society by supporting fair trade, ethical labour practices, and charitable causes (The World Pursuit, n.d.).

Finally, TANGS also focused on building a strong brand reputation to differentiate itself from competitors (Khan, 2020). The company leveraged its rich heritage and legacy to create a unique brand identity and story. TANGS also engaged with customers and the community through philanthropic initiatives and social media campaigns to build brand awareness and loyalty. Some prominent activities include

- Shop for Good: donating part of sales to charity causes; donating to Community Chest having four social cause ambassadors
- Breast Cancer Foundation (BCF): Raising funds through various activities; launching tote bags with local artists; supporting BCF since 2006
- Social media: Sharing products, promotions, events, and content; using interactive features; partnering with influencers and celebrities

In summary, TANGS succeeded in catering to changing consumer preferences by enhancing its product offerings, improving its omnichannel retail capabilities, improving its in-store experience, working closely with vendors and suppliers, and building a strong brand reputation. These strategies helped TANGS adapt to changing consumer preferences and stay relevant in the market while maintaining its position as a leading retailer in Singapore.

References

Briedis, H., Gregg, B., Heidenreich, K., & Liu, W.W. (2021). *Omnichannel: the path to value.* Mckinsey & Company [Online]. Available at: www.mckinsey.com/capabilit ies/growth-marketing-and-sales/our-insights/the-survival-guide-to-omnichannel-and-the-path-to-value (Accessed: 23 May 2023).

Jones, H. (2022). *33 Best sustainable products for simple, eco-friendly switches.* Country Living [Online]. Available at: www.countryliving.com/shopping/g39375176/best-sustainable-products/ (Accessed: 23 May 2023).

Khan, M.A. (2020). How does corporate social responsibility transform brand reputation into brand equity? An empirical study of the banking sector in Pakistan. *Global Business Review*, 21(6), 1479–1497.

Lobaugh, K., Simpson, B., & Schmid, J. (2019). *The consumer is changing, but perhaps not how you think.* Deloitte Insights [Online]. Available at: www2.deloitte.com/us/en/insights/industry/retail-distribution/the-consumer-is-changing.html (Accessed: 23 May 2023).

TANGS Singapore (n.d.). *River Home: sustainable bedding exclusively at TANGS* [Online]. Available at: https://tangs.com/tangs-editor/home/river-home-sustainable-bedding-exclusively-at-tangs (Accessed: 23 May 2023).

The World Pursuit (n.d.). *38 Eco-friendly products that are sustainable & GREEN!* [Online]. Available at: https://theworldpursuit.com/list-of-eco-friendly-products/ (Accessed: 23 May 2023).

8 Osim International evolving customer preferences

Dimitrios N. Koufopoulos
Director of the Online Global MBA Programs, Visiting Professor Queen Mary University, Honorary Research Fellow at Birkbeck University, United Kingdom

Osim International is a company that specialises in the design, manufacture, and retail of massage chairs and other health and wellness products. The company operates in more than 20 countries across Asia, Oceania, Africa, and the Middle East. The company faced challenges in evolving customer preferences and shifting market trends, but it has succeeded in adapting to these changes through various strategies that are briefly discussed.

Changing customer preferences: Osim has adapted its product offerings to meet evolving customer needs. This requires constant research and development to create innovative products that appeal to customers. Osim has also conducted market research and customer feedback surveys to understand customer preferences and satisfaction levels. Osim has used this information to improve its existing products and develop new ones that meet customer demands (Lobaugh et al., 2019).

Competition: The health and wellness market is highly competitive, with many established players competing for market share. Osim has had to differentiate itself from competitors and offers unique value propositions to customers. For example, the company has focused on creating high-quality products that provide health and wellness benefits to customers. It has also had to cope with the threat of new entrants and substitutes that could erode its market position. Osim has done this by investing in innovation and branding to create customer loyalty and awareness (Porter, 2008).

Economic downturns: Economic downturns can impact consumer spending on luxury items like massage chairs. Osim has had to adjust its pricing strategies and marketing campaigns to address these challenges. It has offered discounts, promotions, trade-in specials, and extended warranty plans to attract and retain customers who are looking for value and quality. The company has also had to manage its costs and cash flows to ensure its financial sustainability in the face of reduced revenues and increased competition (Kotler & Keller, 2016). Osim has optimised its operations, supply chain, and distribution channels to reduce expenses and improve efficiency. It has also invested in research and development to innovate its products and services, as well as in customer service and loyalty programmes to enhance customer satisfaction and retention.

DOI: 10.4324/9781032660547-9

The company has responded to these challenges as follows:

Diversified product offerings: Osim has diversified its product offerings beyond just massage chairs to include other health and wellness products, such as air purifiers, humidifiers, fitness devices, beauty devices, and gaming chairs (OSIM Singapore, 2022). This has helped the company to appeal to a wider customer base and reduce its reliance on a single product category. It has also collaborated with global partners to create massage chairs and sofas with attractive designs and features. These strategies have helped Osim to enhance its brand image and customer loyalty, as well as to expand its market share and reach in the competitive wellness industry even during recessions.

Innovative product designs: Osim has invested heavily in research and development to create innovative product designs that meet the changing needs and preferences of customers. For example, the company introduced a massage chair that can be controlled through a smartphone app, which appeals to tech-savvy consumers. This demonstrates Osim's originality and ingenuity in providing comprehensive wellness solutions to its customers. The company has also won several awards for its product designs, among many is the Red Dot Design Award for its uPamper 2 handheld massager (Red Dot Design Award, 2016), and Silver Award for Best eCommerce Campaign – Cross Border/ MultiMarket at the Asia eCommerce Awards 2020 (SmartOSC, 2020).

Strong branding and marketing: Osim has built a strong brand image through its marketing campaigns, which emphasise the health and wellness benefits of its products. The company has also focused on creating a unique in-store experience that appeals to customers and sets them apart from competitors. It has also engaged celebrities as brand ambassadors to enhance its brand awareness and credibility (Keller et al., 2012). Osim has devoted resources to research and development to enhance and upgrade its product quality and features, which boosts its brand image and customer loyalty (Osim, 2022).

Overall, Osim has successfully adapted to changing customer preferences and shifting market trends through diversified product offerings, innovative product designs, and strong branding and marketing. These strategies have helped the company to differentiate itself from competitors, appeal to a wider customer base, and position itself for long-term growth in a highly competitive industry.

References

Keller, K.L., Parameswaran, M.G., & Jacob, I. (2012). *Strategic Brand Management: Building, Measuring, and Managing Brand Equity.* Pearson Education India.

Kotler, P., & Keller, K.L. (2016). *Marketing Management* (15th ed.). Pearson Education Limited.

Lobaugh, K., Stephens, B., & Simpson, D. (2019). *The New Digital Divide: The Future of Digital Influence in Retail.* Deloitte Insights.

OSIM Singapore (2022). *Shop online for healthy living products* [Online]. Available at: https://sg.osim.com/ (Accessed: 19 May 2023).

Porter, M.E. (2008). The five competitive forces that shape strategy. *Harvard Business Review, 86*(1), 25–40.

Red Dot Design Award (2016). *Honourable mention – OSIM International – uPamper 2* [Online]. Available at: www.red-dot.org/project/upamper-2-11419/ (Accessed: 19 May 2023).

SmartOSC (2020). *SmartOSC and OSIM Take Home Silver Award for best ecommerce campaign* [Online]. Available at: www.smartosc.com/smartosc-and-osim-take-home-silver-award-for-best-ecommerce-campaign/ (Accessed: 20 May 2023).

9 How Mapletree Investments diversified its portfolio and expanded globally

Krishnamoorthy Renganathan
Director, Wise Consulting, Singapore

Mapletree Investments is a real estate development, investment, and management company headquartered in Singapore. Founded in 2000, the company has diversified its portfolio across various asset classes, including office, retail, industrial, logistics, residential, and data centres. Mapletree has also expanded globally, with assets in the United States, Europe, Australia, and Asia. According to its website, Mapletree's vision is to be a leading real estate company with a global footprint and a focus on sustainability. The company's mission is to create value for its stakeholders through its business model that maximises capital efficiency. As of March 2023, Mapletree owns and manages S$78.7 billion of office, retail, logistics, industrial, data centre, residential, and lodging properties across 13 markets (Mapletree Investments, 2023).

One of the biggest challenges faced by Mapletree was the regulatory hurdles that come with expanding globally. Each country has its laws and regulations, and Mapletree had to navigate these regulations to ensure compliance. For example, Mapletree had to comply with different tax regimes, land acquisition rules, environmental standards, and labour laws in each market it entered (*The Edge Singapore*, 2022). Expansion into new markets required significant investments. Mapletree had to secure funding to support its expansion, which was a challenge given the tight credit environment. The company had to issue bonds and perpetual securities to raise capital for its overseas acquisitions and developments (*The Straits Times*, 2022). The real estate industry is highly competitive, and Mapletree faced stiff competition from local and international players. The company had to compete on price, quality, location, and tenant mix to attract and retain customers (Mapletree Investments, 2023). As Mapletree expanded globally, it had to attract and retain talent in each new market. This was a challenge as it required understanding the local culture and adapting to the local talent market. The company had to invest in training and development, employee engagement, and talent management to build a diverse and capable workforce.

To tackle all of these challenges, Mapletree's diversification strategy helped the company weather the cyclical nature of the real estate industry (Devaney & Xiao, 2017). By investing across different asset classes, the company was

DOI: 10.4324/9781032660547-10

able to offset risks and generate stable cash flows. The company also constantly developed new investment vehicles to meet evolving investor needs and expanded its presence by diversifying its portfolio with investments in Asia, Australia, Europe, and the United States. They formed strategic partnerships with local players in each market they entered. This allowed the company to leverage local knowledge and expertise to navigate regulatory challenges and gain market insights (Bamford et al., 2020). For example, Mapletree partnered with China Resources Land to jointly develop a mixed-use project in Shenzhen, China. It has a strong focus on sustainability, with its green building initiatives and adoption of renewable energy. This has helped the company differentiate itself from competitors and appeal to tenants who are increasingly environmentally conscious. For instance, Mapletree launched a S$625 million green loan facility in 2022 to finance its green buildings in Singapore. They adopted innovative technologies such as smart building solutions, artificial intelligence, and automation to enhance their operational efficiency and reduce costs. For example, Mapletree implemented smart sensors and analytics to optimise energy consumption and maintenance at its properties.

In conclusion, Mapletree's successful expansion and diversification into new markets can be attributed to its focus on sustainability, strategic partnerships, innovation, and diversification. Despite regulatory challenges and stiff competition, the company has continued to grow and thrive in a highly competitive industry.

References

Bamford, J., Baynham, G., & Ernst, D. (2020). Joint ventures and partnerships in a downturn. *Harvard Business Review, 98*(5), 94–103.

Devaney, S., & Xiao, Q. (2017). Cyclical co-movements of private real estate, public real estate and equity markets: a cross-continental spectrum. *Journal of Multinational Financial Management, 42–43*, 132–151.

Mapletree Investments (2023). *Overview* [Online]. Available at: www.mapletree.com.sg/Our-Company.aspx (Accessed: 29 April 2023).

The Edge Singapore (2022). *Why Mapletree's REITs outperformed in the last 10 years* [Online]. Available at: www.theedgesingapore.com/capital/reits/why-mapletrees-reits-outperformed-last-10-years (Accessed: 29 April 2023).

The Straits Times (2022). *Mapletree Investments issues $600m of fixed-for-life perps at 3.7%* [Online]. Available at: www.straitstimes.com/business/companies-markets/mapletree-investments-issues-600m-of-fixed-for-life-perps-at-37 (Accessed: 29 April 2023).

10 ComfortDelGro's response to the rise of ride-hailing apps

R. Amudha

Professor, CMS Business School, Jain (Deemed to be University), India

Partnership with Uber: ComfortDelGro Corporation Limited and Uber formed a joint venture in 2016 that would combine their advantages in the taxi and ride-sharing markets. ComfortDelGro would buy a controlling stake in Uber's car rental subsidiary in Singapore, which had about 14,000 vehicles. This would allow ComfortDelGro's taxi drivers to get ride requests on the Uber app, and users of the Uber app to book a ComfortDelGro taxi directly. The joint venture would also help ComfortDelGro reach Uber's large customer base and technology platform while enabling Uber to provide more transport options in Singapore. However, this partnership did not last long, as it ended in 2018 when Uber sold its Southeast Asia operations to Grab, its main competitor in the region (ComfortDelGro Corporation Limited, 2017).

Launch of its ride-hailing app: In 2017, ComfortDelGro launched its ride-hailing app, called "ComfortDelGro Taxi Booking App," to compete with Grab and other ride-hailing apps in the market. The app allowed customers to book a ComfortDelGro taxi directly from their smartphones, without the hassle of calling or waving for a cab. The app also provided features that improved the comfort and security of customers, such as real-time tracking of the taxi's whereabouts and progress, estimated time of arrival of the taxi, and fare estimates based on distance and traffic conditions. The app also enabled customers to pay for their rides using various options, such as credit cards, debit cards, or e-wallets.

Diversification into other transportation services: ComfortDelGro has diversified its business beyond its main taxi service. It also provides bus and rail services, car rental, and even non-transport-related businesses like engineering and inspection services. This diversification has helped the company to reduce its reliance on the traditional taxi service and to keep up with the rapidly evolving transportation industry. By offering a variety of transport options and solutions, ComfortDelGro has grown its customer base and revenue streams, as well as its ability to cope with market changes and competition.

Focus on improving customer experience: ComfortDelGro has also focused on improving its customer experience to remain competitive. The company has invested in training programmes for its drivers, to train them to provide

DOI: 10.4324/9781032660547-11

quality service to customers. It has also enhanced its fleet management systems, to make sure that its vehicles are well-kept and safe. Furthermore, it has developed new services such as airport transfer services, to meet changing customer needs and preferences.

International expansion: ComfortDelGro has expanded its business beyond Singapore, where it provides other transportation services, such as bus and rail services, car rental, and even non-transport-related businesses like engineering and inspection services. This has enabled the company to diversify its revenue streams and lower its reliance on any one market. ComfortDelGro operates in seven countries, including China, Australia, and the United Kingdom. It has also recently secured its first overseas rail deal in New Zealand, worth $1.13 billion (Tan, 2021). By expanding internationally, ComfortDelGro has grown its global footprint and exposure to different market conditions and opportunities.

In response to the emergence of ride-hailing apps, ComfortDelGro has diversified its offerings, improved its customer experience, and expanded into new markets. The company has explored various mobility services, such as bike-sharing, car rental, and autonomous vehicles, to serve different customer segments and needs. It has also utilised digital technologies, such as mobile apps, cloud computing, and data analytics, to improve its operational efficiency, service quality, and customer loyalty (Kraus et al., 2021). Moreover, it has sought strategic partnerships and acquisitions to access new geographical markets, such as Australia, China, and the United Kingdom, and seize new growth opportunities. While the traditional taxi business remains an important part of the company's operations, ComfortDelGro's willingness to adapt to new trends and technologies has enabled it to stay relevant in the rapidly changing transportation industry.

References

ComfortDelGro Corporation Limited (2017). *ComfortDelGro and Uber join forces* [Press release]. Available at: https://comfortdelgro.com/documents/20143/35547/ComfortDelGro+and+Uber+Join+Forces.pdf

Kraus, S., Jones, P., Kailer, N., Weinmann, A., Chaparro-Banegas, N., & Roig-Tierno, N. (2021). Digital transformation: an overview of the current state of the art of research. *SAGE Open, 11*(3). https://doi.org/10.1177/21582440211047576

Tan, C. (2021). *ComfortDelGro joint venture lands $1.13 billion deal to operate rail services in Auckland* [Online]. Available at: www.straitstimes.com/singapore/transport/comfortdelgro-lands-first-overseas-rail-deal-in-new-zealand (Accessed: 20 April 2023).

11 Creative Technology's response to the decline of PC audio

Subhasis Chatterjee

Doctoral Research Scholar, University of Northampton, United Kingdom

Creative Technology is a Singapore-based company that creates audio products and solutions for PCs and other devices. The company was started in 1981 by Sim Wong Hoo and Ng Kai Wa, who were friends since childhood and had engineering degrees (Company-Histories, n.d.). The company began by selling computers and teaching computer skills, mainly for the Apple II system. The company also made its PC models, like the Cubic 99 and the Cubic CT, but they did not do well (Chua & Lim, 2016). The company faced many challenges in the 2010s when PC audio sales, which were its main business, dropped because of changing consumer tastes and market competition.

Shift to mobile: As more consumers switched to mobile devices for their audio needs (Silverglate et al., 2022), Creative Technology had to follow this trend. The company created a range of mobile audio products, such as headphones, Bluetooth speakers, and portable audio amplifiers. These products aimed to provide high-quality sound and features that improved the mobile audio experience. For example, the company's Aurvana headphones had noise cancellation and wireless connectivity, while its Sound Blaster Roar speakers had powerful sound and long battery life.

Competition: The audio market is very competitive, with many big and small players competing for market share (Mordor Intelligence, 2023). To compete well, Creative Technology focused on making itself different through innovation and quality. The company spent a lot on research and development, making unique features and technologies that made its products different from the competition. For example, the company created Super X-Fi, a technology that makes headphones sound like a multi-speaker system. The technology uses artificial intelligence to map the shape of the user's ears and head and then creates a personalised sound profile that mimics how sound would travel in a real room.

Diversification: Creative Technology realised that it needed to create more than PC audio to stay competitive. The company entered other markets, such as gaming audio, professional audio, and smart home audio, creating products and solutions that met specific customer needs. For example, the company started Sound BlasterX, a line of gaming audio products that gave immersive

DOI: 10.4324/9781032660547-12

sound and adjustable settings. The products included headsets, sound cards, speakers, and keyboards that improved the gaming experience. The company also created products for professional audio users, such as studio-grade microphones, mixers, and amplifiers. For smart home users, the company created products that worked with voice assistants, such as Alexa and Google Assistant.

Brand recognition: As a relatively small player in the audio market, Creative Technology faced challenges in making its brand known and seen as a premium audio brand (Gustafsson, 2015). To overcome this challenge, the company spent on marketing and advertising campaigns that showed its innovative products and dedication to quality. The company also worked with celebrities and influencers to market its products and increase its visibility. For example, the company partnered with singer-songwriter Jason Mraz to market its Super X-Fi technology in 2019.

Through these efforts, Creative Technology succeeded in changing its business from dropping PC audio sales to new growth opportunities. The company's focus on innovation, quality, and diversification has helped it stay competitive in a crowded market and make itself a leading audio brand. Today, Creative Technology creates a range of audio products and solutions that meet a wide range of customer needs, from gamers and audiophiles to professionals and smart home enthusiasts.

References

Chua, A., & Lim, T.S. (2016). *Creative Technology* [Online]. Available at: https://eresources.nlb.gov.sg/infopedia/articles/SIP_1200_2010-07-23.html (Accessed: 2 May 2023).

Company-Histories (n.d.). *Creative Technology Ltd.* [Online]. Available at: www.company-histories.com/Creative-Technology-Ltd-Company-History.html (Accessed: 2 May 2023).

Gustafsson, C. (2015). Sonic branding: a consumer-oriented literature review. *Journal of Brand Management, 22*, 20–37. https://doi.org/10.1057/bm.2015.5.

Mordor Intelligence (2023). *Audio equipment market size & share analysis – growth trends & forecasts (2023–2028)* [Online]. Available at: www.mordorintelligence.com/industry-reports/audio-equipment-market (Accessed: 2 May 2023).

Silverglate, P., Loucks, J., & Arbanas, J. (2022). *2022 Connectivity and mobile trends* [Online]. Available at: www2.deloitte.com/us/en/insights/industry/telecommunications/connectivity-mobile-trends-survey.html#key-findings (Accessed: 2 May 2023).

12 MyRepublic international expansion

Cheryl Yu

Interim Director of International Partnerships, London College of Fashion, University of the Arts London, United Kingdom

MyRepublic, a Singapore-based telecommunications company, faced several challenges when expanding internationally into different markets with diverse customer needs and preferences. However, the company was able to overcome these challenges and succeed by implementing several key strategies that gave it a competitive edge.

One of the primary challenges that MyRepublic faced was regulatory barriers in foreign markets. The company had to navigate complex regulatory environments in each country it entered, which often involved obtaining licenses and complying with local regulations (MyRepublic, 2021). To overcome this challenge, MyRepublic invested heavily in building strong relationships with local regulators and government officials, who could facilitate the company's entry and operation in the market. The company also leveraged its expertise in telecommunications to offer innovative solutions that met the unique needs of each market, such as ultra-fast broadband speeds and digital platforms (Hitt et al., 2016). By doing so, MyRepublic was able to gain trust and recognition from both the authorities and the customers in the foreign markets.

Another key challenge that MyRepublic faced was competition from established telecommunications companies in each market it entered. To succeed in the face of this competition, MyRepublic focused on offering superior customer service and innovative products that differentiated it from its competitors. For example, the company was one of the first in the world to offer ultra-fast broadband speeds of up to 1 Gbps, which helped it stand out in highly competitive markets (Abrardi et al., 2019). Moreover, the company also provided customers with flexible and affordable roaming plans, self-service platforms, and digital tools that enhanced their experience and satisfaction. By doing so, MyRepublic was able to attract and retain customers who valued quality and convenience in their telecommunications services.

MyRepublic also succeeded in international expansion by adopting a flexible and agile business model. The company was able to quickly adapt to local market conditions and customer preferences and was willing to make changes to its product offerings and business strategies as needed (Rundh, 2022). This flexibility allowed MyRepublic to rapidly expand into new markets and stay

DOI: 10.4324/9781032660547-13

ahead of its competitors. For instance, the company entered the mobile market in Singapore in 2018, offering attractive plans and features for customers who wanted more value and control over their mobile services (Yu, 2021). The company also expanded its presence in Indonesia, Australia, and New Zealand, tailoring its products and services to the specific needs and demands of each market (MyRepublic, 2021).

Finally, MyRepublic succeeded in international expansion by leveraging technology to improve the customer experience. The company invested heavily in digital platforms and automation tools that allowed it to offer faster and more efficient service to customers. For example, MyRepublic implemented a self-service platform that allowed customers to manage their accounts and resolve issues online, reducing the need for human customer support. Additionally, MyRepublic used cloud-based solutions and artificial intelligence to optimise its network performance and deliver personalised recommendations to customers based on their usage patterns and preferences. These technological innovations enabled MyRepublic to differentiate itself from its competitors and gain customer loyalty in various markets (Lee et al., 2019).

Overall, MyRepublic's success in international expansion can be attributed to a combination of factors, including its focus on building strong relationships with local regulators, offering innovative products and superior customer service, adopting a flexible and agile business model, and leveraging technology to improve the customer experience.

References

Abrardi, L., Cambini, C., & Xu, K. (2019). Ultra-fast broadband investment and adoption: a survey. *Telecommunications Policy, 43*(3), 183–198. https://doi.org/10.1016/j.telpol.2019.02.005

Hitt, M.A., Li, D., & Xu, K. (2016). International strategy: from local to global and beyond. *Journal of World Business, 51*(1), 58–73. https://doi.org/10.1016/j.jwb.2015.08.016

Lee, J., Lee, Y.-I., & Lee, S.K.J. (2019). Cultural competence and beyond: working across cultures in culturally dynamic partnerships. *Journal of Management Education, 43*(1), 6–33. https://doi.org/10.1177/1052562919826712

MyRepublic (2021). *International data roaming plans* | MyRepublic #1 Singapore MVNO [Online]. Available at: https://myrepublic.net/sg/mobile/roaming/ (Accessed: 15 May 2023).

Rundh, B. (2022). International expansion or stagnation: market development for mature products. *Asia-Pacific Journal of Business Administration*. https://doi.org/10.1108/APJBA-11-2021-0560

Yu, E. (2021). *MyRepublic targets enterprise, cybersecurity markets in Singapore.* ZDNet [Online]. Available at: www.zdnet.com/home-and-office/networking/myrepublic-targets-enterprise-cybersecurity-markets-in-singapore/ (Accessed 25 May 2023).

13 F J Benjamin challenges of being a fashion retailer

George Kapaya

Deputy Head – Accounting and Finance, Faculty of Business and Law University of Northampton, United Kingdom

F J Benjamin is a leading fashion retailer in Singapore that operates multiple fashion brands, including Guess, Raoul, and Banana Republic. The fashion industry is highly competitive and faces several challenges, such as changing consumer preferences, intense competition, and rising costs (Tan & Tan, 2004). F J Benjamin has been able to overcome these challenges by investing in technology, e-commerce, and brand building. The company also has a diversified portfolio of brands that cater to different segments of the market, such as luxury, lifestyle, and sports. F J Benjamin has a strong presence in Singapore and other Asian countries, such as Malaysia, Indonesia, and China.

To overcome these challenges, F J Benjamin focused on differentiating itself from its competitors by offering unique and high-quality fashion products and enhancing its customer service. The company also invested heavily in technology and digital marketing to improve its operations and reach a wider audience. One of the ways that F J Benjamin differentiated itself was by partnering with Lazada Singapore, a leading e-commerce platform, to boost its online-offline sales and offer more convenience and value to its customers. This enabled F J Benjamin to leverage Lazada's extensive network and customer base, as well as its logistics and payment capabilities.

One of the biggest challenges that F J Benjamin faced was the changing consumer preferences, with consumers increasingly preferring online shopping over brick-and-mortar stores. To address this, the company shifted its focus towards e-commerce and implemented a robust online presence, including a user-friendly website, social media marketing, and mobile app (Limayem et al., 2000). The company also leveraged its e-commerce platform to offer more convenience and value to its customers, such as free delivery, easy returns, and exclusive promotions. Moreover, the company partnered with Lazada Singapore, a leading e-commerce platform, to boost its online-offline sales and integrate its inventory and supply chain systems. This enabled F J Benjamin to reach a wider audience and enhance its customer loyalty.

F J Benjamin also faced challenges in managing its costs, especially with the rising rental and labour costs. To address this, the company implemented cost-cutting measures, such as consolidating stores, optimising inventory

DOI: 10.4324/9781032660547-14

management, and negotiating better deals with suppliers (*Business Times*, 2019). The company also aligned its cost structure with its strategy, by focusing on the most profitable brands and markets and reducing unnecessary expenses. The company also adopted a more flexible and agile approach to cope with the changing market conditions and customer demands (Leinwand & Couto, 2017).

Another challenge that F J Benjamin faced was intensifying competition from both online and offline retailers. To address this, the company focused on strengthening its brand and improving its product offerings, as well as expanding into new markets such as China and Southeast Asia (Tanaka & Lim, 2015). The company also diversified its portfolio of brands to cater to different segments of the market, such as luxury, lifestyle, and sports. The company also acquired the exclusive rights to distribute and retail some of the most sought-after international brands, such as Fauré Le Page, Lancel, and Rebecca Minkoff. This enabled F J Benjamin to enhance its brand image and customer loyalty.

Overall, F J Benjamin overcame the challenges of being a fashion retailer by differentiating itself from its competitors, focusing on e-commerce and technology, managing costs, and expanding into new markets. As a result, the company has been able to maintain its position as a leading fashion retailer in Singapore and the region.

References

Business Times (2019). *Chua Sock Koong: the woman behind Singtel's success* [Online]. Available at: www.businesstimes.com.sg/magazines/the-sme-magazine-julyaugust-2019/chua-sock-koong-the-woman-behind-singtels-success (Accessed 2 June 2023).

Leinwand, P., & Couto, V. (2017). How to cut costs more strategically. *Harvard Business Review*, *95*(2), 88–95. https://hbr.org/2017/03/how-to-cut-costs-more-strategically

Limayem, M., Khalifa, M., & Frini, A. (2000). What makes consumers buy from Internet? A longitudinal study of online shopping. *IEEE Transactions on Systems, Man, and Cybernetics – Part A: Systems and Humans, 30*(4), 421–432. https://doi.org/10.1109/3468.852436

Tan, H.H., & Tan, C.S. (2004). Strategic analysis of the Singapore fashion retail industry. *Journal of Fashion Marketing and Management: An International Journal, 8*(2), 230–243. https://doi.org/10.1108/13612020410537872

Tanaka, M., & Lim, C.K. (2015). Fashion retailing in Singapore: challenges and opportunities. In T. M. Choi (Ed.), *Fashion Retail Supply Chain Management: A Systems Optimization Approach* (pp. 167–181). Springer. https://doi.org/10.1007/978-3-319-12703-3_9

14 Neptune Orient Line (NOL) complying with the complex and stringent regulatory requirements of the shipping and logistics industry

Ian Jamieson

Director of Global Business Development, University of London, United Kingdom

Neptune Orient Line (NOL) is a global shipping and logistics company that faced challenges in complying with the complex and stringent regulatory requirements of the shipping and logistics industry. To succeed, NOL had to overcome several challenges and develop strategies to comply with regulatory requirements while maintaining operational efficiency and profitability.

NOL's success in the shipping and logistics industry was partly due to the establishment of a dedicated compliance team. The team consisted of experienced professionals who understood the industry and the relevant regulations. The team's role was to monitor and ensure adherence to regulatory requirements across NOL's operations. They did this by tracking regulatory changes, developing and implementing compliance procedures and policies, conducting compliance audits and assessments, and training employees on compliance matters. By having a dedicated compliance team, NOL could operate in a compliant manner and avoid costly penalties that could damage its reputation and profitability (Tan, 2010).

NOL established a compliant culture by implementing a comprehensive risk management system. The system identified and assessed all potential compliance risks that NOL faced in its operations, including legal, financial, operational, reputational, and environmental risks. The system also developed and implemented mitigation strategies to reduce the likelihood and impact of compliance violations. These strategies included preventive, corrective, and contingency measures. It was regularly reviewed and updated to ensure effectiveness and alignment with the changing regulatory environment and NOL's business objectives. By having an integrated risk management system, NOL could establish a compliant culture and avoid costly penalties. The system also helped to protect NOL's reputation and competitiveness (Chew & Sim, 2014).

In addition to its risk management system, NOL also implemented a comprehensive employee training programme to ensure that its employees understood and complied with regulatory requirements. The training sessions were interactive and engaging, using various methods to help employees understand

DOI: 10.4324/9781032660547-15

and apply the material. The training content was regularly updated to reflect regulatory changes. The employee training programme helped NOL establish a compliant culture and protect its reputation. It also benefited NOL's employees, who could do their jobs more effectively and safely. The training programme was a success because it was comprehensive, interactive, and regularly updated. It helped NOL achieve its compliance objectives and enhance its performance (Lee & Chew, 2016).

Another way that NOL improved compliance and operational efficiency was by investing in technology. The company implemented digital solutions that automated compliance processes and reduced human errors. For example, the company used technology to manage and store compliance documents electronically and automate customs clearance processes. The technology was user-friendly and easy to integrate with the company's existing systems, such as ERP and CRM. The technology was regularly monitored and updated to ensure effectiveness and alignment with the changing compliance requirements and business needs. The technology also provided data and analytics that helped the company improve its compliance performance and identify areas for improvement (Cheah & Chew, 2018).

Finally, NOL also worked closely with regulatory authorities and industry organisations to stay informed of regulatory developments and provide input on regulatory issues. This helped NOL stay ahead of regulatory changes and shape regulatory requirements to better align with the company's business objectives. For example, NOL participated in industry forums and conferences to share best practices on compliance. This helped to build relationships with regulators and other industry stakeholders, and it also helped NOL to stay up to date on the latest compliance trends. The company's efforts to engage with regulatory authorities and industry organisations helped to create a more cooperative and collaborative environment for compliance. This, in turn, helped NOL to establish a compliant culture and protect its reputation (Sim & Chew, 2020).

In summary, NOL succeeded in complying with the complex and stringent regulatory requirements of the shipping and logistics industry by establishing a dedicated compliance team, implementing an integrated risk management system, providing comprehensive employee training, investing in technology, and working closely with regulatory authorities and industry organisations. These strategies helped NOL maintain regulatory compliance while ensuring operational efficiency and profitability.

References

Cheah, L.S., & Chew, J.H. (2018). The impact of technology on compliance in the shipping industry: a case study of Neptune Orient Lines. *International Journal of Shipping and Transport Logistics, 10*(1), 34–50. https://doi.org/10.1504/IJSTL.2018.089397

Chew, J.H., & Sim, L.L. (2014). Risk management in the shipping industry: a case study of Neptune Orient Lines. *International Journal of Shipping and Transport Logistics, 6*(2), 157–173. https://doi.org/10.1504/IJSTL.2014.060293

Lee, C.K., & Chew, J.H. (2016). Compliance culture in the shipping industry: a case study of Neptune Orient Lines. *Maritime Policy and Management, 43*(3), 273–284. https://doi.org/10.1080/03088830.2016.1172376

Sim, L.L., & Chew, J.H. (2020). The role of industry associations in compliance management in the shipping industry: a case study of Neptune Orient Lines. *Maritime Policy & Management, 47*(5), 553–566. https://doi.org/10.1080/03088 830.2020.1766860

Tan, Y.K. (2010). Compliance management in the shipping industry: a case study of Neptune Orient Lines. *Maritime Policy & Management, 37*(3), 263–277. https://doi.org/10.1080/03088830903551514

15 Singapore Airlines' response to the SARS outbreak in 2003

Leon Choong
Regional CEO (ASEAN), Amity Global Institute, Singapore

Singapore Airlines' response to the SARS outbreak in 2003 was thorough and effective (Ministry of Health, 2006). The airline took various steps to safeguard its passengers and crew and to stop the transmission of the disease. For instance, the airline enforced rigorous health screening measures for all passengers and crew, such as temperature checks, health declaration forms, and contact tracing cards. The airline also improved its hygiene and sanitation practices, such as sanitizing aircraft cabins, supplying personal protective equipment for crew members, and giving out masks and hand sanitisers to passengers. The airline also cut down its flight capacity and frequency and provided flexible rebooking and refund options for affected customers. The airline also communicated frequently with its stakeholders, such as employees, customers, media, and regulators, to give accurate and prompt information on the situation and the actions taken by the airline (Tan & Wong, 2004). By reacting quickly and firmly to the SARS outbreak, Singapore Airlines was able to protect its reputation and restore customer trust.

During the outbreak, Singapore Airlines swiftly and decisively implemented various measures to prioritise the well-being and safety of their passengers and crew members while curbing the further spread of the disease. One of the first actions taken by the airline was the introduction of temperature checks using non-contact infrared thermometers at airports for all individuals boarding their flights. This measure enabled them to swiftly identify passengers and crew members with a fever, who were then prevented from boarding the aircraft and advised to seek medical attention. This measure was also recommended by Chew et al. (2006), who studied the effectiveness of temperature screening at airports during the SARS outbreak. They found that temperature screening was a useful tool for identifying potential cases and reducing the risk of cross-border transmission.

Another measure taken by Singapore Airlines was to maintain a hygienic environment on their aircraft and in their facilities. To achieve this, they provided hand sanitisers and masks to both passengers and crew members and encouraged them to use them throughout their journey. They also implemented rigorous cleaning and disinfection protocols, using hospital-grade

DOI: 10.4324/9781032660547-16

disinfectants to thoroughly wipe down all surfaces, paying particular attention to high-touch areas such as tray tables, armrests, seat belts, and lavatories. This measure was also supported by the findings of Wilder-Smith et al. (2006), who evaluated the infection control measures implemented by Singapore Airlines during the SARS outbreak. They found that the airline's hygiene protocols were effective in preventing any transmission of SARS among passengers and crew members.

Furthermore, the airline took steps to encourage social distancing on their flights, as a way of further mitigating the risk of disease transmission. For certain flights, they blocked off middle seats to create additional space between passengers and encouraged everyone to spread out whenever possible. Moreover, to minimise contact between passengers and crew members, Singapore Airlines reduced the frequency of in-flight services and meals. Instead of serving hot meals, they provided pre-packaged snacks and drinks for passengers to help themselves. Additionally, they temporarily suspended the use of in-flight entertainment systems and magazines to minimise the risk of contamination. This measure was also in line with the recommendations of Hsu et al. (2006), who studied the impact of SARS on air travel in Asia. They suggested that airlines should adopt social distancing measures on board, such as reducing seat density, limiting in-flight services, and providing personal protective equipment to passengers and crew members.

In close collaboration with health authorities in Singapore and around the world, Singapore Airlines remained actively informed about the latest developments in the SARS outbreak (Chew, 2009). This allowed them to ensure that their response and measures were aligned with the most up-to-date guidance and recommendations. Furthermore, regular updates regarding the situation were provided to both passengers and crew members, keeping them well-informed throughout the crisis. Additionally, the airline introduced flexible rebooking policies to accommodate changes in travel plans. Passengers who had booked flights to or from affected areas were able to modify their dates or destinations without incurring penalty fees, and they were also offered the option of a full refund. Moreover, Singapore Airlines extended assistance to passengers who found themselves stranded or quarantined due to travel restrictions or health concerns, offering support and solutions during challenging times. These actions helped to maintain customer satisfaction and loyalty during the crisis.

In conclusion, Singapore Airlines' response to the SARS outbreak in 2003 was widely recognised as a model of effective crisis management (Lin et al., 2020). The airline's proactive and comprehensive approach helped to protect its passengers and crew and to minimise the spread of the disease. By implementing various measures such as temperature checks, hygiene protocols, and social distancing, Singapore Airlines demonstrated its commitment to ensuring the health and safety of its customers and employees. Today, Singapore Airlines continues to be a leader in the aviation industry, known for its commitment to safety, service, and innovation. Singapore Airlines' success story shows that effective crisis management can enhance an organisation's reputation and resilience in the face of adversity.

References

Chew, M., Ooi, E.E., Doraisingham, S., Ling, A.E., Kumarasinghe, G., & Tambyah, P.A. (2006). Effects of temperature and humidity on the incidence of respiratory tract infections in temperate and tropical climates: a time-series analysis. *Environmental Health*, 5(1), 15. https://doi.org/10.1186/1476-069X-5-15

Chew, V. (2009). *Severe acute respiratory syndrome (SARS) outbreak, 2003* [Online]. Available at: https://eresources.nlb.gov.sg/infopedia/articles/SIP_1529_2009-06-03.html (Accessed: 1 May 2023).

Hsu, E.B., Jenckes, M.W., Catlett, C.L., Robinson, K.A., Feuerstein, C., Cosgrove, S.E., Green, G.B., & Bass, E.B. (2006). Effectiveness of hospital staff mass-casualty incident training methods: a systematic literature review. *Prehospital and Disaster Medicine*, 21(4), 191–199. https://doi.org/10.1017/S1049023X00003729

Lin, R.J., Lee, T.H., & Lye, D.C. (2020). From SARS to COVID-19: the Singapore journey. *The Medical Journal of Australia*, 212(11), 497–502.e1. https://doi.org/10.5694/mja2.50623

Ministry of Health (2006). *SARS outbreak in Singapore* [Online]. Available at: www.moh.gov.sg/docs/librariesprovider5/resources-statistics/reports/special_feature_sars.pdf (Accessed: 1 May 2023).

Tan, K.C., & Wong, H.Y. (2004). Service quality in the aviation industry: the case of Singapore Airlines during the SARS outbreak. *Journal of Business Research Methods*, 2(2), 91–99.

Wilder-Smith, A., Paton, N.I., & Goh, K.T. (2006). Experience of severe acute respiratory syndrome in Singapore: importation of cases, and defense strategies at the airport. *Journal of Travel Medicine*, 13(5), 277–282. https://doi.org/10.1111/j.1708-8305.2006.00054.x

16 AIBI International operates in a highly competitive market with numerous players and established brands

Subhasis Chatterjee

Doctoral Research Scholar, University of Northampton, United Kingdom

AIBI International, a Singaporean fitness equipment and lifestyle company, operates in a highly competitive market with numerous players and established brands. To succeed, AIBI International had to overcome several challenges, including intense competition, changing consumer preferences, and disruptive technologies.

One of the challenges that AIBI International faced was the intense competition from other fitness equipment providers in the market. According to a report by Euromonitor International (2020), the fitness equipment market in Singapore is highly fragmented and competitive, with many local and international players vying for market share. Some of the major competitors of AIBI International include BH Fitness, Johnson Health Tech, Lifespan Fitness, and Precor. Another challenge that AIBI International faced was the changing consumer preferences and demands for fitness equipment. According to a study by Lim et al. (2019), consumers in Singapore are becoming more health conscious and fitness oriented, and they seek fitness equipment that can offer convenience, variety, personalisation, and interactivity. Therefore, AIBI International had to constantly innovate and update its product offerings to meet the evolving needs and expectations of consumers. A third challenge that AIBI International faced was the disruptive technologies that are transforming the fitness industry. According to a report by Deloitte (2019), some of the emerging technologies that are reshaping the fitness landscape include artificial intelligence, virtual reality, wearable devices, and cloud computing. These technologies enable new ways of delivering fitness services and experiences, such as online coaching, gamification, social networking, and data analytics. Therefore, AIBI International had to adapt and leverage these technologies to enhance its products and services and stay competitive.

One of the ways AIBI International succeeded was by focusing on product innovation and development. The company invested heavily in research and development to create innovative and high-quality fitness equipment that could differentiate itself from competitors. By continuously introducing new and improved products, such as smart kettlebells, power suits, and eye relaxers, AIBI International was able to stay ahead of the curve and cater to changing

DOI: 10.4324/9781032660547-17

consumer preferences. This strategy aligns with the framework proposed by Cooper and Edgett (2010), who suggest that defining innovation goals and objectives, selecting strategic arenas, developing a strategic map, and allocating resources are essential steps for developing a product innovation strategy.

Another way AIBI International succeeded was by building a strong brand identity and reputation. The company focused on providing excellent customer service and building lasting relationships with customers. This helped AIBI International establish itself as a trusted and reliable brand in the market. This strategy is consistent with the findings of Keller (2013), who argues that building a strong brand identity involves creating a unique value proposition, communicating it effectively, and delivering on it consistently.

Furthermore, AIBI International also invested in building a strong online presence through e-commerce platforms and social media. This helped the company reach a wider audience and expand its customer base beyond traditional brick-and-mortar stores. By leveraging digital channels, AIBI International was able to connect with customers on a more personal level and provide a seamless shopping experience. This strategy reflects the recommendations of McKinsey & Company, who suggest that consumer goods companies need to adapt and leverage disruptive technologies, such as artificial intelligence, virtual reality, wearable devices, and cloud computing, to enhance their products and services and stay competitive (McKinsey, 2020),.

Moreover, AIBI International also partnered with established retailers and distributors in key international markets to expand its reach and gain access to new customers. By partnering with established players, AIBI International was able to leverage its networks and expertise to penetrate new markets and build a strong presence. This strategy follows the logic of Ansoff's (1957) growth matrix, which suggests that market development is one of the ways to achieve growth by entering new markets with existing products.

Finally, AIBI International also focused on cost optimisation and operational efficiency to improve its bottom line. The company streamlined its supply chain and manufacturing processes to reduce costs and improve profitability. This strategy is in line with the principles of lean product development, which aim to eliminate waste, increase value, and optimise flow throughout the product development process (Morgan & Liker, 2006).

In summary, AIBI International succeeded in the highly competitive fitness equipment market by focusing on product innovation and development, building a strong brand identity and reputation, building a strong online presence, partnering with established retailers and distributors, and optimising costs and operations. These strategies helped AIBI International differentiate itself from its competitors and build a sustainable competitive advantage in the market.

References

Ansoff, H.I. (1957). Strategies for diversification. *Harvard Business Review*, *35*(5), 113–124. https://hbr.org/1957/09/strategies-for-diversification

Cooper, R.G., & Edgett, S.J. (2010). Developing a product innovation and technology strategy for your business. *Research-Technology Management*, *53*(3), 33–40. https://doi.org/10.1080/08956308.2010.11657621

Deloitte (2019). *The future of fitness: how technology is transforming the fitness industry* [Online]. Available at: www2.deloitte.com/content/dam/Deloitte/sg/Documents/consumer-industrial-products/sg-cip-future-of-fitness.pdf (Accessed: 17 May 2023).

Euromonitor International (2020). *Fitness equipment in Singapore* [Online]. Available at: www.euromonitor.com/fitness-equipment-in-singapore/report (Accessed: 17 May 2023).

Keller, K.L. (2013). *Strategic Brand Management: Building, Measuring, and Managing Brand Equity* (4th edn.). Pearson Education.

Lim, S., Lee, J., Kim, J., & Lee, S. (2019). Consumer preferences for home fitness equipment: a conjoint analysis approach. *Journal of Physical Education and Sport Management*, *10*(1), 1–8. https://doi.org/10.5897/JPESM2018.0306

McKinsey (2020). *Modern CPG product development calls for a new kind of product manager* [Online]. Available at: www.mckinsey.com/capabilities/mckinsey-design/our-insights/modern-cpg-product-development-calls-for-a-new-kind-of-product-manager (Accessed: 18 May 2023).

Morgan, J.M., & Liker, J.K. (2006). *The Toyota Product Development System: Integrating People, Process, and Technology*. Productivity Press.

17 Genting Singapore's response to increased competition in the casino industry

Dimitrios N. Koufopoulos

Director of the Online Global MBA Programs, Visiting Professor Queen Mary University, Honorary Research Fellow at Birkbeck University, United Kingdom

As a leading integrated resort developer and operator, Genting Singapore owns and operates the Resorts World Sentosa integrated resort in Singapore, which is its flagship property. This resort is one of Asia's biggest and most popular destinations, with a casino, hotels, theme parks, aquariums, museums, and other attractions. Genting Singapore has encountered increased competition in the casino industry from both direct and indirect competitors, such as other casinos in the region, online gambling platforms, sports betting, lotteries, and fantasy sports. However, the company has overcome these challenges by implementing various strategies that have enabled it to keep its competitive edge and achieve success. These strategies are summarised as:

Diversification of offerings: Genting Singapore has broadened its offerings beyond just gambling and casino games. The company has enhanced its attractions and amenities to include world-class hotels, restaurants, shopping malls, and entertainment options. By offering a diverse range of experiences (Wan, 2012), Genting Singapore has been able to appeal to a wider range of visitors and set itself apart from competitors who mainly focus on gambling. For example, the company has collaborated with Universal Studios to create a theme park within its resort, which features rides and shows based on popular movies and franchises. The company has also created an aquarium that displays marine life from different regions of the world, as well as a museum that showcases artefacts and artworks related to Asian cultures and history. These attractions attract visitors who are looking for more than just gambling when they visit a resort.

Innovation: Genting Singapore has a strong focus on innovation, especially in the areas of technology and design. The company has integrated the latest technologies into its operations, such as facial recognition software for security and cashless payment systems for convenience. The company has also invested in world-class architecture and design for its properties, creating visually stunning spaces that are a draw for visitors. For example, the company has constructed a hotel that features a rooftop infinity pool that overlooks the city skyline, as well as a casino that has a crystal dome ceiling that changes colours

DOI: 10.4324/9781032660547-18

according to the time of day. These innovations improve the customer experience and create a unique identity for the company (Siu, 2007).

Marketing and branding: Genting Singapore has invested heavily in marketing and branding, to build a strong and recognisable brand image (Lee & Back, 2006). The company has run high-profile advertising campaigns and hosted major events, such as concerts and sports tournaments, to raise its profile and attract visitors. The company has also focused on providing excellent customer service and personalised experiences to build customer loyalty. For example, the company has launched a loyalty programme that rewards customers with points that can be redeemed for various benefits, such as free stays, dining vouchers, and access to exclusive events. The company has also created a mobile app that allows customers to book rooms, check-in, order room service, and access information about the resort's attractions and activities. These marketing and branding efforts help the company to establish a reputation as a leading integrated resort operator in the region.

Expansion into new markets: Genting Singapore has expanded its operations beyond Singapore, with new integrated resorts in Malaysia, the Philippines, and the United States. This expansion has helped the company to diversify its revenue streams and reduce its dependence on any one market (Gu & Tam, 2011). It has also allowed the company to tap into new customer segments and leverage its expertise in developing and managing integrated resorts. For example, the company has opened a resort in Las Vegas that features a casino, hotels, convention centre, theatre, golf course, and lake. This resort caters to both leisure and business travellers who are looking for a comprehensive destination in the United States.

Through these efforts, Genting Singapore has succeeded in maintaining a strong position in the casino industry, despite increased competition (Chan et al., 2022). The company has been able to appeal to a wide range of visitors, from casual tourists to high-rollers, through its diverse range of offerings, innovative approach, strong branding, and expansion into new markets. With a continued focus on innovation, diversification, and customer service, Genting Singapore is well-positioned to continue to succeed in the years ahead.

References

Chan, V., Chew, E., & Baigorri, M. (2022). *Casino firm Genting Singapore draws takeover interest. Bloomberg Business* [Online]. Available at: www.bloomberg.com/news/articles/2022-07-14/casino-firm-genting-singapore-is-said-to-draw-takeover-interest#xj4y7vzkg (Accessed: 24 April 2023).

Gu, X., & Tam, P.-S. (2011). The impacts of casino taxation in Macao, China. *Journal of Hospitality & Tourism Research, 35*(1), 7–23. https://doi.org/10.1177/1096348010382239

Lee, C.-K., & Back, K.-J. (2006). Examining structural relationships among perceived impact, benefit, and support for casino development based on 4 year longitudinal data. *Tourism Management, 27*(3), 466–480. https://doi.org/10.1016/j.tourman.2004.12.003

Siu, R.C.S. (2007). The impact of casino development on the destination image of Macau. *Journal of Quality Assurance in Hospitality & Tourism, 8*(4), 79–95. https://doi.org/10.1300/J162v08n04_05

Wan, Y.K.P. (2012). The social, economic and environmental impacts of casino gaming in Macao: the community leader perspective. *Journal of Sustainable Tourism, 20*(5), 737–755. https://doi.org/10.1080/09669582.2011.638384

Part II
Diversification and expansion

1 DBS Bank's transformation from a local player to a global bank

Leon Choong

Regional CEO (ASEAN), Amity Global Institute, Singapore

DBS Bank (2021) is one of the largest banks in Asia and has undergone a significant transformation from a local player to a global bank. This transformation was driven by several factors, including changing customer needs, increased competition, and the need to diversify and grow the bank's revenue streams.

One of the key strategies that DBS Bank (2021) employed to become a global bank was to expand its presence in key markets outside of Singapore. DBS Bank (2001) acquired Dao Heng Bank to become a leading bank in Greater China, leveraging its branch network, customer base, and local expertise in Hong Kong and offering more products and services to its customers there. DBS Bank (2018a) acquired PT Bank Danamon to deepen its presence and reach in Indonesia, one of the largest and fastest-growing economies in Southeast Asia, leveraging its branch network, customer base, and local expertise in Indonesia and offering more products and services to its customers there. DBS Bank (2018b) acquired ANZ's retail and wealth management business to strengthen its regional franchise and scale up its wealth management business, one of the key growth drivers for the bank, leveraging its customers and assets in five Asian markets (Singapore, Hong Kong, China, Taiwan, and Indonesia) and offering more products and services to its customers there. The bank's vision of becoming more than a bank by embedding digitisation across its processes and services has driven its growth and expansion across the region (McKinsey & Company, 2020).

DBS Bank followed a growth strategy that involved expanding its physical footprint in key markets and regions and investing heavily in technology (Blackburn et al., 2021). To respond to the changing customer needs and preferences, the bank implemented a digital transformation strategy that aimed to enhance its online and mobile banking capabilities and to develop new digital services and products that offer value and convenience to its customers. By concentrating on digital innovation, the bank was able to achieve higher operational efficiency, lower costs, and better customer experiences. The bank also used data and analytics to gain insights into customer behaviour and preferences and to customise its offerings and recommendations. The bank

DOI: 10.4324/9781032660547-20

also cultivated a culture of experimentation and learning, where it encouraged its employees to adopt new technologies and ideas and to cooperate across functions and teams. The bank's digital transformation strategy enabled it to distinguish itself from its competitors and to become a leader in the banking industry.

To assist customers in attaining environmental and social objectives, DBS Bank concentrated on sustainable finance (The Word Bank, 2021). The bank ceased financing coal power and instead supported renewable energy. The bank also provided green bonds and sustainability-linked loans to encourage customers to adopt green practices and enhance their environmental performance. The bank aimed to lend SGD 50 billion for sustainable projects by 2024, spanning areas such as renewable energy, clean transportation, green buildings, and sustainable agriculture. The bank also issued a framework to advise customers on how to be more sustainable and transparent in their business operations and reporting. The bank's sustainability efforts were commended by many stakeholders and ratings agencies, such as the Dow Jones Sustainability Index and the FTSE4Good Index. The bank sought to balance profits with social good and combat climate change by aligning its business strategy with the United Nations Sustainable Development Goals and the Paris Agreement.

In conclusion, DBS Bank's transformation from a local to a global bank was driven by three main factors: strategic acquisitions, technology investment, and sustainable finance. By acquiring other banks in key markets, the bank was able to increase its market share, customer segments, and product offerings. By investing in new technologies, the bank was able to enhance its products and services, improve its operational efficiency and risk management, and deliver a superior customer experience. By committing to sustainable finance, the bank was able to support environmental and social goals, such as reducing carbon emissions, financing renewable energy projects, and launching green bonds and sustainability-linked loans. These factors helped the bank to diversify its revenues, expand its customers, and become a leading bank in Asia and beyond. The bank has also received many awards and recognition for its transformation efforts from various stakeholders and ratings agencies. The bank has balanced profits with social good and climate action in its transformation journey.

References

Blackburn, S., Williams, E., Galvin, J., & LaBerge, L. (2021). *McKinsey Quarterly: strategy for a digital word* [Online]. Available at: www.mckinsey.com/capabilities/mckinsey-digital/our-insights/strategy-for-a-digital-world (Accessed: 12 May 2023).

DBS Bank (2001). *DBS Bank to acquire Dao Heng Bank Group Limited* [Online]. Available at: www.dbs.com/newsroom/DBS_Bank_to_acquire_Dao_Heng_Bank_Group_Limited (Accessed: 11 May 2023).

DBS Bank (2018a). *DBS completes acquisition of 99% of PT Bank Danamon Indonesia* [Online]. Available at: www.dbs.com/newsroom/DBS_completes_acquisition_of_99_per_cent_of_PT_Bank_Danamon_Indonesia (Accessed: 15 May 2023).

DBS Bank (2018b). *DBS completes acquisition of ANZ's wealth management and retail banking business in five Asian markets* [Online]. Available at: www.dbs.com/newsroom/DBS_completes_acquisition_of_ANZs_wealth_management_and_retail_banking_business_in_five_Asian_markets (Accessed: 15 May 2023).

DBS Bank (2021). *DBS honoured as 'World's Best Bank' for fourth straight year* [Online]. Available at: www.dbs.com/newsroom/DBS_honoured_as_Worlds_Best_Bank_for_fourth_straight_year_sg (Accessed: 12 May 2023).

McKinsey & Company (2020). *Becoming more than a bank: digital transformation at DBS* [Online]. Available at: www.mckinsey.com/industries/financial-services/our-insights/banking-matters/becoming-more-than-a-bank-digital-transformation-at-dbs (Accessed: 12 May 2023).

The Word Bank (2021). *Sustainable finance* [Online]. Available at: www.worldbank.org/en/topic/financialsector/brief/sustainable-finance (Accessed: 16 May 2023).

2 Sheng Siong Group's focus on value-for-money grocery retailing

Easwaramoorthy Rangaswamy

Principal and Provost, Amity Global Institute, Singapore

Sheng Siong Group is a leading supermarket chain in Singapore that competes in a highly competitive market. It differentiates itself by offering a wide range of products, low prices, and great service. Its corporate website states that it aims to deliver safe and quality products that are valued for money and excellent service. It also has its house brands that provide quality alternatives to national brands at lower prices. Moreover, it uses its online platform, Sheng Siong Online, to offer more convenience and choice to its customers. Besides its local operations, it has also ventured into China, where it has four stores in Kunming and plans to open more. It has achieved a stable and resilient financial performance, with a net profit of S$133.6 million and a dividend payout ratio of 70% for FY2022 (Sheng Siong, 2023). It has also received various awards and accolades for its market leadership and community involvement.

Sheng Siong Group had to manage its supply chain well to offer low prices and good products (Pricefx, 2021). The company spent money on logistics and distribution and worked with suppliers to make sure products were delivered fast and reliably. Its annual report said that Sheng Siong Group used cold chain management to store and handle its fresh produce since 2011, which kept the fresh and chilled food safe, fresh, long-lasting, and of good quality. The company also checked the quality of products and fresh produce by sending samples to an outside lab for tests on germs, chemicals, and pesticides. Moreover, the company made its house brands with its suppliers, which gave customers good choices at cheap prices. The company also kept a good relationship with its suppliers (Earls, 2021), choosing them based on how good, how much they sell, and how well they fit with Sheng Siong's values.

Sheng Siong Group had to keep up with the changing preferences and behaviours of consumers to stay relevant (*Harvard Business Review*, 2022). To do this, the company spent money on market research and analysis and updated its products to suit the changing consumer demands. A report by RHB Invest said that Sheng Siong Group did regular surveys with focus groups to find out what customers wanted and thought, and used data analytics to improve its product mix and pricing. The company also added new

DOI: 10.4324/9781032660547-21

products and categories, such as ready-to-eat meals, organic products, and health supplements, to meet the changing needs and lifestyles of its customers. Moreover, the company used its online platform, Sheng Siong Online, to give more convenience and choice to its customers, especially during the COVID-19 pandemic. The company's market research and analysis helped it to keep its market share and customer loyalty (Huang & O'Toole, 2020) in a very competitive industry.

Sheng Siong Group wanted to grow by opening more stores and reaching more places. To do this, the company chose good locations, made its stores nice and easy to use, and made its operations more efficient to make sure new stores made money and did well. Its annual report said that Sheng Siong Group opened three more stores in Singapore and one more store in China in FY2022, adding 40,000 square feet of space to sell things. The company also got two more places in Singapore that will start selling things in FY2023. The company picked places where it was not there before and where people wanted its products. The company also made its stores big, bright, and friendly and gave them new things like self-checkout counters and electronic shelf labels. Moreover, the company made its operations better by spending money on logistics and distribution (Banker, 2021), such as machines that store and move things, conveyor belts, and cold chain management. The company's efforts to open more stores have helped it to make more money and get more customers in both Singapore and China.

Through these efforts, Sheng Siong Group succeeded in establishing itself as a leading value-for-money grocery retailer in Singapore. The company has a strong reputation for quality and reliability and has expanded its business into other areas, such as e-commerce and wholesale distribution, to broaden its revenue base and drive growth. As a result, Sheng Siong Group is well-positioned to continue to succeed in the highly competitive grocery retail market in Singapore in the years ahead.

References

Banker, S. (2021). *Walmart's massive investment in a supply chain transformation* [Online]. Available at: www.forbes.com/sites/stevebanker/2021/04/23/walmarts-massive-investment-in-a-supply-chain-transformation/ (Accessed: 7 April 2023).

Earls, A.R. (2021). *8 key supplier relationship management strategies* [Online]. Available at: www.techtarget.com/searcherp/feature/8-key-supplier-relationship-management-strategies (Accessed: 7 April 2023).

Harvard Business Review (2022). *Keeping up with customers' increasingly dynamic needs* [Online]. Available at: https://hbr.org/2022/09/keeping-up-with-customers-increasingly-dynamic-needs (Accessed: 7 April 2023).

Huang, J., & O'Toole, T. (2020). Customer loyalty: the new generation. *Harvard Business Review*. Available at: https://hbr.org/2020/09/keeping-up-with-customers-increasingly-dynamic-needs

Pricefx (2021). *8 strategies to manage price fluctuations & supply chain problems* [Online]. Available at: www.pricefx.com/learning-center/8-strategies-to-manage-price-fluctuations/ (Accessed: 7 April 2023).

Sheng Siong (2023). *Sheng Siong Group delivers a stable net profit of S$133.6 million for FY2022* [Online]. Available at: https://corporate.shengsiong.com.sg/sheng-siong-group-delivers-a-stable-net-profit-of-s133-6-million-for-fy2022/ (Accessed: 7 April 2023).

3 Sustainability initiatives and outcomes of Mapletree Commercial Trust

Ian Jamieson

Director of Global Business Development, University of London, United Kingdom

Mapletree Commercial Trust (MCT) is a real estate investment trust (REIT) that is based in Singapore and focuses on commercial properties. MCT owns and manages a diversified portfolio of assets that includes office buildings, business parks, and retail malls across Singapore. MCT has also made sustainability a key priority in its operations and has implemented several initiatives to reduce its environmental footprint. MCT is committed to adopting green building standards and practices for its properties, such as obtaining green certifications, installing energy-efficient features, and promoting waste reduction and recycling. MCT also engages with its stakeholders, such as tenants, customers, employees, and community partners, to raise awareness and foster collaboration on sustainability issues. MCT believes that sustainability is not only a social responsibility but also a source of competitive advantage and long-term value creation for its business.

MCT faced the challenge of low stakeholder awareness and understanding of sustainability. It tackled this challenge by engaging its stakeholders in various sustainability activities (Shook et al., 2022). Stakeholder engagement is essential for sustainability (Sustenuto, n.d.), as it helps organisations to align with stakeholder expectations and needs, gain insights, build trust, foster collaboration, and create impact. MCT's stakeholder engagement programme improved its sustainability performance and value proposition, as well as its stakeholder relationships (National Center for Education Statistics, 2012).

Another challenge faced by MCT was to improve the energy efficiency of its buildings. Energy efficiency is an important aspect of sustainability, as it helps to reduce greenhouse gas emissions, lower operating costs, and enhance occupant comfort and productivity (IEA, 2020). To tackle this challenge, MCT implemented several energy-saving measures across its portfolio of properties, such as installing energy-efficient lighting and air conditioning systems that use less electricity and generate less heat, implementing building automation systems that monitor and control the energy usage of different building functions and adjust them according to occupancy and weather conditions, and upgrading the building envelope by replacing windows, doors, roofs, and walls to improve the thermal performance and insulation of the buildings.

DOI: 10.4324/9781032660547-22

These measures helped MCT to reduce its energy consumption and carbon footprint, as well as to achieve green certifications for its buildings (Ministry of Sustainability and the Environment, n.d.).

MCT also implemented waste reduction initiatives to minimise the amount of waste generated and disposed of by its properties. One of the initiatives was the adoption of a recycling programme that encouraged tenants and customers to segregate and recycle their waste, such as paper, plastic, metal, and glass. MCT also provided recycling bins and collection services in its retail malls to facilitate the recycling process. Another initiative was the installation of food waste digesters in its retail malls that converted food waste into water and organic fertiliser. This reduced the amount of food waste sent to landfills and incinerators, as well as the associated greenhouse gas emissions and disposal costs. In addition, MCT sourced materials from sustainable sources and adopted green building materials to reduce the environmental impact of its building operations. MCT ensured that the materials used for construction and renovation were certified by recognised green labels, such as the Singapore Green Building Product Certification Scheme and the Singapore Green Label Scheme. MCT also used materials that had low embodied energy and carbon, high recycled content, and low volatile organic compound emissions. These measures helped MCT to conserve natural resources, reduce waste generation, and improve indoor environmental quality. By implementing these waste reduction initiatives, MCT demonstrated its commitment to being a responsible and environmentally friendly organisation that cares about the well-being of its tenants, customers, and communities.

MCT's focus on sustainability has resulted in several accolades, including the Green Mark Platinum Award for its Mapletree Business City and the Building and Construction Authority Green Mark Gold Award for its VivoCity mall. These awards recognise MCT's commitment to sustainable practices and its efforts to reduce its environmental impact.

References

IEA (2020). *Energy efficiency 2020* [Online]. Available at: www.iea.org/reports/energy-efficiency-2020 (Accessed: 14 May 2023).

Ministry of Sustainability and the Environment (n.d.). *Energy* [Online]. Available at: www.mse.gov.sg/policies/energy (Accessed: 12 May 2023).

National Center for Education Statistics (2012). *Stakeholder engagement & sustainability* [Online]. Available at: https://nces.ed.gov/Programs/SLDS/pdf/Stakeholderengagement_Sustainability.pdf (Accessed: 4 May 2023).

Shook, E., Lacy, P., Suntook, C., & Rademacher, J. (2022). How stakeholder alignment on sustainability unlocks a competitive advantage. *World Economic Forum*. Available at: www.weforum.org/agenda/2022/02/how-to-strengthen-sustainability-by-engaging-with-stakeholders/.

Sustenuto (n.d.). *Stakeholder engagement is key to sustainable development* [Online]. Available at: https://sustenuto.com/insights/stakeholder-engagement-an-essential-part-of-sustainable-development/ (Accessed: 12 May 2023).

4 Fraser and Neave's diversification into food and beverage

Melvin Goh Kim Ho

Associate Dean, Amity Global Institute, Singapore

Fraser and Neave (F&N) is a Singapore-based conglomerate that started as a beverage company and later diversified into food and beverage. The food and beverage market is highly competitive, with many established players and new entrants vying for market share. To compete effectively, F&N had to differentiate itself through innovation and quality. The company responded by developing new products, improving existing products, and investing in marketing and advertising campaigns.

F&N was a newcomer in the food and beverage market and struggled to create a strong brand image and position itself as a high-quality brand. The company responded to this challenge by launching marketing and advertising campaigns that highlighted its quality and innovation. F&N adopted various strategies (Nawaz et al., 2020), such as introducing new and varied products, such as halal food, ice cream, and confectionery, using its existing brands and licenses to cater to different consumer needs and occasions, such as 100PLUS, F&N SEASONS, F&N MAGNOLIA, and SUNKIST, and connecting with consumers through digital platforms and social media, such as Facebook, Instagram, and YouTube. These strategies aimed to boost F&N's brand value, awareness (Sharma et al., 2018), and loyalty (Fetscherin et al., 2019) among consumers, especially teenagers who are a major target group for food and beverage marketers.

F&N overcame the challenge of managing the complex and demanding supply chain for food and beverage products by building strong relationships with suppliers and enforcing strict quality control standards across the supply chain. Effective food supply chain management (FSCM) brought F&N various benefits, such as waste reduction, food safety improvement, customer satisfaction enhancement, and profitability increase (Zhong et al., 2017). However, F&N also faced several challenges in FSCM, such as demand uncertainty, environmental sustainability, traceability, and transparency issues (Palazzo & Vollero, 2022). To cope with these challenges, F&N used data-driven IT systems to facilitate its FSCM, such as enterprise resource planning, radio frequency identification, and block chain technology. These systems helped F&N to make optimal decisions on inventory, transportation, and distribution, as

DOI: 10.4324/9781032660547-23

well as to track and monitor its products throughout the supply chain (Zhong et al., 2017).

To diversify into food and beverage, F&N had to acquire new skills and competencies beyond its core beverage business. The company achieved diversification by buying well-known food and beverage companies with strong brands and products that complemented its own, such as Yeo Hiap Seng and Nestle's Malaysian beverage business. The diversification strategy brought F&N several benefits in the food and beverage industry, such as improving competitive advantage, lowering business risk, expanding market share and profitability, and benefiting from synergies and economies of scale (Jallow, 2021; Oyewole et al., 2019). However, the diversification strategy also entailed some challenges, such as dealing with cultural differences, merging operations and systems, ensuring quality standards, and addressing regulatory and environmental issues (Palazzo & Vollero, 2022). Therefore, F&N followed a strategic approach to diversification, by choosing the target companies that aligned with its vision and values, performing due diligence and valuation analysis, agreeing on fair and reasonable terms, and executing effective post-acquisition integration plans (Jallow, 2021).

F&N adapted to the dynamic consumer preferences in food and beverage by investing in research and development and creating new products that met the changing tastes and dietary preferences. F&N considered various factors that influence consumer preferences, such as sensory attributes, health and nutrition claims, environmental and ethical concerns, social and cultural norms, convenience, and price (Sogari et al., 2019). F&N researched the needs and wants of its target segments, such as teenagers, health-conscious consumers, and ethnic minorities. F&N introduced new products with novel ingredients, flavours, and formats, such as plant-based beverages, functional drinks, and ready-to-eat meals. F&N also used innovative packaging and labelling to communicate the benefits and values of its products (Mughal et al., 2021).

Through these efforts, F&N succeeded in diversifying into food and beverage and becoming a leading player in the market. The company's focus on innovation, quality, and diversification has allowed it to remain competitive in a crowded market and establish itself as a premium brand. Today, F&N offers a range of food and beverage products that cater to a wide range of customer needs, from traditional beverages to packaged foods and snacks.

References

Fetscherin, M., Boulanger, M., Gonçalves Filho, C., & Quiroga Souki, G. (2019). How well do consumer-brand relationships drive customer brand loyalty? Generalizations from a meta-analysis of brand relationship elasticities. *Journal of Consumer Research, 46*(3), 435–459. https://doi.org/10.1093/jcr/ucz006

Jallow, A. (2021). A strategic case study on PepsiCo. *SSRN Electronic Journal*. https://doi.org/10.2139/ssrn.3828353

Mughal, A.J., Faisal, F., & Khokhar, M.N. (2021). Exploring consumer's perception and preferences towards purchase of non-certified organic food: a qualitative perspective. *Cogent Business & Management, 8*(1), 1984028. https://doi.org/10.1080/23311975.2021.1984028

Nawaz, S., Jiang, Y., Alam, F., & Nawaz, M.Z. (2020). Role of brand love and consumers' demographics in building consumer–brand relationship. *SAGE Open, 10*(4), 2158244020983005. https://doi.org/10.1177/2158244020983005

Oyewole, A., Adegbite, T., & Ogunnaike, O. (2019). Diversification strategy and profitability of selected food and beverage firms in Lagos State, Nigeria. *Journal of Strategic Management Studies, 4*(1), 1–13. https://stratfordjournals.org/journals/index.php/journal-of-strategic-management/article/view/1440

Palazzo, M., & Vollero, A. (2022). A systematic literature review of food sustainable supply chain management (FSSCM): building blocks and research trends. *The TQM Journal, 34*(7), 54–72. https://doi.org/10.1108/TQM-10-2021-0300

Sharma, P., Davcik, N.S., & Pillai, K.G. (2018). Promoting customer brand engagement and brand loyalty through customer brand identification and value congruity. *Spanish Journal of Marketing–ESIC, 22*(3), 362–379. https://doi.org/10.1108/SJME-06-2018-0030

Sogari, G., Brecchi, D., & Menozzi, D. (2019). Consumer behavior and food choice: a systematic review of sensory science methodologies applied in experimental studies. *Foods, 8*(12), 669. https://doi.org/10.3390/foods8120669

Zhong, R., Xu, X., & Wang, L. (2017). Food supply chain management: systems, implementations, and future research. *Industrial Management & Data Systems, 117*(9), 2085–2114. https://doi.org/10.1108/IMDS-09-2016-0391

5   CapitaLand's expansion into China

Lim Keai

Academic Director (Senior), Amity Global Institute, Singapore

CapitaLand has faced several challenges in its expansion into China, including regulatory hurdles, cultural differences, competition, economic uncertainty, and environmental regulations. Here are some examples of how CapitaLand has succeeded in overcoming these challenges:

Regulatory hurdles: One of the challenges that CapitaLand has faced in its expansion into China is the complex and evolving regulatory environment (Deloitte, 2021) that affects its real estate activities. However, CapitaLand has been able to overcome this challenge by building strong and long-term relationships with the local governments and authorities in China (S&P Global, 2022), and by securing the necessary approvals and permits (McKinsey Global Institute, 2021) for its real estate projects. For example, in 2017, CapitaLand's joint venture in China, Raffles City Chongqing, received the green light from the Chongqing Municipal Government to proceed with the development of the project, which is one of the largest integrated developments in China and features a unique horizontal skyscraper.

Cultural differences: By employing local professionals and collaborating with Chinese firms, CapitaLand has managed to overcome cultural differences. This has enabled CapitaLand to gain a deeper insight into the local market and customise its products to suit the needs (Shoham, 2015) of Chinese customers. China is a very diverse and complex country, with various regions, segments, and preferences that demand adjustment and localisation. Beijing, the capital and cultural hub of China, has a splendid legacy of traditional arts and crafts, such as Peking opera, calligraphy, and painting. CapitaLand has utilised its local knowledge and network to pursue special situation opportunities in Beijing and other cities, such as integrated developments, business parks, logistics, and data centres.

Competition: CapitaLand has been successful in differentiating itself in the highly competitive Chinese real estate market by offering unique value propositions. For example, CapitaLand's Ascott brand provides serviced residences that cater to the needs of business travellers and families, which has helped it stand out from other players in the market. China's real estate market is highly fragmented and dynamic, with many local and foreign competitors vying for

DOI: 10.4324/9781032660547-24

market share and customer loyalty. The market is also affected by various factors such as economic growth, policy changes, consumer preferences, and technological innovations (Liu & Liang, 2016). CapitaLand has leveraged its strong capabilities in asset management, fund management, and capital recycling to create value for its stakeholders and customers (CapitaLand Investment Limited, 2022). CapitaLand has also established various onshore and offshore funds to invest in special situation opportunities in China, such as integrated developments, business parks, logistics, and data centres (CapitaLand Investment Limited, 2023).

Economic uncertainty: CapitaLand diversified its portfolio and focused on long-term growth to cope with China's economic uncertainties (CNBC, 2022). For example, it invested in logistics and data centre projects, which are more resilient to economic fluctuations than other real estate sectors (Liu & Liang, 2016). China's economy faced various uncertainties, such as the trade war, the pandemic, the debt crisis, and the regulatory crackdown. These uncertainties challenged the real estate sector, which depended on demand, supply, prices, and financing conditions. CapitaLand is diversified across different asset classes, geographies, and tenants. It also increased its exposure to new economy assets, such as logistics and data centres, which had strong growth potential and stable cash flows in the digital era.

Environmental regulations: CapitaLand has complied with China's environmental regulations by applying sustainable design to its projects. For instance, its Raffles City Chongqing project has a "sky park" that lowers heat and enhances air quality. China has tough environmental standards and policies to reduce carbon emissions and foster green development. These regulations impact the real estate sector, which consumes much energy and resources. CapitaLand has adhered to environmental regulations and boosted its environmental performance. CapitaLand has adopted sustainable design principles in its projects, such as energy efficiency, water conservation, waste management, green materials, and biodiversity.

Overall, CapitaLand's success in China can be attributed to its ability to navigate regulatory hurdles, bridge cultural differences, differentiate itself in a competitive market, focus on long-term growth, and incorporate sustainable design principles into its projects.

References

CapitaLand Investment Limited (2022). *CLI establishes its first onshore RMB fund in China* [Online]. Available at: www.capitaland.com/en/about-capitaland/newsroom/news-releases/international/2022/jun/Capitaland-investment-establishes-first-onshore-rmb-fund-in-China.html (Accessed: 13 April 2023).

CapitaLand Investment Limited (2023). *CapitaLand Investment establishes CapitaLand China Opportunistic Partners Programme to invest in special situation opportunities in China* [Online]. Available at: www.capitaland.com/en/about-capitaland/newsroom/news-releases/international/2023/february/CLI_establishes_CL_China_Opportunistic_Partners_Programme_to_invest_in_special_situation_opportunities_in_China.html (Accessed: 13 April 2023).

CNBC (2022). *CapitaLand Investment says investments slowing amid economic red flags* [Online]. Available at: www.cnbc.com/2022/08/12/capitaland-investment-says-investments-slowing-amid-economic-red-flags.html (Accessed: 13 April 2023).

Deloitte (2021). *Behind the headlines: China's regulatory environment* [Online]. Available at: www2.deloitte.com/us/en/pages/consulting/articles/behind-the-headlines-china-regulatory-environment.html (Accessed: 13 April 2023).

Liu, H., & Liang, L. (2016). China's real estate industry: a decade in review and prospects for the future. *International Journal of Housing Markets and Analysis*. https://doi.org/10.1108/IJHMA-03-2015-0015

McKinsey Global Institute (2021). *The new challenges for MNCs in China landscape* [Online]. Available at: www.mckinsey.com/mgi/our-research/the-china-imperative-for-multinational-companies (Accessed: 13 April 2023).

S&P Global (2022). *Perspectives from China: the shifting regulatory landscape* [Online]. Available at: www.spglobal.com/marketintelligence/en/news-insights/blog/perspectives-from-china-the-shifting-regulatory-landscape (Accessed: 13 April 2023).

Shoham, A. (2015). The EPRG framework: does it affect managerial perceptions of export success? In: Manrai, A., Meadow, H. (eds.) *Global Perspectives in Marketing for the 21st Century. Developments in Marketing Science: Proceedings of the Academy of Marketing Science*. Springer. https://doi.org/10.1007/978-3-319-17356-6_112

6 Hutchison Port Holdings' expansion into new markets

Cheryl Yu

Interim Director of International Partnerships, London College of Fashion, University of the Arts London, United Kingdom

As a leading port operator and developer, Hutchison Port Holdings (HPH) had a strong presence in many regions around the world. However, when HPH tried to enter new markets, it encountered various difficulties and obstacles. Some of these challenges included adapting to different cultures and regulations, competing with local rivals, and managing complex logistics and operations. HPH had to overcome these challenges to establish itself as a successful and reliable port operator in new markets.

One of the biggest challenges for HPH when expanding into new markets was navigating complex regulatory environments. To address this challenge, the company invested in local partnerships and established strong relationships with regulatory authorities to ensure compliance with local laws and regulations. This strategy was crucial for HPH to avoid or mitigate the potential negative consequences of innovation, such as market disruption, consumer protection issues, environmental impacts, and ethical dilemmas (OECD, 2020). Moreover, by engaging with regulators and policymakers, HPH was able to influence the design of governance and regulatory approaches that supported its business objectives and innovation potential (PwC, n.d.). However, HPH also faced the risk of regulatory uncertainty and inconsistency across different jurisdictions, which could affect its operational efficiency and competitiveness (KPMG, 2021). Therefore, HPH had to monitor and adapt to the changing regulatory landscape and adopt a proactive and flexible approach to managing regulatory risk.

Port development entails substantial infrastructure investment, encompassing the construction of terminals, berths, and related facilities. To address this challenge, HPH invested considerably in infrastructure and established partnerships with local governments and private investors to share the costs and risks of port development. This approach enabled HPH to operate market-leading, best-in-class, and deep-water container terminals in the Pearl River Delta of South China. HPH also expanded its inland port portfolio to enlarge its catchment area and provide customers with efficient and green logistics solutions (HPH, 2023). Furthermore, by collaborating with local governments and private investors, HPH was able to participate in

DOI: 10.4324/9781032660547-25

public-private partnership (PPP) projects that offered attractive returns and long-term concessions (Ng, 2022). However, HPH also faced the challenge of managing complex contractual arrangements and ensuring the alignment of interests among multiple stakeholders (HPH, 2022). Therefore, HPH had to adopt a rigorous governance framework and a transparent communication strategy to ensure the success of its infrastructure investment.

The port industry is very competitive, with many big companies fighting for business. HPH tried to win by offering good services, fair prices, and great customer service. The port industry is also changing a lot with new technologies that make things faster and better. HPH spent money and work on finding and using new technologies to improve its work and services (McKinsey & Company, 2017). For example, HPH used machines to move containers, smart systems to run terminals, and online platforms to connect with customers. HPH also used green technologies to protect the environment and reduce pollution. HPH also made new products and services that were different from its competitors and got more customers. But HPH still had to deal with the fast changes in technology and make sure its systems were safe and reliable (ABB, 2019). So HPH had to keep learning and improving and follow strong rules to make its technology investment work.

Through these efforts, HPH succeeded in expanding its business into new markets and establishing itself as a leading port operator and developer. The company has a strong reputation for quality and reliability and has diversified its business into other areas, such as logistics and real estate, to broaden its revenue base and drive growth. As a result, HPH is well-positioned to continue to succeed in the highly competitive port industry in the years ahead.

References

ABB (2019). *Smart port, smart nation: Singapore builds on spectrum of strengths* [Online]. Available at: https://new.abb.com/news/detail/78949/smart-port-smart-nation-singapore-builds-on-spectrum-of-strengths (Accessed: 3 April 2023).

HPH Trust (2022). *Annual report 2022* [Online]. Available at: www.hphtrust.com/annual_report.html (Accessed: 3 April 2023).

HPH Trust (2023). *HPH Trust* [Online]. Available at: www.hphtrust.com/ (Accessed: 3 April 2023).

KPMG (2021). *Ten key regulatory challenges of 2022* [Online]. Available at: https://advisory.kpmg.us/articles/2021/ten-key-financial-services-regulatory-challenges-2022.html (Accessed: 3 April 2023).

McKinsey & Company (2017). *The future of port automation* [Online]. Available at: www.mckinsey.com/industries/travel-logistics-and-infrastructure/our-insights/the-future-of-automated-ports (Accessed: 3 April 2023).

Ng, K.S. (2022). *Public-private partnerships: balancing project opportunities and risk* [Online]. Available at: www.infrastructureasia.org/en/Insights/Public-Private-Partnerships (Accessed: 3 April 2023).

OECD (2020). *Case Studies on the Regulatory Challenges Raised by Innovation and the Regulatory Responses.* OECD Publishing. https://doi.org/10.1787/70df2cab-en.

PwC (n.d.). *Risk and regulatory challenges for health industries* [Online]. Available at: www.pwc.com/us/en/industries/health-services/navigate-risk-and-regulatory-complexity.html (Accessed: 3 April 2023).

7 Mapletree Investments' diversification into logistics and data centres

Nishad Nawaz

Associate Professor, Kingdom University, Kingdom of Bahrain

Mapletree Investments is a Singapore-based real estate company that has ventured into logistics and data centres. It started as a subsidiary of Temasek Holdings, a state-owned investment company, in 2000. Since then, it has expanded its global presence with a range of assets in Asia Pacific, Europe, and the United States. Some of the challenges that Mapletree overcame and how they achieved success are:

Regulatory environment: Mapletree faced complex regulatory environments when it diversified into logistics and data centres. The company tackled this challenge by partnering with local firms and building strong ties with regulators to comply with local laws and regulations. For instance, in China, Mapletree joined forces with local partners to buy and develop logistics properties and also got the required approvals from the Ministry of Commerce and the State Administration of Foreign Exchange (Wang & Li, 2016). In the United States, Mapletree bought 29 data centres from Sila Realty Trust, a real estate investment trust (REIT) that focuses on data centre properties (Forbes Asia, 2021). By buying the properties through a REIT structure, Mapletree avoided corporate income tax on the rental income from the data centres (Chaney et al., 2019).

Technological innovation: Mapletree had to keep up with technological innovation in the logistics and data centre industries. This meant investing a lot in research and development and working with technology companies to create and apply cutting-edge solutions. For instance, in Singapore, Mapletree teamed up with NTT Communications Corporation, a global leader in information and communications technology solutions, to build a high-performance data centre with advanced security systems, energy-efficient cooling technologies, and smart building management systems (Mapletree, 2019). In China, Mapletree joined forces with Cainiao Smart Logistics Network, Alibaba Group's logistics arm, to construct a modern logistics park that uses artificial intelligence, big data, and cloud computing to improve operational efficiency and customer service (Mapletree, 2020a). In Japan, Mapletree bought a stake in a logistics facility that uses automated storage and retrieval systems,

DOI: 10.4324/9781032660547-26

robotics, and the Internet of Things to make the best use of space and inventory management (Mapletree, 2021).

Competition: The logistics and data centre industries are very competitive, with many big players competing for market share. Mapletree tried to stand out by offering high-quality services, fair pricing, and great customer service. For instance, in Singapore, Mapletree offered tailored solutions for its tenants, such as flexible lease terms, extra services, and integrated facilities management (Tan et al., 2017). In the United States, Mapletree used its strong tie with NTT Communications Corporation, a global leader in information and communications technology solutions, to get long-term leases for its data centres (Forbes Asia, 2021). In Europe, Mapletree improved the quality and efficiency of its data centres by upgrading the power supply, cooling systems, and security features (Mapletree, 2020b).

Infrastructure investment: Mapletree had to invest a lot in infrastructure to build and run logistics and data centre facilities like many real estate companies. The company tackled this challenge by investing a lot in infrastructure and partnering with local governments and private investors to split the costs and risks of development. For instance, in Vietnam, Mapletree built a big integrated logistics park with help from the local authorities, who gave land clearance, tax incentives, and infrastructure improvements. In Australia, Mapletree bought a portfolio of logistics properties from Propertylink Group, an Australian real estate investment trust, with co-investment from a group of institutional investors. In Japan, Mapletree got a long-term loan from the Japan Bank for International Cooperation, a state-owned financial institution, to fund the development of a data centre in Osaka.

Through these efforts, Mapletree succeeded in diversifying its business into logistics and data centres and has established itself as a leading provider of real estate services in these areas. The company has won numerous awards for its logistics and data centre offerings and has expanded its business into other areas, such as student housing and senior living, to broaden its revenue base and drive growth. As a result, Mapletree is well-positioned to continue to succeed in the highly competitive real estate industry in the years ahead.

References

Chaney, P.K., Erickson, M., & Wang, W. (2019). Tax avoidance and real estate investment trusts: An agency perspective. *Journal of Accounting and Economics, 67*(2–3), 535–557. https://doi.org/10.1016/j.jacceco.2018.12.005

Forbes Asia (2021). *Singapore's Mapletree industrial to buy U.S. data centers for $1.3 billion* [Online]. Available at: www.forbes.com/sites/jonathanburgos/2021/05/21/singapores-mapletree-industrial-to-buy-us-data-centers-for-13-billion/ (Accessed: 23 April 2023).

Mapletree (2019). *Mapletree partners NTT Communications Corporation to develop its first data centre in Singapore* [Online]. Available at: www.mapletree.com.sg/en/Newsroom/Press-Releases/2019/November/Mapletree-partners-NTT-Communications-Corporation-to-develop-its-first-data-centre-in-Singapore (Accessed: 23 April 2023).

Mapletree (2020a). *Mapletree signs agreement with Cainiao Smart Logistics Network to lease 200,000 sqm of warehouse space in China* [Online]. Available at: www.mapletree. com.sg/en/Newsroom/Press-Releases/2020/August/Mapletree-signs-agreem ent-with-Cainiao-Smart-Logistics-Network-to-lease-200000-sqm-of-warehouse-space-in-China (Accessed: 23 April 2023).

Mapletree (2020b). *Annual report 2019/2020* [Online]. Available at: www.maplet ree.com.sg/en/MLT/Investor-Relations/Financial-Information/Annual-Reports (Accessed: 23 April 2023).

Mapletree (2021). *Mapletree acquires a 98.47% stake in a freehold logistics facility in Greater Tokyo for JPY37 billion* [Online]. Available at: www.mapletree.com.sg/en/Newsroom/Press-Releases/2021/May/Mapletree-acquires-a-9847-stake-in-a-freehold-logistics-facility-in-Greater-Tokyo-for-JPY37-billion (Accessed: 23 April 2023).

Tan, G.W.-H., Lee, V.H., Lin, B., & Ooi, K.-B. (2017). Mobile applications in tourism: The future of the tourism industry? *Industrial Management & Data Systems, 117*(3), 560–581. https://doi.org/10.1108/IMDS-12-2015-0490

Wang, Y., & Li, L.H. (2016). The development of modern logistics industry and urbanization: a case study of China. *Habitat International, 53,* 274–283. https://doi.org/10.1016/j.habitatint.2015.11.036

8 Ascendas-Singbridge's diversification into logistics and industrial real estate

George Kapaya

Deputy Head – Accounting and Finance, Faculty of Business and Law University of Northampton, United Kingdom

Ascendas-Singbridge is a leading developer and operator of sustainable urban and business space solutions in Asia. The company has diversified into logistics and industrial real estate to capture the growing demand for high-quality logistics and industrial properties in the region. This means that Ascendas-Singbridge not only creates and manages eco-friendly and innovative spaces for living, working, and leisure but also provides integrated solutions for warehousing, manufacturing, and distribution activities. By expanding its portfolio of logistics and industrial properties, Ascendas-Singbridge aims to meet the needs of its customers and partners in various sectors, such as e-commerce, consumer goods, pharmaceuticals, and technology. Ascendas-Singbridge is committed to delivering excellence and value to its stakeholders through its expertise and experience in developing and operating sustainable urban and business spaces in Asia. Some of the challenges that Ascendas-Singbridge faced during this diversification process include:

Land and property acquisition: A major challenge for Ascendas-Singbridge was to find and buy land and properties in desirable locations. This was especially difficult in markets where land was limited or sought-after. The company had to locate and negotiate with landowners to purchase the land. For instance, in 2019, Ascendas-Singbridge bought Ascendas Pte Ltd and Singbridge Pte Ltd from Temasek Holdings for S$11 billion, which expanded its portfolio of assets in different sectors and regions (*The Straits Times*, 2019; *The Business Times*, 2019). This was one of the biggest deals in Asia's real estate sector and a key milestone for Ascendas-Singbridge's growth plan (Financial Horse, 2019). However, such deals also required complicated legal and financial procedures, as well as integration efforts with the existing business units (CapitaLand, 2019).

Regulatory compliance: Ascendas-Singbridge had to deal with different regulatory requirements in the various countries where it operates. The company had to understand and follow the local laws and regulations in each market it entered. For example, the company had to meet different environmental, social, and governance (ESG) standards and reporting frameworks in Singapore, China, India, Australia, and other countries where it owns properties

DOI: 10.4324/9781032660547-27

(CapitaLand Ascendas REIT, 2020). The company also had to obey the rules and regulations of the Singapore Exchange Securities Trading Limited (SGX-ST) and the Monetary Authority of Singapore (MAS) as a sponsor of three real estate investment trusts (REITs) listed on SGX-ST. In addition, the company faced regulatory hurdles when it was bought by CapitaLand Limited in 2019, which needed approvals from various authorities and shareholders (*The Straits Times*, 2019). The acquisition also required harmonising the operational and governance processes of both entities to ensure a smooth integration (CapitaLand Ascendas REIT, 2019).

Managing risks: Ascendas-Singbridge invested a lot of money in logistics and industrial real estate. The company had to handle the risks related to these investments, such as changes in property prices, market situations, and regulations. For instance, the company had to deal with the effect of the COVID-19 pandemic on its properties in different countries and sectors, which reduced its occupancy rates, rental income, and valuation. The company also had to watch out for and prevent the risks of fraud, corruption, and bribery in its operations, especially in developing markets where it operates. The company also had to face the risks of ESG issues, such as climate change, health and safety, and stakeholder engagement, which could harm its reputation and performance. In addition, the company had to handle the risks of integration and alignment with CapitaLand Limited, which bought it in 2019, which required harmonising the operational and governance processes, systems, and culture of both entities.

Despite these challenges, Ascendas-Singbridge has succeeded in its diversification into logistics and industrial real estate by leveraging its expertise in real estate development and management. The company has a strong track record of delivering high-quality properties that meet the needs of its tenants. It has also established strong partnerships with logistics and industrial companies to provide integrated solutions that meet their specific requirements. In addition, Ascendas-Singbridge has adopted sustainable practices in its developments, which have helped to differentiate it from its competitors and appeal to environmentally conscious tenants.

References

CapitaLand (2019). *CapitaLand and Ascendas-Singbridge complete transaction to form one of Asia's largest diversified real estate groups* [Online]. Available at: www.capitaland.com/en/about-capitaland/newsroom/news-releases/international/2019/jun/capitaland-asb-complete-transaction-to-form-unified-group.html (Accessed: 2 April 2023).
CapitaLand and Ascendas REIT (2019). *Singbridge complete transaction to form one of Asia's largest diversified real estate groups* [Online]. Available at: www.capitaland.com/en/about-capitaland/newsroom/news-releases/international/2019/jun/capitaland-asb-complete-transaction-to-form-unified-group.html (Accessed: 2 April 2023).

CapitaLand and Ascendas REIT (2020). *Sustainability* [Online]. Available at: https://investor.capitaland-ascendasreit.com/sustainability.html (Accessed: 2 April 2023).

Financial Horse (2019). *5 quick thoughts on CapitaLand's S$11.3 billion acquisition of Ascendas Singbridge* [Online]. Available at: https://financialhorse.com/capitaland-ascendas-singbridge/ (Accessed: 2 April 2023).

The Business Times (2019). *CapitaLand's acquisition of Ascendas-Singbridge completed* [Online]. Available at: www.businesstimes.com.sg/companies-markets/capitalands-acquisition-of-ascendas-singbridge-completed (Accessed: 2 April 2023).

The Straits Times (2019). *CapitaLand completes $11b acquisition of Ascendas-Singbridge, to operate as unified entity* [Online]. Available at: www.straitstimes.com/business/companies-markets/capitaland-completes-11b-acquisition-of-ascendas-singbridge-from-temasek (Accessed: 2 April 2023).

9 ARA Asset Management's diversification into real estate funds

Desti Kannaiah
Associate Lecturer, Newcastle University, Singapore

ARA Asset Management is a top real estate firm in Singapore that helps its clients invest and manage properties, such as private and public funds, real estate investment trusts (REITs), and property management. The company has overcome many difficulties while expanding into real estate funds, like rules, risks, and rivals. They have done well by using a smart plan and their skills in the industry. They have looked for good deals in various markets and areas, made solid connections with investors and partners, and increased the worth of their properties by managing them well and being creative.

One of the challenges that ARA Asset Management faced was to create a diversified portfolio of real estate assets that could generate stable returns for investors. The company responded by focusing on both income-generating and growth assets across different asset classes, including retail, office, industrial, hospitality, and residential properties. This enabled them to offer a broad range of investment options for investors and mitigate risks through diversification. According to Chen et al. (2019), diversification is an important strategy for real estate fund managers to reduce portfolio volatility and enhance performance. ARA Asset Management has diversified its portfolio not only by asset class but also by geography and sector. The company has invested in various markets across Asia Pacific, Europe, and the United States, and has exposure to different sectors such as logistics, data centres, infrastructure, and credit. By doing so, ARA Asset Management has been able to capture the growth opportunities in the new economy and provide resilient returns for its investors (Tan, 2021).

ARA Asset Management wanted to create a varied portfolio of real estate assets that could give steady returns to investors. The company did this by focusing on both assets that generate income and assets that grow in value across different types of properties, such as retail, office, industrial, hospitality, and residential. This allowed them to offer many investment choices for investors and lower risks by diversifying. Chen et al. (2019) said that diversifying is a key strategy for real estate fund managers to make their portfolios less volatile and more profitable. ARA Asset Management has varied its portfolio not just by type of property but also by location and sector. The company has

DOI: 10.4324/9781032660547-28

invested in different markets in Asia Pacific, Europe, and the United States, and has invested in different sectors like logistics, data centres, infrastructure, and credit. By doing this, ARA Asset Management has taken advantage of the growth opportunities in the new economy and had given strong returns to its investors (Tan, 2021).

ARA Asset Management aimed to build a strong distribution network for their real estate funds. They worked with financial institutions and other channels to reach more investors. They also used their relationships with institutional investors to get capital for their funds. Lee and Lee (2018) said that distribution channels are important for real estate fund managers to access different investors and markets, and to improve their reputation and trust. ARA Asset Management made partnerships with different financial institutions to sell their real estate funds to retail and wealthy investors (ARA Asset Management Limited, 2021). They also kept ties with institutional investors to get capital for their private funds and REITs. This helped ARA Asset Management create a varied and loyal investor base for their real estate funds.

Overall, ARA Asset Management's success in diversifying into real estate funds can be attributed to its strategic approach, extensive experience and knowledge in the industry, and strong partnerships and distribution networks. By addressing the challenges they faced and leveraging their strengths, the company was able to build a strong portfolio of real estate assets and deliver value to investors.

References

ARA Asset Management Limited (2021). *FY2021 audited financials* [Online]. Available at: https://links.sgx.com/FileOpen/ARA%20Asset%20Management%20Limited%20-%20Audited%20Financials%20FY2021_Final.ashx?App=Announcement&FileID=711098 (Accessed: 10 March 2023).

Chen, J., Hoesli, M., & Oikarinen, E. (2019). Diversification benefits of REIT preferred and common stock: new evidence from a utility-based framework. *Journal of Real Estate Finance and Economics, 58*(4), 633–655.

Lee, S., & Lee, C. (2018). Distribution channel strategies for real estate investment trusts. *Journal of Property Investment & Finance, 36*(4), 367–381.

Tan, J. (2021, August 5). *ESR to buy Singapore-based ARA for $7b, creating Asia's biggest real estate fund manager* [Online]. Available at: www.straitstimes.com/business/property/hong-kongs-esr-to-buy-real-estate-fund-manager-ara-asset-for-7-billion (Accessed: 10 March 2023).

10 Charles & Keith's adaptation to the rise of e-commerce and the emergence of new digital platforms

Krishnamoorthy Renganathan
Director, Wise Consulting, Singapore

Charles & Keith, a Singapore-based fashion brand that specialises in women's footwear and accessories, faced significant challenges due to the rise of e-commerce and the emergence of new digital platforms. However, the company was able to adapt and succeed by implementing several key strategies. These strategies included creating a unique and compelling brand identity, investing in omnichannel retail, adopting new technology and digital platforms, and being agile and responsive to changing market conditions. By applying these strategies, Charles & Keith was able to differentiate itself from other fast-fashion retailers and expand its customer base and global presence.

One of the primary strategies that Charles & Keith used to succeed in the face of e-commerce competition was to focus on creating a unique and compelling brand identity. The company invested heavily in creating a strong visual aesthetic and in building a loyal community of customers who identified with the brand's values and style. According to Roll (2019), a global business and brand strategist, Charles & Keith was able to differentiate itself from other fast-fashion retailers by offering "relevant fashion designs available at affordable and accessible price points." The brand also leveraged its Asian roots and global reach to appeal to modern Asian women who were looking for fashionable products that suited their lifestyles and preferences.

Another key strategy that helped Charles & Keith succeed was its investment in omnichannel retail. The company recognised that customers were increasingly shopping across multiple channels, including online, in-store, and via mobile devices. To address this trend, Charles & Keith worked to create a seamless and integrated shopping experience across all channels, allowing customers to browse and purchase products in whatever way was most convenient for them (Asmare & Zewdie, 2022). The brand was also one of the pioneers in launching an e-commerce store in Singapore in 2004 when e-commerce was still new. By offering online shopping options, Charles & Keith was able to expand its customer base and reach new markets as highlighted in Rangaswamy et al. (2022).

In addition to its omnichannel strategy, Charles & Keith also invested in new technology and digital platforms to improve the customer experience.

DOI: 10.4324/9781032660547-29

For example, the company implemented virtual try-on technology, which allowed customers to see how shoes would look on their feet before making a purchase. Charles & Keith also invested in personalisation technology, which allowed the company to offer tailored product recommendations and personalised promotions to individual customers (ReferralCandy, 2016). These innovations helped the brand to enhance customer satisfaction and loyalty. Furthermore, the company also capitalised on social media platforms such as Instagram, Facebook, and YouTube to engage with its customers and showcase its products and brand stories. The company also collaborated with celebrities and influencers to promote its products and increase its brand visibility and credibility. The company's use of technology and digital platforms enabled it to create a more interactive and immersive customer experience and to reach a wider and more diverse audience.

Finally, Charles & Keith was able to succeed in the face of e-commerce competition by being agile and responsive to changing market conditions. The company constantly monitored trends and customer feedback and was willing to make changes to its product offerings, marketing strategies, and other key aspects of its business to stay ahead of the competition (Chai, 2022). The brand also strategically planned and rapidly executed its global expansion strategy, opening stores in prominent fashion cities such as Seoul, Shanghai, Dubai, Paris, London, and more (Charles & Keith SG, 2021). By doing so, the brand was able to increase its brand awareness and recognition, tap into new markets and customer segments, and leverage the cultural diversity and fashion influence of these cities. The brand's global expansion strategy also demonstrated its ambition and confidence to compete with other international fashion brands.

Charles & Keith achieved success in the e-commerce era by applying various strategies. The company created a unique and appealing brand identity for modern Asian women, invested in omnichannel retail to reach more customers, adopted new technology and digital platforms to improve customer experience and satisfaction, and stayed agile and responsive to market changes. These strategies helped Charles & Keith overcome e-commerce challenges and become a global fashion brand.

References

Asmare, A., & Zewdie, S. (2022). Omnichannel retailing strategy: a systematic review. *The International Review of Retail, Distribution and Consumer Research, 32*(1), 59–79. https://doi.org/10.1080/09593969.2021.2024447.

Chai, A. (2022). The rise and rise of Charles & Keith: from humble shoe store to S'pore's most successful fashion export. *The Straits Times* [Online]. Available at: www.straitstimes.com/life/style/the-rise-and-rise-of-charles-keith-a-case-study-of-singapores-most-successful-fashion-export (Accessed: 15 May 2023).

Charles & Keith SG (2021). *Brand profile | About us* [Online]. Available at: www.charleskeith.com/sg/information/about-us/brand-profile.html (Accessed: 15 May 2023).

Rangaswamy, E., Nawaz, N., & Changzhuang, Z. (2022). The impact of digital technology on changing consumer behaviors with special reference to the home furnishing sector in Singapore. *Humanities and Social Sciences Communications*, *9*(1), Article 83. DOI: 10.1057/s41599-022-01102-x

ReferralCandy (2016). *4 ways Charles & Keith became an internationally known brand* [Online]. Available at: www.referralcandy.com/blog/charles-and-keith-marketing-strategy/ (Accessed: 15 May 2023).

Roll, M. (2019). *Charles & Keith – a truly successful Asian global fast fashion retail brand* [Online]. Available at: https://martinroll.com/resources/articles/asia/charles-keith-a-truly-successful-asian-global-fast-fashion-retail-brand/ (Accessed: 15 May 2023).

11 ComfortDelGro's expansion into new markets through partnerships and acquisitions

Katalin Illes

Associate Head of College – External Relations at the University of Westminster, United Kingdom

ComfortDelGro is a transportation company based in Singapore that has encountered various difficulties and obstacles in its efforts to enter and grow in new markets through forming partnerships and making acquisitions. In this article, we will discuss some of the challenges that ComfortDelGro had to overcome and the strategies that it adopted to achieve success in its expansion plans.

Cultural differences: A major challenge that ComfortDelGro encountered in its expansion into new markets was the cultural differences that existed between different regions and countries. Cultural differences can have an impact on various aspects of business operations, such as customer preferences, communication styles, and management practices (Hofstede et al., 2010). To overcome this challenge, the company invested in building local partnerships and hiring local talent with experience and knowledge of the local market. For instance, in China, ComfortDelGro partnered with local taxi operators and bus companies to leverage their networks and expertise in the Chinese market (ComfortDelGro, 2019). In Australia, ComfortDelGro hired local managers and drivers who understood the local culture and regulations in the Australian market (ComfortDelGro, 2020). By doing so, ComfortDelGro was able to adapt to the different cultural contexts and expectations of its customers and stakeholders in the new markets.

Regulatory environment: A significant challenge that ComfortDelGro faced in its expansion into new markets was the different regulatory environments that existed in different countries and regions. Regulatory environments can have an impact on various aspects of business operations, such as licensing requirements, taxation policies, and environmental standards (Peng et al., 2017). ComfortDelGro addressed this challenge by working closely with local regulators and stakeholders to ensure compliance with local regulations and laws. For instance, in the United Kingdom, ComfortDelGro obtained the necessary licenses and permits to operate bus and rail services in various cities, such as London, Liverpool, and Sheffield (ComfortDelGro, 2019). In Singapore, ComfortDelGro participated in competitive tenders to secure bus contracts under the new bus contracting model, which gave the

DOI: 10.4324/9781032660547-30

company more flexibility and incentives to improve service quality and effi-ciency (ComfortDelGro, 2019). By doing so, ComfortDelGro was able to adapt to the different regulatory contexts and expectations of its customers and stakeholders in the new markets.

Integration of acquisitions. Another challenge that ComfortDelGro faced was the integration of acquisitions into its existing business. Integration of acquisitions can involve various challenges, such as aligning strategies, cultures, and systems; managing human resources; and achieving synergies (Haspeslagh & Jemison, 1991). ComfortDelGro addressed this challenge by implementing a rigorous due diligence process to assess potential acquisition targets and developed a comprehensive integration plan to ensure a smooth transition. For example, in 2017, ComfortDelGro acquired a majority stake in Uber's car rental subsidiary Lion City Holdings (LCH), which was later rebranded as ComfortDelGro Rent-A-Car (CDGRC) (ComfortDelGro, 2018). ComfortDelGro conducted thorough due diligence on LCH's assets, liabil-ities, and operations before finalising the deal. ComfortDelGro also developed an integration plan that involved transferring LCH's drivers to CDGRC's plat-form, streamlining LCH's fleet management system with CDGRC's system, and enhancing LCH's customer service standards (ComfortDelGro, 2018). Through this integration process, ComfortDelGro was able to leverage the strengths of both companies and create value for its customers and shareholders.

Financial risks. Expanding into new markets through partnerships and acquisitions can also pose financial risks, including currency risks, funding risks, and liquidity risks. Currency risks refer to the potential losses or gains arising from fluctuations in exchange rates. Funding risks refer to the potential difficul-ties or costs of obtaining financing for business expansion. Liquidity risks refer to the potential inability or difficulty of converting assets into cash or meeting financial obligations (Madura & Fox, 2011). ComfortDelGro addressed this challenge by implementing a robust risk management framework to iden-tify, assess, and manage financial risks. For example, ComfortDelGro hedged its currency exposure by using forward contracts and natural hedges, which are transactions that offset the currency risk of another transaction (Madura & Fox, 2011). ComfortDelGro diversified its sources of funding by using a mix of debt and equity financing from various financial institutions, such as banks, bond markets, and shareholders. ComfortDelGro maintained a healthy cash flow by optimising its working capital management and capital expend-iture planning, which involved managing its current assets and liabilities and planning its long-term investments (ComfortDelGro, 2019).

As a result of these efforts, ComfortDelGro has managed to achieve success in entering and growing in new markets through forming partnerships and making acquisitions. The company has built a strong foothold in markets such as Australia, the United Kingdom, and China, where it operates various transport services and businesses. ComfortDelGro also continues to explore new possibilities for further growth and expansion in other regions and coun-tries. The key factors that have contributed to ComfortDelGro's success are its emphasis on developing strong partnerships with local players, its investment in local talent and knowledge to understand and serve the local markets, and its adherence to compliance and risk management standards to ensure smooth and sustainable operations.

References

ComfortDelGro (2018). *Annual report 2017: moving ahead together* [Online]. Available at: www.comfortdelgro.com/documents/20143/0/CDG+AR+2017.pdf (Accessed: 18 May 2023).

ComfortDelGro (2019). *Annual report 2018: driving change for tomorrow* [Online]. Available at: www.comfortdelgro.com/documents/20143/0/CDG+AR+2018.pdf (Accessed: 18 May 2023).

ComfortDelGro (2020). *Annual report 2019: driving change for tomorrow* [Online]. Available at: www.comfortdelgro.com/documents/20143/0/CDG+AR+2019.pdf (Accessed: 18 May 2023).

Haspeslagh, P.C., & Jemison, D.B. (1991). *Managing Acquisitions: Creating Value through Corporate Renewal.* New York, NY: Free Press.

Hofstede, G., Hofstede, G.J., & Minkov, M. (2010). *Cultures and Organizations: Software of the Mind* (3rd edn.). New York, NY: McGraw-Hill.

Madura, J., & Fox, R. (2011). *International Financial Management* (2nd edn.). Andover, UK: Cengage Learning.

Peng, M.W., Wang, D.Y., & Jiang, Y. (2017). An institution-based view of international business strategy: a focus on emerging economies. *Journal of International Business Studies, 39*(5), 920–936. https://doi.org/10.1057/palgrave.jibs.8400377

12 How Fullerton Health expanded its network of clinics across Asia

Gemini V. Joy

Associate Professor, VIT Business School, VIT University, India

Fullerton Health is a Singapore-based healthcare provider that operates a network of clinics across Asia. The company was founded in 2010 and has since grown rapidly, expanding its presence to more than 500 healthcare facilities in 9 countries. Here are some of the challenges and opportunities Fullerton Health faced during its expansion, as well as how it succeeded:

Challenges

Regulatory hurdles: One of the biggest challenges Fullerton Health faced was navigating the complex regulatory landscape in each of the countries it operates in. Healthcare regulations and laws vary widely across different jurisdictions, and complying with them can be a significant barrier to entry for new players in the industry (Chen et al., 2019). Of course, there are new opportunities and market needs in the area of eldercare due to ageing population (Rangaswamy et al., 2021). Fullerton Health had to understand and adhere to the different regulatory requirements and standards in each market, such as licensing, accreditation, quality assurance, data protection, and taxation.

Talent acquisition: Healthcare is a people-intensive industry, and recruiting and retaining skilled medical professionals is essential to delivering quality care. Fullerton Health had to compete with other established players to attract top talent, particularly in markets where there is a shortage of medical professionals (Tan et al., 2019). Fullerton Health had to offer competitive compensation and benefits, provide training and development opportunities, and foster a positive work culture and environment.

Funding and investment: Building and scaling a network of clinics requires significant investment, and securing funding can be challenging, especially for a new player in the industry. Fullerton Health had to raise funds from investors and financial institutions to finance its growth, which required a convincing business plan and a strong track record (Fullerton Health Group, 2021). Fullerton Health had to balance its capital structure, manage its debt obligations, and ensure its profitability and sustainability.

DOI: 10.4324/9781032660547-31

Successes

Rapid expansion: Fullerton Health has grown rapidly since its inception, expanding its network of clinics across Asia and establishing a strong presence in key markets. The company's aggressive expansion strategy has helped it capture a significant share of the growing healthcare market in Asia. The company has also leveraged its expertise and experience in Singapore to enter new markets such as Vietnam, Cambodia, Laos, China, Hong Kong SAR, and Papua New Guinea (PR Newswire, 2021). By expanding its geographical footprint and market coverage, the company has increased its economies of scale and scope and enhanced its competitive advantage.

Diversification of services: Fullerton Health has diversified its service offerings beyond primary care to include speciality care, diagnostics, digital health solutions, insurance services, occupational health services, and corporate health management. This diversification has helped the company capture a broader range of healthcare needs and positioned it for long-term growth (Fullerton Health Group, 2021). The company has also developed innovative solutions such as telemedicine, online appointment booking, electronic medical records, and health analytics. Machine learning tools are to be used even to address and analyse issues like ageing population (Periyasamy et al., 2023). These solutions have enabled the company to improve the quality and efficiency of healthcare delivery and to meet the evolving needs and preferences of patients.

Strong partnerships: Fullerton Health has formed strategic partnerships with hospitals, insurance companies, employers, government agencies, and other healthcare providers, which has helped it expand its network and provide more comprehensive healthcare solutions to patients (Fullerton Health Group, 2021). These partnerships have also helped the company position itself as a key player in the healthcare ecosystem in Asia. For example, the company partnered with Ping An Good Doctor in China to provide online consultation services to more than 300 million users. The company also partnered with WeDoctor in Singapore to create a health management platform that integrates online and offline healthcare services in the region.

In summary, Fullerton Health faced significant challenges in navigating the complex regulatory landscape, recruiting and retaining skilled talent, and securing funding for growth. However, the company has successfully leveraged growing demand for healthcare, technology and innovation, and strategic partnerships to establish itself as a leading healthcare provider in Asia. The company has also demonstrated its resilience and adaptability in responding to the COVID-19 pandemic, which has accelerated the adoption of telemedicine and digital health solutions. The company's vision of transforming healthcare in the Asia Pacific by making it affordable and accessible to all has driven its growth and expansion across the region.

References

Chen C., Chou Y., Lin I., & Huang C. (2019). Regulatory barriers for internationalization of healthcare service providers: the case of Taiwan. *International Journal of Healthcare Management, 14*(3), 215–224. https://doi.org/10.1080/20479 700.2019.1697208

Fullerton Health Group (2021). *Fullerton Health focuses on ASEAN in its growth strategy* [Online]. Available at: www.fullertonhealth.com/fullerton-health-focuses-on-asean-in-its-growth-strategy/ (Accessed: 28 May 2023).

Periyasamy, G., Rangaswamy, E., & Srinivasan, U.R. (2023). A study on impact of ageing population on Singapore healthcare systems using machine learning algorithms. *World Review of Entrepreneurship, Management and Sustainable Development, 19*(1–2), 47–70. DOI: 10.1504/WREMSD.2023.10051345

PR Newswire (2021). *Fullerton Health focuses on ASEAN in its growth strategy* [Online]. Available at: https://en.prnasia.com/releases/apac/fullerton-health-focu ses-on-asean-in-its-growth-strategy-335001.shtml (Accessed: 28 May 2023).

Rangaswamy, E., Periyasamy, G., & Nawaz, N. (2021). A study on Singapore's ageing population in the context of eldercare initiatives using machine learning algorithms. *Big Data and Cognitive Computing*, 5(4), Article 51. DOI: 10.3390/bdcc5040051

Tan S., Goh C., & Wong J. (2019). Healthcare workforce management: a systematic literature review. *International Journal of Manpower, 40*(8), 1446–1470. https:// doi.org/10.1108/IJM-03-2018-0087

13 How BreadTalk grew from a single bakery to a global brand

Katalin Illes

Associate Head of College, External Relations at the University of Westminster, United Kingdom

BreadTalk started as a humble bakery in Singapore, but over the years, it has transformed into a global brand with outlets in more than 16 countries. Along the way, BreadTalk faced many challenges that tested its resilience and adaptability. In this article, we will explore some of these challenges and how BreadTalk overcame them with its innovative and strategic approach.

Brand recognition: As a relatively unknown brand outside of Singapore, BreadTalk had to build brand recognition in new markets. To do this, the company focused on creating unique and innovative products that would stand out in the crowded bakery market. They also invested in advertising and marketing campaigns to raise awareness of the brand. For example, BreadTalk launched a series of limited-edition buns inspired by popular movies, celebrities, and events, such as the Harry Potter bun, the Michael Jackson bun, and the SARS bun (Tan & Devi, 2020). These products generated buzz and attracted customers who were curious about the taste and appearance of the buns. Moreover, BreadTalk leveraged its social media platforms and online influencers to promote its products and engage with its target audience. They also participated in various events and festivals to showcase their brand and products to the local communities.

Cultural differences: As BreadTalk expanded into new markets, it had to navigate cultural differences and adapt its products to local tastes. To address this challenge, BreadTalk hired local staff to help with product development and marketing and made adjustments to its menu to appeal to local preferences. For instance, BreadTalk introduced more savoury buns and halal-certified products in Muslim-majority countries like Indonesia and Malaysia, while offering more sweet buns and cakes in China and Taiwan (Tay, 2017). BreadTalk also leveraged its local partners' knowledge and expertise to understand consumer behaviour and preferences in different markets. Furthermore, BreadTalk respected the local customs and traditions and incorporated them into their products and packaging. For example, they offered special buns for festive occasions such as Chinese New Year, Ramadan, and Christmas. They also used local ingredients and flavours to create products that reflected the local culture and identity.

DOI: 10.4324/9781032660547-32

Supply chain management: Managing a global supply chain can be complex and challenging, especially for a company like BreadTalk which relies on fresh ingredients. To overcome this challenge, the company implemented a centralised supply chain management system that allowed them to monitor inventory levels and streamline logistics operations. The system also enabled them to standardise the quality and consistency of their products across different outlets and regions. Additionally, BreadTalk piloted frozen dough in some of its recipes, which reduced wastage and transportation costs while maintaining freshness (EMBA Pro, 2022). Besides, BreadTalk adopted a blockchain-based supply chain management solution that enhanced the transparency and traceability of its products. This solution allowed them to track the origin and movement of their ingredients and products throughout the supply chain, as well as to verify the quality and safety of their products. This solution also improved the efficiency and security of their transactions and data sharing with their suppliers and customers.

Competition: The bakery industry is highly competitive, with many established players and new entrants constantly emerging. To stand out in this crowded market, BreadTalk focused on innovation and differentiation, introducing unique products like their famous "Flosss" buns and collaborating with international brands and chefs to create new flavours and products. BreadTalk also diversified its brand portfolio by venturing into other F&B segments, such as Din Tai Fung (a Taiwanese restaurant chain), Toast Box (a coffee shop chain), Food Republic (a food court operator), and Thye Moh Chan (a traditional Teochew bakery) (Tan & Devi, 2020). These brands helped BreadTalk to cater to different customer segments and occasions, as well as to leverage its economies of scale and cross-selling opportunities.

Despite these challenges, BreadTalk has succeeded in growing into a global brand by leveraging its strengths in product innovation and differentiation, strategic partnerships, and a strong supply chain. The company has also been successful in expanding through franchising, allowing them to rapidly expand their footprint and enter new markets with minimal risk. Today, BreadTalk is recognised as a leading bakery brand in Asia and beyond, with a strong reputation for quality, innovation, and creativity. It has demonstrated its social responsibility and commitment to giving back to the community by supporting various charitable causes and initiatives. The company has also embraced sustainability and environmental protection by reducing its carbon footprint and waste generation.

References

EMBA Pro (2022). *BreadTalk (Singapore) blockchain based supply chain management* [Online]. Available at: https://embapro.com/frontpage/bcscmcoanalysis/21339-breadtalk (Accessed: 27 April 2023).

Tan, J., & Devi, U. (2020). *Saving BreadTalk*. The Edge Singapore [Online]. Available at: www.theedgesingapore.com/issues/company-news/saving-breadtalk (Accessed: 27 April 2023).

Tay, S. (2017). *How BreadTalk's strategy earns $3.8mil in 6 months*. AsiaOne [Online]. Available at: www.asiaone.com/business/how-breadtalks-strategy-earns-38mil-6-months (Accessed: 27 April 2023).

14 Food Empire Holdings expanding its business to new markets

Melvin Goh Kim Ho

Associate Dean, Amity Global Institute, Singapore

Food Empire Holdings is a global food and beverage company that specialises in the production, distribution, and marketing of instant beverages and snacks. The company has faced several challenges in expanding its business to new markets but has managed to succeed through a range of strategies. The following are some of the strategies that the company has employed to address the challenges:

Challenges

Cultural differences: Food Empire Holdings has faced challenges in adapting its products and marketing strategies to different cultures and consumer preferences. This can include differences in taste preferences, dietary habits, and packaging requirements. For instance, the company had to modify its coffee products to suit the local preferences of consumers in Vietnam, Russia, and Ukraine (Nguyen & Nguyen, 2015). The company also had to adjust its marketing campaigns to reflect the cultural values and norms of different markets (Kuznetsova & Kuznetsov, 2017).

Regulatory compliance: Expanding into new markets requires compliance with different regulatory frameworks and standards, which can be complex and time-consuming. Food Empire Holdings has had to invest in research and development to ensure that its products meet the requirements of different markets. For example, the company had to obtain halal certification for its products to enter the Muslim markets in Indonesia and Malaysia (Food Empire Holdings Limited, 2020). The company also had to comply with various food safety and quality standards in different countries (Food Empire Holdings Limited, 2019).

Competition: The food and beverage industry is highly competitive, with many established players competing for market share. Food Empire Holdings has had to find ways to differentiate itself from competitors and build a strong brand presence in new markets. For example, the company has leveraged its flagship brand MacCoffee to create a loyal customer base and increase its market share in Eastern Europe (Kuznetsova & Kuznetsov, 2017). The company

DOI: 10.4324/9781032660547-33

has also introduced innovative products and packaging formats to appeal to different consumer segments (Food Empire Holdings Limited, 2020).

Successes

Market research and localisation: Food Empire Holdings has invested in market research to better understand the needs and preferences of consumers in different markets. The company has also localised its products and marketing strategies to better resonate with local consumers. For example, the company has conducted extensive consumer surveys and focus group discussions to identify the gaps and opportunities in different markets (Food Empire Holdings Limited, 2020). The company has also customised its products and packaging designs to suit the local tastes and preferences of consumers (Hinrichs, 2003).

Strategic partnerships and collaborations: Food Empire Holdings has formed strategic partnerships and collaborations with local distributors, retailers, and manufacturers to expand its reach and distribution network. This has helped the company to navigate regulatory requirements and gain a foothold in new markets. For example, the company has partnered with local distributors such as PT Sinar Niaga Sejahtera in Indonesia, CJ CheilJedang Corporation in South Korea, and Al Maya Group in Dubai (Food Empire Holdings Limited, 2020). The company has also collaborated with local manufacturers such as PT Sari Incofood Corporation in Indonesia, Vinacafe Bien Hoa Joint Stock Company in Vietnam, and ZAO Klassno Rusland in Russia (Food Empire Holdings Limited, 2019).

Innovation and product development: Food Empire Holdings has created new products and packaging to cater to various consumer segments and needs. The company has launched a wide range of instant beverages and snacks with different flavours and ingredients, such as coffee, chocolate, tea, cheese, nuts, fruits, and vegetables. The company has also used different packaging designs to enhance convenience and appeal, such as stand-up pouches, resealable bags, single-serve sachets, and easy-open cans. These innovations have helped the company to differentiate itself from competitors and meet the changing demands of consumers (Food Empire Holdings Limited, n.d.).

Overall, Food Empire Holdings has successfully expanded its business to new markets by investing in market research and localisation, forming strategic partnerships and collaborations, and focusing on innovation and product development. These strategies have helped the company to overcome the challenges of cultural differences, regulatory compliance, and competition, and establish a strong global presence in the food and beverage industry.

References

Food Empire Holdings Limited (2019). *Sustainability report 2019* [Online]. Available at: www.foodempire.com/wp-content/uploads/2020/06/Food-Empire-Sustainability-Report-2019.pdf (Accessed: 25 May 2023).

Food Empire Holdings Limited (2020). *Annual report 2020* [Online]. Available at: www.foodempire.com/wp-content/uploads/2021/04/Food-Empire-Annual-Report-2020.pdf (Accessed: 25 May 2023).

Food Empire Holdings Limited (n.d.). *Our brands & products* [Online]. Available at: https://www.foodempire.com/our-brands/ / (Accessed: 25 May 2023).

Hinrichs, C.C. (2003). The practice and politics of food system localization. *Journal of Rural Studies, 19*(1), 33–45. https://doi.org/10.1016/S0743-0167(02)00040-2

Kuznetsova, I.V., & Kuznetsov, N.A. (2017). Marketing strategies of foreign companies in Russia: the case of Food Empire Holdings Ltd. In *Proceedings of the 30th International Business Information Management Association Conference*, IBIMA 2017-Vision 2020: Sustainable Economic Development, Innovation Management, and Global Growth (pp. 1441–1450).

Nguyen, T.T., & Nguyen, T.D. (2015). Factors influencing consumer behavior: a study of the instant coffee market in Vietnam. *International Journal of Business and Management, 10*(10), 81–90. https://doi.org/10.5539/ijbm.v10n10p81

15 Singapore Technologies Electronics' diversification into defence technology

Leon Choong

Regional CEO (ASEAN), Amity Global Institute, Singapore

As a subsidiary of Singapore Technologies Engineering (ST Engineering), Singapore Technologies Electronics (ST Electronics) specialises in offering advanced electronics solutions for various sectors and applications. However, when the company decided to diversify its portfolio and enter the defence technology market, it encountered several difficulties and obstacles. This market is characterised by high levels of regulation and competition, which pose significant challenges for new entrants.

Compliance with regulations was one of the major challenges that ST Electronics faced when it diversified into defence technology. Defence technology products and solutions have to adhere to strict regulations and certifications that vary across different countries and defence organisations, depending on their security, quality, and performance requirements. These regulations and certifications are often complex and costly to obtain, as they involve rigorous testing, verification, and documentation processes. They also require a lot of time and effort to maintain, as they are subject to frequent updates and audits. ST Electronics had to ensure that its offerings met all the relevant regulations and standards to operate in the defence technology market, which was a challenging and resource-intensive task (Wong et al., 2019).

Another challenge that ST Electronics faced was intense competition: The defence technology industry is highly competitive, with many established players and new entrants vying for contracts from various defence organisations and governments. ST Electronics had to differentiate itself from competitors by offering innovative, reliable, and cost-effective solutions that met customer requirements and expectations. ST Electronics also had to prove its capabilities to win contracts by demonstrating its track record, expertise, and reputation in the industry. This was a difficult and demanding task, as the company had to compete with global and regional players who had more experience and resources in the defence technology market (Amyx, 2020).

The third challenge that ST Electronics faced was changing customer requirements: Defence technology customers have evolving requirements, as they face new threats, challenges, and opportunities in the modern warfare environment. These requirements can be challenging for suppliers to keep up

DOI: 10.4324/9781032660547-34

with, as they demand constant innovation, adaptation, and customisation of products and solutions. ST Electronics had to invest in research and development to develop new technologies and solutions that met these changing requirements, such as artificial intelligence, cybersecurity, robotics, biotech, and aerospace. ST Electronics also had to collaborate with customers to understand their needs and expectations, and provide them with tailored solutions that enhanced their capabilities and performance (Chen et al., 2020).

Despite these challenges, ST Electronics has succeeded in diversifying into defence technology. The company has a strong reputation in the industry, with a track record of delivering high-quality solutions to defence organisations. For example, ST Electronics has provided advanced communication systems, command and control systems, cyber defence solutions, and satellite communication solutions to various defence customers in Singapore and abroad (ST Engineering, 2021). ST Electronics has also invested heavily in research and development, which has allowed it to stay at the forefront of technological innovation in the industry. For instance, ST Electronics has developed new capabilities in artificial intelligence, big data analytics, cloud computing, and robotics, which have enabled it to offer smart and integrated solutions for defence applications (Chen et al., 2020). Additionally, the company has formed strategic partnerships with other defence industry players, which has helped it to expand its reach and capabilities. For example, ST Electronics has collaborated with Boeing, Airbus, Lockheed Martin, and Thales to jointly develop and deliver defence solutions for various markets and customers (Wong et al., 2019).

In conclusion, ST Electronics has achieved remarkable success in diversifying into defence technology, despite the challenges and difficulties that it faced in this highly regulated and competitive industry. The key factors that contributed to its success were its strong focus on innovation, compliance, and customer satisfaction. By investing in research and development, ensuring compliance with regulations and standards, and delivering high-quality and tailored solutions to its customers, ST Electronics has established itself as a reputable and reliable defence technology provider in the global market.

References

Amyx, S. (2020). *The technological innovation challenges in defense* [Online]. Available at: www.forbes.com/sites/forbesbusinesscouncil/2020/07/14/the-technological-innovation-challenges-in-defense/ (Accessed: 27 June 2023).

Chen, C., Lee, J., Lee, J., Lee, S., & Park, J. (2020). Defense innovation: a case study of Singapore. *Journal of Open Innovation: Technology, Market, and Complexity, 6*(4), 128. https://doi.org/10.3390/joitmc6040128.

ST Engineering (2021). *Annual report 2020* [Online]. Available at: www.stengg.com/media/4627/st-engineering-annual-report-2020.pdf (Accessed: 27 June 2023).

Wong, K., Tan, C., Tan, K., Tan, S., & Yeo, W. (2019). Strategic partnerships for defense innovation: A case study of Singapore. *Journal of Open Innovation: Technology, Market, and Complexity, 5*(4), 87. https://doi.org/10.3390/joitmc5040087

16 ST Engineering's expansion into defence technology

David Bell

Pro Vice-Chancellor (International), Amity Global Institute, Singapore

As a leading technology, engineering, and defence company based in Singapore, Singapore Technologies Engineering (ST Engineering) has four main business segments: aerospace, electronics, land systems, and marine (ST Engineering, 2021). The company faced various challenges when it decided to expand its operations and capabilities in the field of defence technology, which is a highly competitive and complex industry. The company also succeeded in overcoming these challenges by adopting various strategies and measures.

Developing expertise in new technology: One of the biggest challenges that ST Engineering faced was developing expertise in new and emerging defence technologies, such as unmanned systems and cybersecurity. These technologies are essential for enhancing the capabilities and performance of defence forces in the modern warfare environment (Chen et al., 2020). To overcome this challenge, the company invested heavily in research and development and hired experts in the field to help develop new products and technologies. The company also collaborated with universities, research institutes, and other industry partners to leverage their knowledge and resources (Wong et al., 2020; MINDEF, 2021). For example, the company worked with Nanyang Polytechnic to provide cyber defence training for its personnel, and with DSTA to develop the Hunter Armoured Fighting Vehicle (MINDEF, 2019).

Meeting the needs of diverse customers: ST Engineering also faced the challenge of meeting the needs of diverse customers in the defence industry, such as militaries, governments, and commercial clients in various sectors and regions. The company had to understand the unique requirements and expectations of each customer segment, such as their security, operational, and budgetary needs, and provide them with customised solutions that met their specifications and standards. The company also had to adapt to the changing customer preferences and demands, such as increased emphasis on sustainability, digitalisation, and innovation (ST Engineering, 2021). For example, the company developed green solutions for its aerospace and marine customers, such as hybrid propulsion systems and biofuel technologies. The company also leveraged digital technologies such as artificial intelligence and

DOI: 10.4324/9781032660547-35

big data analytics to enhance its products and services for its defence and security customers.

Ensuring safety and reliability. Another critical factor in the development and deployment of defence technology is safety and reliability. The company had to ensure that its products and services met the highest standards of quality, safety, and reliability, as any failure or malfunction could have serious consequences for its customers and stakeholders, such as compromising their security and performance. The company had to develop rigorous testing and quality control procedures to verify and validate its products and services before delivery. The company also had to comply with various industry standards and certifications, such as ISO 9001 and AS9100, to demonstrate its quality management system. The company also had to ensure that its products and services were resilient against cyberattacks and other threats, such as electromagnetic interference and jamming, by implementing robust cybersecurity measures and countermeasures (Chen et al., 2020). For example, the company developed a secure cloud platform for its defence and security customers, which provides encryption, authentication, and access control features.

Overcoming regulatory and legal barriers. The defence industry is highly regulated, with complex laws and regulations governing the development, production, and export of defence products and services. The company had to navigate the legal and regulatory landscape of different countries and regions and ensure compliance with relevant laws and regulations. For example, the company had to obtain export licenses and authorisations from various authorities for its defence products and services, such as the US Department of State and Singapore Customs (ST Engineering iDirect, n.d.). The company also had to invest in export controls and compliance programmes to manage the risks associated with international sales, such as potential violations of sanctions or embargoes. The company also had to deal with ethical issues and social responsibilities related to its defence business, such as ensuring that its products and services were not used for human rights abuses or environmental damage (ST Engineering, 2021).

To sum up, ST Engineering has successfully overcome various challenges and difficulties in diversifying into the field of defence technology and has achieved outstanding success in this highly competitive and complex industry. The company has created a range of products and services that are used by militaries and governments, as well as commercial clients in sectors such as aerospace, marine, and electronics. By prioritising quality, safety, and customer needs, ST Engineering has secured its position for continued success in the future. The company has also shown its commitment to innovation, compliance, and social responsibility, which are vital for creating value and enhancing trust in the defence industry. ST Engineering is thus a leader and an example for other defence technology providers in Singapore and around the world.

References

Chen, C., Lee, J., Lee, J., Lee, S., & Park, J. (2020). Defence innovation: a case study of Singapore. *Journal of Open Innovation: Technology, Market, and Complexity*, 6(4), 128. https://doi.org/10.3390/joitmc6040128.

MINDEF (2019). *Fact sheet: Hunter armoured fighting vehicle* [Online]. Available at: www.mindef.gov.sg/web/portal/mindef/news-and-events/latest-releases/article-detail/2019/june/11jun19_fs (Accessed: 27 May 2023).

MINDEF (2021). *Defence science & technology* [Online]. Available at: www.mindef.gov.sg/web/portal/mindef/defence-matters/defence-topic/defence-topic-detail/defence-science-and-technology (Accessed: 27 May 2023).

ST Engineering iDirect. (n.d.). *Export classifications* [Online]. Available at: https://www.idirect.net/partner-resources/export-classifications/ (Accessed: 27 May 2023)

ST Engineering (2021). *Annual report 2020* [Online]. Available at: www.stengg.com/media/4627/st-engineering-annual-report-2020.pdf (Accessed: 27 May 2023).

Wong, K., Tan, C., Tan, K., Tan, S., & Yeo, W. (2019). Strategic partnerships for defence innovation: a case study of Singapore. *Journal of Open Innovation: Technology, Market, and Complexity*, 5(4), 87. https://doi.org/10.3390/joitmc5040087

17 Global expansion and service diversification

A case study of SIA Engineering Company

Matthew Sullivan

*Distinguished Global Educator and Former Head of School at
NPS International School, Singapore*

SIA Engineering Company (SIAEC) is a leading aircraft maintenance, repair, and overhaul (MRO) company based in Singapore. SIAEC succeeded in diversifying into aircraft maintenance and repair and establishing itself as a leader in the industry. By focusing on quality, innovation, compliance, and global expansion, SIAEC has become a trusted partner for airlines and MRO companies around the world, and is well-positioned to succeed in the future.

SIAEC was formed in 1992 as a subsidiary of Singapore Airlines (SIA), which had invested heavily in building capabilities, facilities, and equipment to support the most modern aircraft operated by SIA. This enabled SIAEC to develop MRO capabilities and experience in the newest aircraft in the market before other MRO companies. In 2000, SIAEC was listed on the Singapore Exchange, gaining greater autonomy to pursue new business opportunities globally (SIA Engineering Company, n.d.).

SIAEC offers extensive MRO services on current and new-generation widebody and narrowbody aircraft. Its maintenance facilities provide complete MRO services in the airframe, line, cabin, fleet management, components, and engines. SIAEC also provides line maintenance services to more than 60 airlines passing through Singapore Changi Airport, ensuring a high level of punctuality for all its customers' flight departures.

SIAEC has also collaborated with leading original equipment manufacturers (OEMs) and strategic partners in the airframe, component, engine, and modification to complement and strengthen its core competencies and market reach. Today, with its MRO network of joint ventures and subsidiaries, SIAEC broadens and deepens its suite of integrated MRO services and network support to airlines worldwide.

SIAEC has achieved several awards and recognitions for its excellence in MRO services. For instance, it was named Asia-Pacific MRO of the Year 2022 by Aviation Week Network (Aviation Week Network, 2021), Asia MRO of the Year – Airframe by Aviation Week Network (Aviation Week Network, 2020), and Best Airframe MRO Provider – Asia by Aircraft Technology Engineering and Maintenance Awards (Aircraft Commerce, 2019).

DOI: 10.4324/9781032660547-36

SIAEC has also demonstrated its commitment to quality, innovation, and compliance by obtaining certifications from more than 20 airworthiness authorities implementing digital transformation initiatives (Lee & Lim, 2019) such as predictive maintenance and smart inspection, and adhering to environmental, social, and governance (ESG) standards such as reducing carbon emissions and waste generation.

By leveraging its competitive advantages, SIAEC has become a trusted partner for airlines and MRO companies around the world. According to its annual report for FY2020/21, SIAEC served more than 600 customers from over 80 countries. SIAEC has also established strategic alliances with major airlines such as Air France-KLM, Lufthansa Technik, and Nippon Airways.

As the aviation industry recovers from the impact of the COVID-19 pandemic, SIAEC is well-positioned to succeed in the future. SIAEC has maintained its financial resilience by implementing cost-control measures, securing new contracts, and diversifying its revenue streams. SIAEC has also continued to invest in its human capital, technology, and infrastructure to enhance its capabilities and competitiveness (Deloitte, 2021). Moreover, SIAEC has seized opportunities arising from the growing demand for cargo conversion, cabin retrofitting, and green aviation solutions.

In conclusion, SIAEC is a leading aircraft MRO company based in Singapore that has succeeded in diversifying into aircraft maintenance and repair and establishing itself as a leader in the industry. By focusing on quality, innovation, compliance, and global expansion, SIAEC has become a trusted partner for airlines and MRO companies around the world, and is well-positioned to succeed in the future.

References

Aircraft Commerce (2019). *Aircraft Technology Engineering & Maintenance Awards* [Online]. Available at: www.aircraft-commerce.com/conferences/Awards2019/winners.asp (Accessed: 29 April 2023).

Aviation Week Network (2020). *Winners of Aviation Week Network announces winners of 2022* [Online]. Available at: https://aviationweek.com/shows-events/mro-asia/winners-aviation-week-networks-mro-asia-pacific-awards-2022 (Accessed: 29 April 2023).

Aviation Week Network (2021). *Aviation Week Network announces winners of 2022 Aviation Week Laureate Awards* [Online]. Available at: https://aviationweek.com/press-releases/aviation-week-network-announces-winners-2022-aviation-week-laureate-awards (Accessed: 29 April 2023).

Deloitte (2021). *Powering human impact with technology.* Deloitte Insights [Online]. Available at: www2.deloitte.com/us/en/insights/focus/human-capital-trends/2023/human-capital-and-productivity.html (Accessed: 29 April 2023).

Lee J., & Lim W.M. (2019). Digital transformation at Singapore Airlines Engineering Company: a case study. *Journal of Air Transport Management, 81,* 101755.

SIA Engineering Company (n.d.). *Our company profile* [Online]. Available at: www.siaec.com.sg/company_profile.html (Accessed: 29 April 2023).

Part III
Sustainability

1 Banyan Tree Holdings challenges on being a global leader in sustainable tourism

Easwaramoorthy Rangaswamy

Principal and Provost, Amity Global Institute, Singapore

Banyan Tree Holdings is a Singapore-based multinational hospitality company that operates resorts, hotels, and spas in various countries around the world. The company is well known for its strong commitment to sustainability and responsible tourism practices. According to its sustainability report, Banyan Tree was founded with the core value of driving sustainable development and creating long-term value for multiple stakeholders and destinations (Banyan Tree Holdings Limited, 2016).

Banyan Tree faced the challenge of meeting high sustainability standards across its properties, which required significant investment in eco-friendly technology and infrastructure. The company invested in renewable energy, water conservation systems, and waste management programmes to reduce its environmental impact (Moise et al., 2021). For example, Banyan Tree Vabbinfaru in Maldives installed a solar photovoltaic system that generates up to 40% of the resort's electricity needs (Banyan Tree Holdings Limited, 2016). Banyan Tree also established a strong corporate social responsibility programme that focuses on supporting local communities and preserving cultural heritage. The company supports various social and environmental causes through its Banyan Tree Global Foundation, which funds projects such as marine conservation, wildlife protection, education and empowerment, health and protection, and culture and livelihood (Banyan Tree Hotels & Resorts, n.d.).

To promote sustainability and responsible tourism practices, Banyan Tree had to inform and persuade its customers and stakeholders about the significance and benefits of these practices. The company initiated a "Greening Communities" programme that invites guests to join in eco-friendly activities such as planting trees and cleaning up the beaches. These activities not only help to conserve the natural environment but also create a sense of connection and responsibility among the guests and the local communities. Banyan Tree also collaborates with local communities to provide sustainable tourism experiences that highlight local culture and traditions (Han, 2021). For example, Banyan Tree Ringha in China enables guests to visit Tibetan villages and learn about their way of life, customs, and beliefs (Banyan Tree Holdings Limited, 2010). Guests can also enjoy authentic Tibetan cuisine, music, and

DOI: 10.4324/9781032660547-38

dance, and participate in local festivals and ceremonies. These experiences allow guests to appreciate the rich and diverse culture of the region while also supporting the local economy and preserving the cultural heritage.

Banyan Tree faced the challenge of balancing its commitment to sustainability with the need to generate profits. The company achieved this by targeting the high-end, luxury tourism market and developing unique, experiential offerings (Lee et al., 2022) that set it apart from other hospitality providers. Banyan Tree offered its guests distinctive and memorable experiences, such as staying in villas with private pools, enjoying panoramic views of nature, and indulging in personalised spa treatments. Banyan Tree also launched a range of sustainable lifestyle products and services, such as spa products and organic food, that appeal to environmentally conscious consumers. These products and services not only enhance the guest experience but also generate additional revenue streams for the company (Chen et al., 2019).

By creating value for its guests and stakeholders through sustainability, Banyan Tree was able to achieve both financial and environmental goals.

Despite facing various challenges, Banyan Tree has emerged as a global leader in sustainable tourism. The company's sustainability efforts have earned it widespread recognition and acclaim, as well as numerous awards from prestigious organisations, such as the Sustainable Hotel Awards and the Global Green Economic Forum's Green Champion Award. Banyan Tree has also expanded its global presence, with properties in over 25 countries across Asia, Africa, America, and Europe, and continues to innovate with new sustainability initiatives, such as its "Rewilding Communities" programme that focuses on restoring natural habitats and ecosystems. By embracing sustainability as a core value and a competitive advantage, Banyan Tree has created value for the hospitality industry and society, as well as contributed to environmental and social change.

References

Banyan Tree Holdings Limited (2010). *Banyan Tree Holdings Limited sustainability report 2010 global reporting initiative G3 application level* C+ [Online]. Available at: https://investor.banyantree.com/PDF/Annual_Reports/2010/BTH_SR2010.pdf (Accessed: 13 April 2023).

Banyan Tree Holdings Limited (2016). *Banyan Tree Holdings Limited – sustainability report 2016* [Online]. Available at: https://investors.banyantree.com/PDF/Annual_Reports/2016/BTH_SR2016.pdf (Accessed: 13 April 2023).

Banyan Tree Hotels & Resorts (n.d.). *Sustainability impact* | Banyan Tree Hotels & Resorts [Online]. Available at: www.banyantree.com/sustainability (Accessed: 13 April 2023).

Chen, J., Liu, X., Liang, Y., & Chen, H. (2019). Sustainable development of hotel industry based on green marketing: a case study of Banyan tree hotels & resorts. *Journal of Cleaner Production, 237*(1), 117–726. https://doi.org/10.1016/j.jclepro.2019.117726

Han, H. (2021). Consumer behavior and environmental sustainability in tourism and hospitality: a review of theories, concepts, and latest research. *Journal of Sustainable Tourism, 29*(7), 1021–1042. https://doi.org/10.1080/09669582.2021.1903019

Lee, J., Kim, H.J., & Kim, S. (2022). Consumer adoption of green hotels: understanding the role of value congruence. *Journal of Hospitality Marketing & Management, 31*(1), 1–21. https://doi.org/10.1080/19368623.2022.2071370

Moise, M.S., Gil-Saura, I., & Ruiz Molina, M.E. (2021). The importance of green practices for hotel guests: does gender matter?. *Economic Research - Ekonomska Istraživanja, 34*(1), 3508–3529. https://doi.org/10.1080/13316 77X.2021.1875863

2 Mapletree Commercial Trust's focus on sustainable office buildings

Gemini V. Joy
Associate Professor, VIT Business School, VIT University, India

Mapletree Commercial Trust (MCT) is a Singapore-based real estate investment trust that owns and manages a portfolio of commercial properties including office buildings, business parks, and retail malls. MCT has made sustainability a key priority in its operations and has implemented several initiatives to reduce its environmental footprint.

One of the challenges MCT faced in implementing sustainable practices was the lack of awareness and understanding among its tenants and stakeholders. To address this challenge, MCT embarked on an extensive stakeholder engagement programme to educate and raise awareness on sustainability issues. This included organising sustainability workshops, seminars, and events to encourage tenants to adopt sustainable practices in their operations. According to MCT's (2020) sustainability report, the trust conducted 14 sustainability workshops for its tenants in FY19/20, reaching out to more than 200 participants. MCT also collaborated with various partners such as the Building and Construction Authority (BCA), National Environment Agency (NEA), Singapore Green Building Council (SGBC), and WWF Singapore to organise events such as the BCA-NEA Green Mark Awards Ceremony, SGBC Green Mark Awards Ceremony, Earth Hour, and World Environment Day. These events aimed to showcase MCT's sustainability achievements, share best practices, and inspire action among its stakeholders. Stakeholder engagement is a key business concept that can help businesses to understand their stakeholders' needs, expectations, and concerns, as well as build trust and collaboration (Freeman et al., 2010).

Another challenge faced by MCT was to improve the energy efficiency of its buildings. To tackle this, MCT implemented several energy-saving measures, such as installing energy-efficient lighting and air conditioning systems, implementing building automation systems to optimise energy usage, and upgrading the building envelope to improve thermal performance. MCT also invested in renewable energy sources such as solar photovoltaic (PV) systems to reduce its reliance on grid electricity. As a result of these measures, MCT achieved a 9.4% reduction in energy consumption intensity and a 10.8% reduction in carbon emissions intensity across its portfolio in FY19/20 compared

DOI: 10.4324/9781032660547-39

with FY18/19 (MCT, 2020). MCT's efforts to improve its energy efficiency were recognised by the BCA with the Green Mark Platinum Award for its Mapletree Business City (MBC) property and the Green Mark Gold Award for its VivoCity mall. Energy efficiency is another important business concept that can help businesses to reduce their energy consumption, costs, and greenhouse gas emissions, including improving their productivity, competitiveness, and resilience (IEA, 2018).

MCT also implemented waste-reduction initiatives, including the adoption of a recycling programme and the installation of food waste digesters in its retail malls. In addition, MCT sourced materials from sustainable sources and adopted green building materials to reduce the environmental impact of its building operations. For instance, MCT used recycled concrete aggregates for the construction of MBC II, which reduced the use of natural resources and minimised waste generation (MCT, 2020). MCT also ensured that its contractors complied with environmental regulations and standards during the construction and renovation of its properties. Waste reduction is another relevant business concept that can help businesses to conserve resources, save money, and reduce their environmental impact. Waste reduction can also support circular economy principles, which aim to keep materials and products in use for as long as possible and regenerate natural systems (Ellen MacArthur Foundation, 2017).

By making sustainability a key priority in its operations, MCT has not only reduced its environmental footprint but also gained recognition and reputation in the market. MCT has been awarded the prestigious Green Mark Platinum Award for its Mapletree Business City and the Green Mark Gold Award for its VivoCity mall, which demonstrates its excellence in green building design and management. MCT has also impressed various environmental, social, and governance (ESG) rating agencies such as GRESB, Sustainalytics, ISS ESG, and FTSE4Good Index Series, which have given MCT positive ratings for its outstanding performance in ESG aspects. These achievements show that MCT is a leader in sustainability and a responsible corporate citizen that creates long-term value for its stakeholders.

References

Ellen MacArthur Foundation (2017). *What is a circular economy?* [Online]. Available at: www.ellenmacarthurfoundation.org/circular-economy/concept (Accessed: 7 June 2023).

Freeman, R.E., Harrison, J.S., Wicks, A.C., Parmar, B.L., & de Colle, S. (2010). *Stakeholder Theory: The State of the Art.* Cambridge University Press.

IEA (2018). *Energy efficiency 2018: analysis and outlooks to 2040* [Online]. Available at: www.iea.org/reports/energy-efficiency-2018 (Accessed: 7 June 2023). https://doi.org/10.1787/9789264311632-en

MCT (2020). *Sustainability report FY19/20* [Online]. Available at: www.mapletree commercialtrust.com/en/Investor-Relations/Sustainability.aspx (Accessed: 7 June 2023).

3 Sembcorp Industries' focus on sustainable energy solutions

Lim Chin Guan

Consultant, PowerTECH Innovations, Singapore

Sembcorp Industries is a Singapore-based company that provides sustainable energy solutions, including urban development, water and wastewater treatment, and marine and offshore engineering. Here are some of the challenges the company faced in its focus on sustainable energy solutions and how it overcame them to succeed:

Regulatory and policy challenges: One of the biggest challenges for Sembcorp Industries in its focus on sustainable energy solutions was navigating the complex regulatory and policy environment. Governments play a crucial role in setting policies and regulations that incentivise the adoption of renewable energy sources (World Bank, 2018), and Sembcorp had to work closely with regulators to ensure that its projects complied with local regulations and policies. To overcome this challenge, Sembcorp built strong relationships with regulators and policymakers and actively engaged with them to ensure its projects aligned with government goals and objectives.

Technical challenges: Another challenge for Sembcorp was overcoming the technical challenges associated with adopting renewable energy solutions. It included developing and implementing new technologies and processes to capture and store energy and ensuring its projects were reliable and cost-effective. To address this challenge, Sembcorp invested heavily in research and development and collaborated with technology partners to develop innovative solutions for renewable energy storage and distribution (McKinsey, 2021).

Workforce transformation challenges: Sembcorp needs to grow its workforce in sustainability-related fields and ensure they have the right competencies. It provides learning opportunities for all employees to promote sustainability and the skills for the energy transition. The energy transition requires talent to solve complex problems and build greener businesses. Many energy companies struggle to balance hiring new talent and retaining existing talent (Blair et al., 2022). The energy sector also faces retiring professionals, a talent drain, and a need to diversify its workforce (Deloitte, 2021).

Financial challenges: A third challenge for Sembcorp was securing the necessary financing to support its sustainable energy projects. Renewable energy solutions are often capital-intensive, and Sembcorp had to find creative

DOI: 10.4324/9781032660547-40

ways to finance its projects, such as partnering with investors and securing government grants and subsidies (IEA, 2021). Sembcorp also leveraged its financial strength and reputation to secure favourable financing terms from banks and other lenders (United Nations, 2021).

Despite these challenges, Sembcorp Industries has succeeded in its focus on sustainable energy solutions by taking a long-term, strategic approach to its business. The company has built a strong reputation as a reliable and innovative sustainable energy solutions provider. It has developed a diverse portfolio of projects across various geographies and technologies. By investing in research and development, building strong relationships with regulators and policymakers, and leveraging its financial strength, Sembcorp has established itself as a leader in transitioning to a more sustainable energy future.

References

Blair, B., Bruhn, A., & Emmett, E. (2022). *Developing talent strategies for the energy transition*. Bain & Company [Online]. Available at: www.bain.com/insights/developing-talent-strategies-for-energy-transition-enr-report-2022/ (Accessed: 7 April 2023).

Deloitte (2021). *Work toward net zero* [Online]. Available at: www.deloitte.com/global/en/issues/climate/work-toward-net-zero.html (Accessed: 7 April 2023).

IEA (2021). *Financing clean energy transitions in emerging and developing economies* [Online]. Available at: www.iea.org/reports/financing-clean-energy-transitions-in-emerging-and-developing-economies (Accessed: 7 April 2023).

McKinsey (2021). *Net-zero power: long-duration energy storage for a renewable grid* [Online]. Available at: www.mckinsey.com/capabilities/sustainability/our-insights/net-zero-power-long-duration-energy-storage-for-a-renewable-grid (Accessed: 7 April 2023).

United Nations (2021). *The trillion dollar climate finance challenge (and opportunity)* [Online]. Available at: https://news.un.org/en/story/2021/06/1094762 (Accessed: 7 April 2023).

World Bank (2018). *Policy matters: regulatory indicators for sustainable energy* [Online]. Available at: https://openknowledge.worldbank.org/handle/10986/30970 (Accessed: 7 April 2023).

4   City Developments Limited's focus on sustainable urban development

Lim Keai

Academic Director (Senior), Amity Global Institute, Singapore

Imagine a city where buildings are designed to conserve energy and water, where green spaces are abundant and accessible, where waste is minimised and recycled, and where people live in harmony with nature. This is the vision of sustainable urban development that City Developments Limited (CDL), a leading real estate company in Singapore, has been pursuing for over two decades. But achieving this vision is not easy. It requires a shift in mindsets and behaviours, both within the company and among stakeholders (Keith et al., 2023). How did CDL overcome this challenge? How did CDL educate and engage its employees, customers, and partners on the importance of sustainability? How did CDL integrate sustainability principles into its business operations? This case will explore some of the examples of CDL's sustainability journey and its key success factors.

To create sustainable developments, CDL had to focus on resource efficiency, which was not easy in a market that usually valued cost and speed over environmental impact (World Resources Institute, 2016). Resource efficiency means using fewer resources, such as energy, water, and materials, to achieve the same or better results while reducing waste and pollution. CDL achieved this by adopting new and better building technologies and materials, such as green roofs and rainwater harvesting systems, which benefit the environment and save money in the long run. Green roofs are roofs that are covered with plants, which help to regulate the building temperature and provide a habitat for wildlife. Rainwater harvesting systems are systems that collect and store rainwater for reuse, which decreases the demand for potable water and the risk of flooding.

Sustainable urban development often involves meeting rigorous regulatory standards and guidelines, which can be challenging and time-consuming to comply with (Lowe et al., 2022). These standards and guidelines aim to make urban development projects more environmentally friendly, more resource efficient, and more beneficial for society and the economy. CDL tackled these challenges by collaborating with government bodies and industry partners to develop best practices and standards for sustainable building practices. By doing so, CDL achieved high levels of sustainability excellence and innovation

DOI: 10.4324/9781032660547-41

in its projects, while also contributing to the growth of the green building industry in Singapore and other markets.

Sustainable urban development also needs to consider social equity, ensuring that communities are inclusive and accessible to all (Evans et al., 2019). This means that urban development projects should not create or worsen social inequalities, but rather promote social justice and diversity. They should also foster social cohesion and harmony among people. CDL achieved this by designing developments that make it easy and enjoyable for people to access and use, such as public spaces and green areas. These developments enhance the well-being and happiness of the people who live and visit there, by providing them with various facilities and services, and opportunities to interact and connect with others. Moreover, these developments improve the urban environment's eco-friendliness, by adding more plants and animals, lowering the temperature, and cleaning the air and water.

CDL has shown that sustainable urban development is not only possible but also profitable. By educating and engaging its stakeholders on the importance of sustainability, and by incorporating sustainability principles into its business operations, CDL has created a portfolio of green buildings and developments that have set the benchmark for the industry. These green buildings and developments have not only improved the environmental and social well-being of the cities they are in but they have also enhanced the financial performance of the company by lowering operating costs and increasing property values. CDL is not resting on its laurels. The company is constantly innovating and promoting sustainable urban development through partnerships, research and development, and community engagement (CDL Sustainability, 2021). CDL's vision is to create a better future for everyone, and it is well on its way to achieving that goal.

References

CDL Sustainability (2021). *Advancing change resilience – integrated sustainability report 2021* [Online]. Available at: www.cdlsustainability.com/pdf/CDL_ISR_2 021.pdf (Accessed: 7 May 2023).

Evans, J., Karvonen, A., Luque-Ayala, A., Martin, C., McCormick, K., Raven, R., & Palgan, Y.V. (2019). Smart and sustainable cities? Pipedreams, practicalities and possibilities. *The International Journal of Justice and Sustainability, 24*(7), 557–564. https://doi.org/10.1080/13549839.2019.1624701

Keith, M., Birch, E., Buchoud, N.J.A., et al. (2023). A new urban narrative for sustainable development. *Nature Sustainability, 6*, 115–117. https://doi.org/10.1038/s41893-022-00979-5

Lowe, M., Adlakha, D., Sallis, J.F., Salvo, D., Cerin, E., Moudon, A.V., et al. (2022). City planning policies to support health and sustainability: an international comparison of policy indicators for 25 cities. *The Lancet Global Health, 10*(6), E882-E894. https://doi.org/10.1016/S2214-109X(22)00069-9

World Resources Institute (2016). *Accelerating building efficiency: eight actions for urban leaders* [Online]. Available at: https://publications.wri.org/buildingefficiency/ (Accessed: 17 May 2023).

5 Wilmar International's focus on sustainable palm oil production

Jakia Rajoana
Senior Lecturer, Teesside University, United Kingdom

Purpose: The key aim of this case study is to examine the sustainable palm oil production practices of Wilmar International. Wilmar International is a Singapore-based agribusiness company that is one of the world's largest producers and traders of palm oil. The company has made sustainable palm oil production a key focus of its business, as it recognises the environmental and social impacts of the palm oil industry. Sustainable palm oil production means that the company strives to produce palm oil in a way that does not harm the environment, wildlife, or local communities. This involves avoiding deforestation, protecting biodiversity, reducing greenhouse gas emissions, respecting human rights, and supporting smallholders.

Problem statement: To protect forests, peatlands, and people from the impacts of palm oil production, Wilmar adopted a zero-deforestation policy. This policy is part of its broader No Deforestation, No Peat, No Exploitation (NDPE) policy (Wilmar International Limited, 2019a), which applies to all its activities and suppliers since 2013 (Poynton, 2014). Wilmar's NDPE policy is a landmark in the palm oil sector and has received praise from environmental groups. However, Wilmar still has many difficulties in putting its NDPE policy into practice, such as checking, involving, resolving, and disclosing issues (Wilmar International Limited, 2020a).

Strategies: Wilmar took action to address the poor labour practices, such as forced labour and child labour, that the palm oil industry has faced criticism for. Some of the actions that Wilmar took to enhance labour practices in its supply chain are (1) collaborating with Verité, Mars, and Nestlé to create a Toolkit for Palm Oil Producers on Labor Rights (Verité Southeast Asia, 2021); (2) establishing a Human Rights Policy and a way for workers and stakeholders to report any human rights issues or complaints (Wilmar International Limited, 2019b); (3) becoming a member of the Fair Labor Association (FLA) and participating in other multi-stakeholder initiatives to support and safeguard workers' rights and improve working conditions (Wilmar International Limited, 2020a).

Sustainability practices: Wilmar implemented a traceability system to ensure that its palm oil is produced sustainably. The system allows Wilmar to track the

DOI: 10.4324/9781032660547-42

origin of its palm oil and its compliance with its sustainability policies. Some of the system's features are: Wilmar can identify the mills and their locations that supply 98.2% of its palm oil as of 2020 (China Dialogue, 2021). Wilmar can identify the plantations and smallholders and their locations that grow 54% of its palm fruits and 40% of its suppliers' palm fruits as of 2020 conditions (Wilmar International Limited, 2020a).

Stakeholders' engagement: Addressing the complex challenges of sustainable palm oil production requires collaboration and engagement with stakeholders, including suppliers, customers, and civil society organisations. Wilmar succeeded in engaging stakeholders by establishing partnerships with NGOs and other organisations, and by participating in multi-stakeholder initiatives such as the Roundtable on Sustainable Palm Oil (RSPO). Wilmar has a policy that guides its engagement with different stakeholders through various methods (Wilmar International Limited, 2019c), works with NGOs on projects that support its sustainability goals, and joins multi-stakeholder initiatives that address sustainability challenges in the palm oil sector (Wilmar International Limited, 2020a).

Conclusion: Wilmar has become a leader in sustainable palm oil production through its efforts to address the environmental and social challenges of the industry. The company has achieved a range of certifications and recognition for its sustainability practices, such as the Roundtable on Sustainable Palm Oil (RSPO) certification (Wilmar International Limited, 2020b), the Palm Oil Innovation Group (POIG) verification (Wilmar International Limited, 2020c), and the Green Supply Chain CITIC Award (Wilmar International Limited, 2020a). The company's commitment to sustainability has not only helped to address environmental and social challenges but it has also contributed to the bottom line by increasing customer demand for sustainably produced palm oil. Today, Wilmar continues to innovate and promote sustainable palm oil production through partnerships, research and development, and community engagement.

References

China Dialogue (2021). *Palm oil derivatives: are sustainability promises lost in the supply chain?* [Online]. Available at: https://chinadialogue.net/en/business/palm-oil-derivatives-are-sustainability-promises-lost-in-the-supply-chain/ (Accessed: 13 March 2023).

Poynton, S. (2014). *Wilmar's 'no deforestation' goal could revolutionise food production.* The Guardian [Online]. Available at: www.theguardian.com/sustainable-business/wilmar-no-deforestation-commitment-food-production (Accessed: 13 March 2023).

Verité Southeast Asia (2021). *Toolkit for palm oil producers on labor rights* [Online]. Available at: www.verite.org/wp-content/uploads/2021/04/Verite-Palm-oil-toolkit-English.pdf (Accessed: 13 March 2023).

Wilmar International Limited (2019a). *No deforestation, no peat, no exploitation policy* [Online]. Available at: www.wilmar-international.com/docs/default-source/defa ult-document-library/sustainability/policies/wilmar-ndpe-policy—2019.pdf?sfv rsn=7870af13_2 (Accessed: 13 March 2023).

Wilmar International Limited (2019b). *Human rights policy* [Online]. Available at: www.wilmar-international.com/docs/default-source/default-document-library/ sustainability/policies/wilmar-human-rights-policy.pdf?sfvrsn=8f8aaf13_2 (Accessed: 13 March 2023).

Wilmar International Limited (2019c). *Stakeholder engagement policy* [Online]. Available at: www.wilmar-international.com/docs/default-source/default-docum ent-library/sustainability/policies/wilmar-stakeholder-engagement-policy.pdf?sfv rsn=8f8aaf13_2 (Accessed: 13 March 2023).

Wilmar International Limited (2020a). *Sustainability report 2020* [Online]. Available at: www.wilmar-international.com/docs/default-source/default-document-library/ sustainability/sustainability-reports/2020-sustainability-report.pdf?sfvrsn=8f8aaf1 3_2 (Accessed: 13 March 2023).

Wilmar International Limited (2020b). *RSPO certification* [Online]. Available at: www. wilmar-international.com/sustainability/certification/rspo-certification (Accessed: 13 March 2023).

Wilmar International Limited (2020c). *POIG verification* [Online]. Available at: www. wilmar-international.com/sustainability/certification/poig-verification (Accessed: 13 March 2023).

6 Suntec Real Estate Investment Trust's focus on sustainable buildings

David Bell

Pro Vice-Chancellor (International), Amity Global Institute, Singapore

Suntec Real Estate Investment Trust (Suntec REIT) is a leading real estate investment trust in Singapore, with a focus on commercial properties. Below are some of the challenges that the company faced when focusing on sustainable buildings, and how they succeeded:

Balancing sustainability with profitability: One of the biggest challenges for Suntec REIT was to balance its commitment to sustainability with the need to generate profits for its shareholders (Santamarta et al., 2022). To overcome this challenge, the company implemented a range of sustainability initiatives like the use of green building features and technologies in its properties and green initiatives at Suntec City that have helped reduce energy consumption by up to 10%, resulting in significant cost savings for the company. These initiatives reduced their environmental impact but also helped to reduce costs and increase operational efficiency.

Ensuring regulatory compliance: To ensure regulatory compliance, Suntec REIT has established a robust compliance framework (Thomson Reuters, 2021) that includes policies, procedures, and controls to manage risks and ensure that the company operates in a legally compliant manner. The framework covers a wide range of areas, including financial reporting, environmental health and safety, data protection, and anti-bribery and corruption.

Suntec REIT also engages with industry associations and regulatory bodies to stay informed about regulatory changes and requirements. The company participates in industry events and forums to keep up to date with developments and best practices, and it works closely with its legal and accounting advisors to ensure that it is meeting all relevant regulations and standards (Monetary Authority of Singapore, 2019; Allen & Gledhill, 2020; Suntec Real Estate Investment Trust, 2021).

Educating tenants and stakeholders: Suntec REIT also faced challenges in educating their tenants and stakeholders about the importance of sustainability and the benefits of sustainable buildings (Shook et al., 2022). To overcome this challenge, the company engaged in regular communication and education initiatives, such as sustainability workshops and seminars, to raise awareness and build support for their sustainability efforts.

DOI: 10.4324/9781032660547-43

Suntec REIT reduced its environmental impact and increased its profitability and operational efficiency by creating a portfolio of sustainable buildings. The company invested in sustainable infrastructure, such as energy-efficient lighting, water-saving technologies, and renewable energy sources (Ulbrich, 2022). The company also achieved its sustainability targets, such as energy efficiency, water conservation, greenhouse gas emissions, environmental certification, and stakeholder engagement (Lee, 2022). The company obtained Green Mark certification for all its buildings in Singapore, demonstrating its commitment to sustainability (Archistar, 2021). Suntec REIT became a leader in sustainable real estate by focusing on sustainable buildings and is ready for future success (World Economic Forum, 2021).

Investing in sustainable infrastructure: To reduce its carbon footprint they invested in a range of energy-saving technologies and practices, such as upgrading its lighting systems, optimising its air-conditioning systems, and installing energy-efficient equipment which improved their sustainability performance. This helped the company to achieve its sustainability targets like energy efficiency, water conservation, greenhouse gas emissions, environmental certification, and stakeholder engagement while also reducing costs and improving operational efficiency (Suntec Real Estate Investment Trust, 2021).

Through these efforts, Suntec REIT succeeded in creating a portfolio of sustainable buildings that not only reduced their environmental impact but also improved their profitability and operational efficiency. The company was able to achieve Green Mark certification for all of its buildings in Singapore, which is a testament to its commitment to sustainability. By focusing on sustainable buildings, Suntec REIT has established a strong reputation as a leader in sustainable real estate and is well-positioned to succeed in the future.

References

Allen & Gledhill (2020). *Issue of S$200 million perpetual securities by HSBC Institutional Trust Services (Singapore) Limited, in its capacity as trustee of Suntec Real Estate Investment Trust* [Online]. Available at: www.allenandgledhill.com/sg/perspectives/articles/17132/issue-of-s-200-million-perpetual-securities-by-hsbc-institutional-trust-services-limited-in-its-capacity-as-trustee-of-suntec-real-estate-investment-trust (Accessed: 11 May 2023).

Archistar (2021). *What is sustainable real estate development?* [Online]. Available at: www.archistar.ai/blog/what-is-sustainable-real-estate-development/

Lee, K. (2022). *The future of real estate: how sustainable green building is changing the industry* [Online]. Available at: https://stacs.io/sustainable-real-estate-green-building-industry-insights/

Monetary Authority of Singapore (2019). *Compliance toolkit for real estate investment trust managers* [Online]. Available at: www.mas.gov.sg/-/media/MAS/Regulations-and-Financial-Stability/Regulations-Guidance-and-Licensing/Securities-Futures-and-Fund-Management/Guidance/Compliance-Toolkit/Compliance-Toolkit-for-REIT-Managers.pdf?la=en&hash=E76EAA73A48A76F54BE4DF785EFDAB38FC972373 (Accessed: 11 May 2023).

Santamarta, S., Seppä, T., Gruß, C., Bozic Mazzi, A., Cuellar, M., Catchlove, P., & Vikström, A. (2022). *The challenges of a sustainability transformation.* Boston Consulting Group [Online]. Available at: www.bcg.com/publications/2022/the-challenges-of-a-sustainability-transformation (Accessed: 11 May 2023).

Shook, E., Lacy, P., Suntook, C., & Rademacher, J. (2022). *How stakeholder alignment on sustainability unlocks a competitive advantage.* World Economic Forum [Online]. Available at: www.weforum.org/agenda/2022/02/how-to-strengthen-sustainabil ity-by-engaging-with-stakeholders/

Suntec Real Estate Investment Trust (2021). *Annual report 2020* [Online]. Available at: www.suntecreit.com/annual-reports.html (Accessed: 11 May 2023).

Thomson Reuters (2021). *Building a compliance department* [Online]. Available at: https://legal.thomsonreuters.com/en/insights/articles/building-a-compliance-department (Accessed: 11 May 2023).

Ulbrich, C. (2022). *The 10 green building principles aiming to get real estate to net zero* [Online]. Available at: www.weforum.org/agenda/2021/11/10-green-build ing-principles-real-estate-net-zero/ (Accessed: 11 May 2023).

World Economic Forum (2021). *Real estate must become more liveable, sustainable and affordable. Here's how.* [Online]. Available at: www.forbes.com/sites/worldeconom icforum/2021/04/21/real-estate-must-become-more-liveable-sustainable-and-aff ordable-heres-how/ (Accessed: 11 May 2023).

7 Ascendas Real Estate Investment Trust's focus on sustainable business parks

Amin Hosseinian Far

Professor of Systems Thinking, University of Northampton, United Kingdom

Ascendas Real Estate Investment Trust (Ascendas REIT) is one of the largest real estate investment trusts in Asia with a focus on business and industrial parks. As with any real estate investment trust, Ascendas REIT faces challenges related to economic cycles, interest rate fluctuations, and tenant demands. However, the trust has also faced challenges specific to its focus on sustainable business parks.

One of the main challenges Ascendas REIT has faced is the need to constantly update and adapt its properties to meet the evolving needs of its tenants. As businesses become increasingly focused on sustainability, the demand for eco-friendly buildings and green spaces has grown. Ascendas REIT has responded by investing in sustainable building features, such as energy-efficient lighting and water-saving fixtures and creating green spaces for tenants to enjoy. However, these upgrades require significant capital investment and ongoing maintenance, which can be a challenge for a real estate investment trust (CapitaLand Ascendas REIT, 2021). Studies show that green buildings can benefit REITs environmentally and socially, but they also require more investment and costs (Wong et al., 2018). REITs should strategically invest in green buildings, considering the market, tenants, regulations, and stakeholders. REITs should also incorporate sustainability into their strategy and governance and disclose their environmental, social, and corporate governance (ESG) performance to improve their financial performance and risk management (Lee & Chan, 2019).

Another challenge Ascendas REIT has faced is the need to balance the demands of sustainability with the needs of its tenants for affordable space. Sustainable building practices and features can be more expensive to implement and maintain, which can increase rental rates and make it more difficult to attract and retain tenants. Ascendas REIT has responded by focusing on long-term sustainability initiatives that will not only benefit the environment but also provide cost savings for tenants over time. JLL (2022) reports that green-certified office buildings can earn up to 28% higher rents than non-certified ones in some Asian markets like Hong Kong, where green-certified supply is scarce. The report also states that sustainability is a key factor for

DOI: 10.4324/9781032660547-44

corporate tenants, and that demand for green-certified buildings exceeds supply in the region. CBRE (2022) agrees that green-certified buildings have higher rents in the office sector and expects the same for other property types as tenants and end-users want more environmental performance. The report also advises investors to view ESG factors to create value and reduce risk, not as a compromise or a cost.

Despite these challenges, Ascendas REIT has succeeded by adopting a pro-active and innovative approach to sustainable business parks. The trust has invested heavily in research and development to identify new technologies and practices that can improve the sustainability and efficiency of its properties. It has also worked closely with its tenants to understand their evolving needs and incorporate their feedback into its property management and development strategies (CapitaLand Ascendas REIT, 2021).

Overall, Ascendas REIT's focus on sustainable business parks has allowed it to differentiate itself in the competitive real estate market and attract a diverse range of tenants. By embracing innovation and sustainability, the trust has positioned itself for long-term success in a rapidly changing business landscape.

References

CapitaLand Ascendas REIT (2021). *Sustainability reports* [Online]. Available at: www.capitaland-ascendasreit.com/en/sustainability.html (Accessed: 4 May 2023).

CBRE (2022). *ESG and real estate: the top 10 things investors need to know* [Online]. Available at: www.cbre.com.sg/insights/reports/esg-and-real-estate-the-top-10-thi ngs-investors-need-to-know (Accessed: 4 May 2023).

JLL (2022). *The value of sustainability: evidence for a green premium in Asia* [Online]. Available at: www.jll.com.sg/en/trends-and-insights/research/the-value-of-sustain ability-asia-pacifics-green-premium-opportunity (Accessed: 4 May 2023).

Lee, W.L., & Chan, E.H.W. (2019). Green buildings for enhancing financial perform-ance of real estate investment trusts. *Journal of Cleaner Production, 227,* 1006–1017.

Wong, J.K.W., Zhou, J.Y.X., & Deng, M. (2018). Green building investment decisions for real estate investment trusts: a review. *Journal of Cleaner Production, 172,* 1530–1543.

8 Ascott Residence Trust's focus on sustainable serviced apartments

Jonny Munby

Principal Lecturer (International), Teesside University, United Kingdom

Imagine staying in a serviced apartment that is not only comfortable and convenient but also eco-friendly and socially responsible. This is the vision of Ascott Residence Trust (ART), a Singapore-based real estate investment trust that owns and manages serviced residences globally. The trust has been focusing on sustainable serviced apartments in recent years, incorporating environmental, social, and governance (ESG) practices into its operations. By doing so, ART aims to create value for its stakeholders, reduce its environmental footprint, and contribute to the well-being of the communities where it operates.

One of the challenges faced by ART in its sustainable initiatives is the implementation of green technologies and practices across its diverse portfolio of properties. The trust has to ensure that its properties comply with local regulations and building codes while also meeting its sustainability targets. To address this, ART has adopted a comprehensive framework for sustainability, which includes a set of guidelines and best practices that are tailored to each property. The framework covers various aspects of sustainability, such as energy efficiency, water conservation, waste management, biodiversity protection, and stakeholder engagement. ART has also obtained green financing for some properties, such as lyf one-north Singapore and Citadines Islington London, which are designed to meet high standards of environmental performance. In addition, ART issued its first global hospitality trust sustainability-linked bond of S$200 million in April 2021. The bond is linked to ART's GRESB score (≥80) and carbon emissions intensity reduction (25% by 2025 from 2018) (Ascott Residence Trust, 2021a; Ascott Residence Trust, 2021b). These financial instruments reflect ART's commitment to aligning its business strategy with its sustainability vision.

Another challenge faced by ART is the integration of sustainability into its supply chain management. The trust has been working with its suppliers to ensure that they meet its sustainability standards and that their products and services are environmentally friendly. This includes partnering with suppliers who provide sustainable materials and equipment for the construction and operation of its properties. ART follows a procurement policy that

DOI: 10.4324/9781032660547-45

includes sustainability criteria for choosing and working with its suppliers. It also checks and evaluates its suppliers regularly to ensure they follow the policy and improve their practices. ART works with its suppliers to adopt green initiatives for its properties. For example, it has installed energy-saving lighting, water-saving devices, and waste management systems. It also urges its suppliers to use recycled or renewable materials. By adopting practices of sustainable supply chain management (Beske & Seuring, 2014), ART not only minimises the environmental footprint of its operations but also fosters long-term relationships with its suppliers based on mutual trust and respect.

Despite these challenges, ART has overcome these challenges and achieved success in its sustainable initiatives, earning recognition from various sustainability rating agencies. In 2020, ART was included in the Dow Jones Sustainability Asia Pacific Index for the fourth consecutive year, demonstrating its strong performance in ESG criteria. The trust has also received the Green Mark Platinum Award, the highest level of certification for sustainable buildings in Singapore, for several of its properties, such as Ascott Orchard Singapore and lyf Funan Singapore. ART performed well in sustainability and received good ratings from the Global Real Estate Sustainability Benchmark (GRESB) (CapitaLand, 2021a). GRESB assesses the ESG performance of real estate and infrastructure portfolios and assets. ART also secured a green loan of S$50 million for its new project, lyf one-north Singapore, and issued a bond of S$200 million that is linked to its sustainability goals (CapitaLand, 2021b). These financial instruments reflect ART's commitment to aligning its business strategy with its sustainability vision.

In sum, ART's sustainability efforts have not only helped the environment but also improved its financial results. Tenants prefer sustainable and eco-friendly choices, and ART's green initiatives have drawn and kept tenants, leading to higher occupancy and rent. Also, ART's green loans and sustainability-linked bonds have allowed it to broaden its financing options and reduce its interest expenses, increasing its financial adaptability and strength. By matching its sustainability goals with its business aims, ART has added value for its stakeholders and become a leader in the hospitality industry.

References

Ascott Residence Trust (2021a). *Sustainability report 2021* [Online]. Available at https://links.sgx.com/FileOpen/20220531_ART_SustainabilityReport2021.ashx?App=Announcement&FileID=719233. (Accessed: 16 May 2023).

Ascott Residence Trust (2021b). *Ascott Residence Trust sustainability-linked finance framework* [Online]. Available at www.capitalandascotttrust.com/system/misc/ART_%20Sustainability-Linked-Finance-Framework_vf.pdf. (Accessed: 16 May 2023).

Beske, P., & Seuring, S. (2014). Putting sustainability into supply chain management. *Supply Chain Management: An International Journal. 19*(3), 322–331. https://doi.org/10.1108/SCM-12-2013-0432

CapitaLand (2021a). *Ascott Residence Trust recognised for leadership in sustainability as 'Global Sector Leader' in 2021 Global Real Estate Sustainability Benchmark* [Online]. Available at www.capitaland.com/en/about-capitaland/newsroom/news-relea ses/international/2021/oct/ART_Global_Sector_Leader_GRESB_2021.html. (Accessed: 16 May 2023).

CapitaLand (2021b). *Ascott Residence Trust is first hospitality trust globally to issue sustainability-linked bond of S$200 million* [Online]. Available at www.capitaland. com/en/about-capitaland/newsroom/news-releases/international/2022/apr/ Ascott_Residence_Trust_first_hospitality_trust_globally_to_issue_sustainability_li nked_bond_S200m.html. (Accessed: 16 May 2023).

9 SPH REIT's focus on sustainable shopping malls

Lim Chin Guan

Consultant, PowerTECH Innovations, Singapore

SPH REIT is a real estate investment trust that owns and manages a portfolio of retail properties in Singapore. These properties include shopping malls, supermarkets, and other commercial spaces that generate income from rents and leases. The trust is committed to implementing environmentally friendly and socially responsible practices in its daily operations and long-term management of its properties. These practices aim to reduce the trust's environmental impact, enhance its tenants' and customers' well-being, and increase its financial performance and resilience.

One of the main challenges in adopting sustainable practices in real estate is finding a balance between environmental and social responsibility and financial returns (Peiser & Wiegelmann, 2019). SPH REIT successfully addressed this challenge by adopting various technologies and practices that help lower its energy use and environmental impact while improving its cost efficiency and operational performance. For instance, the trust installed lighting systems that use less electricity, air conditioning systems that regulate temperature more effectively, and water-saving features that reduce water wastage in its properties. These measures help the trust minimise its energy consumption and carbon footprint.

Another challenge was meeting sustainability targets set by regulators and investors (Mattison & de Longevialle, 2022). SPH REIT responded by developing a sustainability strategy focusing on four pillars: environment, society, governance, and stakeholders. It uses KPIs to track and improve its ESG performance and value creation. The KPIs have clear goals and deadlines. SPH REIT actively collaborates with its tenants to promote sustainability in their businesses as part of its stakeholder engagement efforts. It provides them with guidance and support (SPH REIT, 2021) on implementing green initiatives in their daily operations, such as energy efficiency, waste reduction, and recycling. It also recognises and rewards tenants demonstrating exemplary environmental performance and innovation through its annual Green Star Awards.

SPH REIT believes working with tenants on sustainability is vital for its success. It supports tenants to go green by saving energy, water, and recycling.

DOI: 10.4324/9781032660547-46

It also keeps tenants informed about its sustainability efforts and achievements. ULI (2022) states that tenant engagement can lower carbon emissions for the whole building, improve tenant loyalty and happiness, and boost property value. GRESB (2019) argues that tenant engagement can help match sustainability goals with stakeholders' interests and enhance collaboration and trust. Hello Energy (2020) gives different examples of engaging tenants on sustainability, such as surveys, events, scorecards, and green leasing.

SPH REIT keeps up with the latest sustainability standards and practices. The trust trains its employees to be sustainable. Mapletree (2021) says that following sustainability trends and benchmarks can help real estate companies adapt and satisfy their stakeholders. Deloitte (2020) argues that ESG factors can benefit real estate companies by improving their image, lowering risks, and drawing investors. The World Economic Forum (2021) guides real estate companies to reach net zero carbon emissions with 10 green building principles for data, design, operations, and reporting.

By embracing sustainability, SPH REIT has created value for investors and stakeholders and supported a greener future for Singapore. To reflect its mission of being the preferred landlord and delivering sustainable long-term growth for unit holders, SPH REIT rebranded itself as Paragon REIT in January 2023 (*The Edge Singapore*, 2022). The name change also goes along with the change of its sponsor from Singapore Press Holdings (SPH) to Cuscaden Peak Investments. This consortium involves Hotel Properties, CLA Real Estate Holdings, and Mapletree (*The Straits Times*, 2022).

References

Deloitte (2020). *The impact of social good on real estate* [Online]. Available at: www2.deloitte.com/ce/en/pages/real-estate/articles/the-impact-of-social-good-on-real-estate.html (Accessed: 8 May 2023).

GRESB (2019). *Tenant engagement – the road to corporate sustainability* [Online]. Available at: www.gresb.com/nl-en/tenant-engagement%e2%80%93the-road-to-corporate-sustainability/ (Accessed: 8 May 2023).

Hello Energy (2020). *How to engage tenants on sustainability* [Online]. Available at: www.hello-energy.com/how-to-engage-tenants-on-sustainability-a-sneak-peak/ (Accessed: 8 May 2023).

Mapletree (2021). *Sustainability report* [Online]. Available at: www.mapletree.com.sg/~/media/Media/Publication/Annual%20Reports/2021%202022/19%20Sustainability%20Report.pdf (Accessed: 8 May 2023).

Mattison, R., & de Longevialle, B. (2022). *Key trends that will drive the ESG agenda in 2022* [Online]. Available at: www.spglobal.com/esg/insights/featured/special-editorial/key-esg-trends-in-2022 (Accessed: 8 May 2023).

Peiser, R., & Wiegelmann, T. (2019). Sustainable investment in real estate. *World Built Environment Forum*. Available at: www.rics.org/news-insights/wbef/sustainable-investment-in-real-estate

SPH REIT (2021). *Sustainability report* [Online]. Available at: https://paragonr eit.listedcompany.com/misc/ar2021/sph_reit_AR2021-Sustainability-Report.pdf (Accessed: 8 May 2023).

The Edge Singapore (2022). *SPH REIT changes its name to Paragon REIT* [Online]. Available at: www.theedgesingapore.com/news/reits/sph-reit-changes-its-name-paragon-reit (Accessed: 8 May 2023).

The Straits Times (2022). *SPH REIT to be renamed Paragon REIT from Jan 3* [Online]. Available at: www.straitstimes.com/business/sph-reit-to-be-renamed-paragon-reit-from-jan-3 (Accessed: 8 May 2023).

ULI (2022). *Working toward net zero: tenant engagement best practices and examples* [Online]. Available at: https://knowledge.uli.org/en/reports/research-reports/2022/working-toward-net-zero-tenant-engagement-best-practices-and-examples (Accessed: 8 May 2023).

World Economic Forum (2021). *The 10 green building principles aiming to get real estate to net zero* [Online]. Available at: www.weforum.org/agenda/2021/11/10-green-building-principles-real-estate-net-zero/ (Accessed: 8 May 2023).

10 CapitaLand Mall Trust's focus on sustainable retail operations

Preethi Thankappan Nair

Lecturer – Business Strategy, Co-Founding Director – Business Advice Centre, University of East London, United Kingdom

CapitaLand Mall Trust (CMT) is one of the largest retail real estate investment trusts (REITs) in Singapore. The company has a strong focus on sustainability and has implemented several initiatives to improve its sustainable retail operations. Here are some of the challenges CMT faced and how they succeeded:

Retrofitting existing properties: One of the main challenges CMT faced was retrofitting existing properties to make them more sustainable. Retrofitting refers to the process of improving the environmental performance of existing buildings by upgrading their systems and equipment (Chua et al., 2013). According to its sustainability report, CMT achieved a 19.1% reduction in energy intensity and a 22.9% reduction in water intensity across its portfolio from 2008 to 2019 (CapitaLand Integrated Commercial Trust, 2020). CMT also secured its first sustainability-linked loan of S$200 million from United Overseas Bank Limited in 2020, which incentivises CMT to achieve certain sustainability performance targets (CapitaLand Mall Trust, 2020).

Educating tenants and shoppers: CMT recognised that it was important to educate tenants and shoppers about sustainability and the impact of their actions. Education for sustainability (EfS) is a process of learning that enables people to develop the knowledge, skills, values, and attitudes needed to contribute to a more sustainable world (UNESCO, 2014). The company launched several campaigns to encourage sustainable behaviour, including recycling programmes, energy-saving initiatives, and awareness campaigns. CMT also collaborated with the Singapore Environment Council to organise the Eco-Shop Challenge, which challenges shoppers to reduce their environmental footprint by choosing eco-friendly products and services (CapitaLand Mall Trust, 2019).

Balancing sustainability with profitability: CMT wanted to be sustainable and profitable. It knew that being green could cost more at first but save money and attract customers later. Elkington (1994) said businesses should care about profit, people, and the planet. CMT helped its tenants cut costs and stay green. For example, it gave them rebates for using less electricity

DOI: 10.4324/9781032660547-47

(CapitaLand Integrated Commercial Trust, 2020). It also got a loan that rewarded it for meeting sustainability goals (CapitaLand Mall Trust, 2020).

Adapting to changing market conditions: CMT had to keep up with the changing market conditions. Customers wanted different things, so CMT had to be flexible and quick to change. This meant using technology to make shopping better, such as mobile apps and online platforms, to keep up with the competition. Grewal et al. (2020) said technology can make customers happier by giving them convenience, personalisation, interactivity, and social connection. CMT used technology to give customers more choices, such as picking up or delivering their orders, to suit their different needs and preferences (CapitaLand Integrated Commercial Trust, 2020). CMT also added new features such as contactless payment, virtual fitting rooms, and interactive digital screens to make shopping smooth and fun (CapitaLand Mall Trust, 2019).

Overall, CMT's focus on sustainable retail operations has helped the company differentiate itself from competitors and appeal to customers who value sustainability. Through its sustainability initiatives, CMT has also been able to reduce operating costs and increase tenant satisfaction, which has contributed to the company's success.

References

CapitaLand Integrated Commercial Trust (2020). *Sustainability report 2019/2020* [Online]. Available at: www.cict.com.sg/pdf/CICT_Sustainability_Report_2019_2 020.pdf (Accessed: 12 April 2023).

CapitaLand Mall Trust (2019). *CapitaLand Mall Trust launches Eco-Shop Challenge 2019* [Online]. Available at: www.capitaland.com/international/en/about-capital and/newsroom/news-releases/international/2019/jul/cmt-launches-eco-shop-challenge-2019.html (Accessed: 15 April 2023).

CapitaLand Mall Trust (2020). *CapitaLand Mall Trust secures its first sustainability-linked loan of S$200 million from UOB* [Online]. Available at: www.capitaland.com/en/about-capitaland/newsroom/news-releases/international/2020/sep/cmt-first-sustainability-linked-loan-UOB.html (Accessed: 14 April 2023).

Chua, K.J., Chou, S.K., Yang, W.M., & Yan, J. (2013). Achieving better energy-efficient air conditioning – a review of technologies and strategies. *Applied Energy, 104*, 87–104. https://doi.org/10.1016/j.apenergy.2012.10.037

Elkington, J. (1994). Towards the sustainable corporation: win-win-win business strategies for sustainable development. *California Management Review, 36*(2), 90–100. https://doi.org/10.2307/41165746

Grewal, D., Roggeveen, A.L., Nordfält, J., & Shankar, V. (2020). The future of retailing: an introduction. *Journal of Retailing, 96*(1), 1–7. https://doi.org/10.1016/j.jretai.2019.12.001

UNESCO (2014). *Roadmap for implementing the Global Action Programme on Education for Sustainable Development* [Online]. Available at: https://unesdoc.une sco.org/ark:/48223/pf0000230514 (Accessed: 14 April 2023).

11 Keppel DC REIT commits to sustainable data centres

R. Amudha

Professor, CMS Business School, Jain (Deemed to be University), India

Keppel DC REIT is a specialised real estate investment trust that focuses on owning and managing data centres. The trust aims to deliver consistent returns to investors while also pursuing environmental sustainability in its operations.

A major challenge for data centres is their large energy demand. Data centres need a lot of power to run the servers and cooling systems that enable their operation. This energy demand can have negative impacts on the environment and the climate. The International Energy Agency (IEA) reported that data centres used about 1% of global electricity in 2018, or around 200 TWh (IEA, 2020). Data centres also produce greenhouse gases, both directly from burning fossil fuels and indirectly from using grid electricity. McKinsey research indicates that data centres can emit up to 80 megatonnes of carbon dioxide a year (McKinsey, 2018).

To address this challenge, Keppel DC REIT has invested in renewable energy sources. The trust has equipped its data centres with solar panels and wind turbines, and it is also buying renewable energy credits from other sources. These investments have lowered Keppel DC REIT's carbon emissions and operating costs. The IEA (2020) reported that renewable energy sources such as solar and wind could meet up to 80% of the electricity needs of data centres by 2030. Renewable energy sources can also improve the reliability and resilience of data centres by cutting their reliance on the grid and fossil fuels (Bhattacharya et al., 2019). These investments have lowered Keppel DC REIT's carbon emissions and operating costs. Renewable energy sources such as solar and wind can supply clean and dependable electricity for data centres, cutting their reliance on fossil fuels and grid power. Renewable energy sources can also boost the resilience and competitiveness of data centres by reducing their exposure to price changes and regulatory risks (Forbes, 2020). Keppel DC REIT is not the only one pursuing renewable energy for its data centres. Many other data centre operators, such as Amazon, Microsoft, Google, and Facebook, have also pledged to use 100% renewable energy for their data centres (ENGIE, 2020).

In addition to investing in renewable energy, Keppel DC REIT has also implemented energy-efficient designs in its data centres. These designs have

DOI: 10.4324/9781032660547-48

features such as low-emissivity glass and free cooling. Low-emissivity glass prevents heat from entering the data centre, which helps to save energy. Free cooling uses the outside air to lower the temperature of the data centre, which also reduces energy costs. Energy-efficient design is an important strategy for enhancing the performance and sustainability of data centres. By following best practices such as low-emissivity glass, free cooling, smart sensors, and high-efficiency lighting, data centres can lower their power usage effectiveness (PUE) and carbon emissions (Koomey et al., 2011). PUE is a metric that shows how well a data centre uses energy. A smaller PUE means a more energy-efficient data centre. Some examples of data centres with low PUEs and energy-efficient designs are the CDC's Arlen Specter Center in Atlanta, with free cooling, variable speed fans, and high-efficiency chillers; the Facebook data centre in Luleå, with free cooling from the Arctic air, evaporative cooling towers, and server heat recovery; and the Google data centre in Hamina, with seawater cooling from the Baltic Sea, high efficiency servers, and machine learning for cooling optimisation (Uptime Institute, 2019).

Keppel DC REIT has also obtained environmental certifications to demonstrate its commitment to sustainability. These certifications include the BCA-IMDA Green Mark for Data Centers, the LEED Gold certification, and ISO 50001 certification. Environmental certifications are voluntary standards that assess the environmental impact and performance of buildings, including data centres. They provide a framework and a benchmark for data centres to improve their environmental management and practices. They also signal to stakeholders and customers that data centres are responsible and trustworthy. Additionally, they can help them save energy and money, reduce environmental risks and impacts, improve their image and marketability, and meet customer and regulatory demands (Wang et al., 2018).

Keppel DC REIT is a pioneer in sustainability in the data centre industry. The trust has invested in renewable energy sources that supply clean and dependable electricity for its data centres. The trust has also implemented energy-efficient designs that lower its energy use and costs. Furthermore, the trust has obtained environmental certifications that display its high standards of environmental performance and management. These actions not only show the trust's commitment to sustainability but also generate value for both investors and the environment. Keppel DC REIT is leading the way for other data centre operators to follow and contribute to a greener future.

References

Bhattacharya, S., Chandan, V., Arya, V., Kishore, N., Agarwal, A., Bhatnagar, S., Choudhary, A., Prakash, A., Gupta, R., Sharma, P., Jain, R., Sharma, M.K., Palit, D., Mathur, S., & Tongia, R. (2019). Renewable energy integration for data centers: a survey. *Renewable and Sustainable Energy Reviews, 113*, 109270. https://doi.org/10.1016/j.rser.2019.109270

ENGIE (2020). *Optimising data center energy consumption for "greener" perform-ance* [Online]. Available at: www.engie.com/en/campaign/green-data-centers (Accessed: 12 May 2023).

Forbes (2020). *How data centers are driving the renewable energy transition* [Online]. Available at: www.forbes.com/sites/siemens-smart-infrastructure/2020/03/13/how-data-centers-are-driving-the-renewable-energy-transition/ (Accessed: 7 May 2021).

IEA (2020). *Data centres and data transmission networks* [Online]. Available at: www.iea.org/reports/data-centres-and-data-transmission-networks (Accessed: 7 May 2023).

Koomey, J.G., Brill, K.G., Turner, W.D., Stanley, J., & Taylor, B. (2011). A simple model for determining true total cost of ownership for data centers. *Uptime Institute White Paper*, 1–15. www.researchgate.net/publication/228569907_A_simple_model_for_determining_true_total_cost_of_ownership_for_data_centers (Accessed: 7 May 2023).

McKinsey (2018). *Capturing value from IT infrastructure modernization* [Online]. Available at: www.mckinsey.com/business-functions/mckinsey-digital/our-insights/capturing-value-from-it-infrastructure-modernization# (Accessed: 7 May 2023).

Uptime Institute (2019). *Data center industry survey* [Online]. Available at: https://uptimeinstitute.com/2019-data-center-industry-survey-results (Accessed: 11 May 2023).

Wang, Y., Wang, Y., Wang, Y., Liang, X.J., & Chen, Q.Y. (2018). Green certification for improving organizational reputation and legitimacy in green building industry. *Journal of Cleaner Production, 195*, 1544–1555. https://doi.org/10.1016/j.jclepro.2018.06.021

12 Hyflux becoming a global leader in desalination and water treatment

Choy Murphy
Director, Alionova Education Pte Ltd, Singapore

Hyflux is a Singaporean company that has a strong focus on water treatment and desalination. The company started its operations in 1989 and soon rose to become a prominent player in the global water industry. However, along the way, it encountered various difficulties and obstacles that threatened its survival and growth.

One of the major hurdles that Hyflux had to overcome was the high expense of research and development. As a company that depends heavily on technology to set itself apart from its rivals, Hyflux had to constantly invest in research and development to maintain its edge. This created pressure on the company's finances, and Hyflux had to repeatedly look for funding from investors. Tan (2020) reported that Hyflux allocated about S$1.1 billion for research and development between 2006 and 2017, which made up about 5% of its revenue. However, the outcomes of these investments were not always evident or timely, as some of the technologies that Hyflux created were not widely used or profitable.

Another challenge Hyflux faced was the complexity of operating in diverse markets with different regulatory environments. Hyflux had to adapt to various regulations in countries such as China, Algeria, and Oman, which made it challenging to standardise operations across its global portfolio. Lim (2005) stated that Hyflux encountered issues such as delayed payments, contractual disputes, and environmental compliance in China. In Algeria, Hyflux faced political instability and social unrest that disrupted its projects. In Oman, Hyflux had to deal with changes in government policies that affected its profitability (Low et al., 2019).

In addition, Hyflux faced challenges related to its debt load. The company had borrowed a large amount of money to fund its expansion, and this became a major problem when the global financial crisis struck in 2008. The crisis led to a decline in demand for Hyflux's products and services, which affected the company's cash flow (Jain & Khandelwal, 2020). Moreover, Hyflux's flagship project, the Tuaspring integrated water and power plant in Singapore, was a financial failure. The project cost more than S$1 billion to construct, but it did

DOI: 10.4324/9781032660547-49

not produce enough revenue due to an excess of electricity in the market. As a result, Hyflux incurred losses of more than S$900 million from Tuaspring between 2017 and 2019 (Chua et al., 2020).

Despite these challenges, Hyflux was able to succeed by leveraging its core strengths. One of the company's key strengths is its ability to develop and commercialise innovative water treatment technologies. Hyflux's expertise in this area has enabled it to secure contracts in many countries around the world. For example, Hyflux built the world's largest membrane-based seawater desalination plant in Magtaa, Algeria, which can produce up to 500 million litres of water per day. Hyflux also developed a proprietary technology called Kristal ultrafiltration membrane that can remove contaminants from water more efficiently and effectively than conventional methods. Furthermore, Hyflux launched a new series of compact, pre-engineered seawater and brackish water reverse osmosis systems that incorporate its Kristal ultrafiltration pre-treatment technology to meet challenging water treatment requirements (WaterWorld, 2016).

Another key strength of Hyflux is its ability to form strategic partnerships with companies in different markets. By working closely with local partners, Hyflux has been able to navigate complex regulatory environments and gain access to new markets. For example, Hyflux partnered with Mitsubishi Heavy Industries and Toyota Tsusho Corporation to construct a seawater reverse osmosis desalination plant in Qurayyat, Oman, which can produce up to 200,000 m³ of water per day. Hyflux also collaborated with Yunnan Water Investment Co., Ltd, a leading water operator in China, to jointly develop water projects in China and other regions, such as Indonesia and Vietnam.

Finally, Hyflux has been able to handle its debt load by taking a proactive approach to financial management. The company has been able to obtain financing from various sources, including government agencies and private investors. For example, the company received a S$100 million loan from the Singapore government's Economic Development Board in 2006 to support its research and development activities. Hyflux also raised S$500 million from retail investors through a perpetual securities offering in 2016, which was oversubscribed by more than three times (Low et al., 2019).

In conclusion, Hyflux's journey to success has not been smooth or easy. The company has faced various obstacles and difficulties related to research and development, regulatory environments, and debt management. However, the company has not given up or compromised its vision and values. The company has used its core strengths and formed strategic partnerships to overcome these challenges and create value for its customers and stakeholders. Therefore, Hyflux was once a recognized global leader in the field of water treatment and desalination, celebrated for its steadfast dedication to pioneering solutions and high standards of quality.

References

Chua, S., Tortajada, C., & Biswas, A.K. (2020). Tuaspring desalination plant: what went wrong? *International Journal of Water Resources Development, 36*(1), 1–17. https://doi.org/10.1080/07900627.2019.1672392

Jain, R., & Khandelwal, R. (2020). Dare to defy the challenges of online business. *International Journal of Case Studies in Business, IT, and Education, 4*(1), 1–13. https://doi.org/10.5281/zenodo.3632799

Lim, G.S. (2005). It's so clear: Hyflux and the success story of a Singapore female entrepreneur. *Journal of Enterprising Culture, 13*(2), 171–192. https://doi.org/10.1142/S0218495805000112

Low, D., Foo, M., & Koh, F. (2019). The Hyflux case and the rights of perpetual securities holders. *Asian Journal of Business Ethics, 8*(2), 215–230. https://doi.org/10.1007/s13520-019-00095-4

Tan, K.F. (2020). The Hyflux saga: a cautionary tale of corporate governance failure. *Singapore Economic Review, 65*(4), 1033–1055. https://doi.org/10.1142/S0217590820500318

WaterWorld (2016). *Hyflux expands membrane bioreactor (MBR) range* [Online]. Available at: www.waterworld.com/home/article/16202802/hyflux-expands-membrane-biorector-mbr-range (Accessed: 2 June 2023).

13 PEC Ltd adaptation to the changing dynamics of the oil and gas industry

Desti Kannaiah

Associate Lecturer, Newcastle University, Singapore

The oil and gas industry is one of the most dynamic and complex sectors in the world, facing constant changes and challenges in its operating environment. To survive and thrive in this industry, companies need to be agile, innovative, and resilient. One such company is PEC Ltd, a Singapore-based firm that provides engineering, procurement, and construction services for the oil and gas industry. PEC Ltd has demonstrated its ability to adapt to the changing dynamics of the industry, by implementing several strategies that have enabled it to overcome various challenges and achieve success. In this case study, some of these challenges and strategies will be examined, and how they have helped PEC Ltd to grow and prosper in a rapidly changing industry.

Challenges

Oil price volatility: The oil and gas industry is highly influenced by fluctuations in oil prices, which can affect the demand for PEC's services and the company's profitability. The International Energy Agency (2020) reported that global oil demand contracted for the first time since the global recession of 2009 due to the COVID-19 pandemic and the lockdown measures that followed. The pandemic also aggravated the existing oversupply situation in the market, leading to a sharp decline in oil prices. PEC has had to cope with the uncertainty and volatility in its operating environment and adjust its business plans accordingly, such as reducing its costs, deferring its investments, and diversifying its services.

Intense competition: The oil and gas industry is highly competitive, with many established players competing for market share. PEC has had to find ways to differentiate itself from competitors and offer unique value propositions to clients. Accenture (2020) stated that one of the main challenges for the industry is to improve its environmental performance, as consumers and investors are increasingly demanding cleaner and greener energy sources. PEC has had to balance its core competencies in the oil and gas sector with its efforts to diversify into renewable energy and other segments, such as infrastructure

DOI: 10.4324/9781032660547-50

and building construction. This has helped PEC to enhance its reputation and increase its revenue streams.

Renewable energy shift: The increasing attention to renewable energy sources has resulted in a shift away from traditional fossil fuels, which can influence the demand for PEC's services. The World Economic Forum (2020) stated that the transportation sector, which accounts for a large share of oil demand, is experiencing a transformation as electric vehicles (EVs) become more cost-effective and convenient than internal combustion engines (ICEs). PEC has had to foresee and react to the changing preferences and needs of its customers and stakeholders. This shift is also backed by the findings of Zhang et al. (2020), who examined the global trends and drivers of EV adoption and its implications for oil demand. They found that EVs have the potential to significantly lower oil consumption and greenhouse gas emissions in the transportation sector, especially in regions with high renewable energy penetration.

Successes

Service diversification: PEC has diversified its services to reduce its dependence on the oil and gas industry. The company has ventured into areas such as renewable energy, infrastructure, and building construction. According to its website (PEC Ltd, n.d.), PEC has completed projects such as solar power plants, waste-to-energy plants, water treatment plants, data centres, and residential buildings. These projects have helped PEC to widen its customer base, boost its reputation, and increase its revenue streams. This strategy of service diversification is also recommended by Ford et al. (2017), who analysed the future directions for the oil and gas industry in Australia. They suggested that oil and gas companies should diversify their products and embrace renewable energy to create value in a low-carbon future.

Strategic partnerships and collaborations: PEC have formed strategic partnerships and collaborations with other companies to expand its service offerings and access new markets. This has helped the company to reduce its reliance on any one market or industry. For example, according to its annual report (PEC Ltd, 2020), PEC has partnered with China Huanqiu Contracting & Engineering Corporation (HQC) to jointly pursue opportunities in Southeast Asia and China. PEC has also collaborated with Singapore Technologies Engineering Ltd (ST Engineering) to provide integrated solutions for smart city development.

Innovation and technology emphasis: PEC has invested in innovation and technology to improve its efficiency and lower its costs. The company has implemented digital solutions to streamline its operations and improve its project management capabilities. For example, according to its website (PEC Ltd, n.d.), PEC has adopted a cloud-based platform called AVEVA E3D Design that enables real-time collaboration among engineers across different locations. PEC has also leveraged artificial intelligence (AI) and data analytics to optimise its processes and enhance its decision-making.

In conclusion, PEC has demonstrated its resilience and agility in the face of the changing dynamics of the oil and gas industry by pursuing service diversification, strategic partnerships and collaborations, and innovation and technology emphasis. These strategies have enabled the company to cope with the uncertainty and volatility of oil prices, enhance its differentiation and value proposition to customers, and prepare itself for long-term growth in a rapidly changing industry. PEC's success story shows that oil and gas companies can create value in a low-carbon future by embracing new opportunities and technologies.

References

Accenture (2020). *Reinventing the oil and gas industry: compounded disruption* [Online] Available at: www.weforum.org/agenda/2020/09/reinventing-the-oil-and-gas-industry-compounded-disruption/ (Accessed: 18 May 2023).

Ford, J.A., Fitz, R., Abel, M., DiPaolo, C., & Appathurai, S. (2017). *Diversification versus discipline: value creation in oil and gas 2021*. Boston Consulting Group [Online]. Available at: www.bcg.com/publications/2021/shareholder-value-creation-strategies-oil-gas-sector

International Energy Agency (2020). *Oil 2020* [Online]. Available at: www.iea.org/reports/oil-2020 (Accessed: 18 May 2023).

PEC Ltd (2020). *Annual report 2020* [Online]. Available at: www.peceng.com/annualreport/2020/ (Accessed: 18 May 2023).

PEC Ltd (n.d.). *Projects Works* [Online]. Available at: http://www.peceng.com/html/business_works.php (Accessed: 18 May 2023).

World Economic Forum (2020). *The oil and gas sector must reinvent itself. Here's one way* [Online]. Available at: www.weforum.org/agenda/2020/12/how-to-reinvent-the-oil-and-gas-sector/ (Accessed: 18 May 2023).

Zhang, X., Bai, X., Chang, Y., Wang, T., & Zhang, L. (2020). Global electric vehicle outlook: drivers and impacts on oil demand. *Energy Policy, 147*, 111864. https://doi.org/10.1016/j.enpol.2020.111864

14 Frasers Centrepoint Trust

Lim Chin Guan

Consultant, PowerTECH Innovations, Singapore

As a real estate investment trust based in Singapore, Ascott Residence Trust (ART) operates a global portfolio of serviced residences that cater to various travellers' needs. In line with its vision of positively impacting the environment and society, the trust has implemented environmental, social, and governance (ESG) practices in its sustainable serviced apartments over the past few years.

ART is challenged to consistently apply green technologies and practices across its various properties in different locations. The trust must comply with each country's local environmental regulations and building codes and achieve sustainability goals (Chen & Chang, 2013). To overcome this challenge, ART has developed a holistic framework for sustainability, which provides specific guidelines and best practices adapted to each property's characteristics and needs (Capital and Ascott Trust, 2022). For example, ART has obtained a green loan from DBS Bank to fund its maiden development project and co-living property in lyf one-north Singapore, fitted with green, energy-efficient, and intelligent building features. It is certified with a Green Mark GoldPLUS rating by the Building and Construction Authority of Singapore.

Another challenge ART faces is the integration of sustainability into its supply chain management. The trust has been working with its suppliers to ensure that they meet its sustainability standards and that their products and services are environmentally friendly. It includes partnering with suppliers who provide sustainable materials and equipment for the construction and operation of its properties (Freeman et al., 2010). For example, ART has used bamboo, a fast-growing and renewable plant, for flooring and furniture in some properties, such as Ascott Raffles City Chengdu and Somerset West Lake Hanoi. ART has also used hempcrete, a natural composite material made from hemp and lime, for insulation and fireproofing in some properties, such as Citadines Barbican London and Ascott Orchard Singapore. These materials are eco-friendly, durable, versatile, and low in maintenance.

Despite these challenges, ART has been successful in its sustainable initiatives, receiving recognition from various sustainability ratings agencies, such as the Dow Jones Sustainability Asia Pacific Index for the fourth consecutive year in 2020 and the Green Mark Platinum Award for several of its

DOI: 10.4324/9781032660547-51

properties in Singapore (Capital and Ascott Trust, 2022). These initiatives have benefited the environment and contributed to its financial performance as tenants increasingly seek sustainable, eco-friendly options. ART's sustainability efforts have helped attract and retain tenants, increasing occupancy rates and rental income.

In addition, ART has pioneered issuing sustainability-linked bonds and loans, which are financial instruments that link the cost of borrowing to achieve predefined sustainability performance targets (SPTs). In April 2021, ART issued its first sustainability-linked bond of S$200 million under its Sustainability-Linked Finance Framework, becoming the first hospitality trust globally to do so. The bond has a tenor of seven years and a coupon rate of 2.15% per annum. Twenty-five basis points will adjust the coupon rate if ART fails to achieve its SPTs by 2026. The SPTs are related to reducing greenhouse gas emissions intensity, increasing renewable energy consumption, and maintaining green building certifications across its portfolio of properties (Bouzidi & Papaioannou, 2021).

ART has shown dedication to pursuing sustainability in every aspect of its business, from its operations and supply chain to its financing and investment decisions. By issuing sustainability-linked bonds and loans, ART reduces borrowing costs and reinforces its accountability to meet its SPTs. These targets are aligned with global sustainability goals and reflect ART's ambition to create long-term value for its stakeholders, including its tenants, investors, employees, and communities (Shapiro et al., 2021). Mr Bob Tan, Chairman of Ascott Residence Trust Management Limited (ARTML) and Ascott Business Trust Management Pte. Ltd (ABTM), the managers of ART, said: "The issuance of our first sustainability-linked bond is a testament to our strong ESG track record as well as our ability to tap on various sources of capital to fund our growth. We will continue to seek opportunities to grow our portfolio through sustainable developments and enhance our existing properties with green features." With its clear sustainability vision and strategy, ART is well-positioned to seize opportunities and overcome the challenges in the hospitality industry while positively impacting the environment and society.

References

Bouzidi, A., & Papaioannou, D. (2021). Sovereign sustainability-linked bonds – opportunities, challenges and pricing considerations. *SSRN Electronic Journal.* https://doi.org/10.2139/ssrn.3919159

Capital and Ascott Trust (2022). *Ascott Residence Trust sustainability-linked finance framework* [Online]. Available at: www.capitalandascotttrust.com/system/misc/ART_%20Sustainability-Linked-Finance-Framework_vf.pdf. (Accessed: 3 May 2023).

Chen, Y.-S., & Chang, C.-H. (2013). Greenwash and green trust: the mediation effects of green consumer confusion and green perceived risk. *Journal of Business Ethics, 114*(3), 489–500. https://doi.org/10.1007/s10551-012-1360-0

Freeman, R.E., Harrison, J.S., Wicks, A.C., Parmar, B.L., & de Colle, S. (2010). *Stakeholder Theory: The State of the Art.* Cambridge University Press.

Shapiro, L., Wilkins, M., Romero Ramirez, A.M., & Fiore, Z.S. (2021). Environmental, social, and governance: how sustainability-linked debt has become a new asset class. *S&P Global Ratings.* https://doi.org/10.2139/ssrn.3919159

15 WOHA Architects designed sustainable and iconic buildings in Singapore and beyond

Vijayakumar Gajenderan

Associate Professor, Sir Theagaraya College, India

WOHA Architects is a Singapore-based practice that focuses on conceiving integrated architectural and urban solutions to tackle the problems of the 21st century such as climate change, population growth, and rapidly increasing urbanisation. Founded by Wong Mun Summ and Richard Hassell in 1994, it has been recognised internationally for its innovative and sustainable design projects that range from interiors and architecture to public spaces and regenerative master plans. Some of their iconic buildings include the Parkroyal Collection Pickering, a hotel that features lush green terraces and gardens; the Oasia Hotel Downtown, a vertical garden tower that hosts a variety of plant species and habitats; and the Kampung Admiralty, a mixed-use complex that integrates housing, healthcare, retail, and community facilities for senior citizens.

As an island state, Singapore poses various challenges for WOHA Architects in designing sustainable and iconic buildings that respond to its unique urban, climatic, and environmental conditions (WOHA, 2018). Some of these challenges are related to the high-density urban environment, the tropical climate, and the rising sea levels that characterise Singapore. As a densely populated country with limited land and space for development, Singapore requires buildings that can accommodate a large number of functions and users within a compact footprint (Department of Statistics Singapore, 2020). For example, WOHA designed the Kampung Admiralty, a mixed-use complex that integrates housing, healthcare, retail, and community facilities for senior citizens within a stepped profile that creates a series of cascading gardens and terraces. As a tropical country with high temperatures, humidity, and rainfall throughout the year, Singapore demands buildings that can provide thermal comfort, energy efficiency, and water management while maintaining the health and well-being of the occupants and the environment. For instance, WOHA designed the Oasia Hotel Downtown, a vertical garden tower that hosts more than 60 plant species and 30 animal species within its red mesh facade. The building uses natural ventilation, cross ventilation, evaporative cooling, and other passive design strategies to achieve thermal comfort without air-conditioning (WOHA, 2018). As a low-lying island nation

DOI: 10.4324/9781032660547-52

vulnerable to climate change, Singapore needs buildings that can protect the city from flooding and erosion caused by sea level rise while enhancing its biodiversity and ecosystem services. This involves building seawalls, dykes, and floating structures, restoring mangroves and wetlands, and creating artificial islands and reefs. To illustrate, WOHA proposed a master plan for Singapore in 2050 that envisions a series of floating islands that provide housing, recreation, agriculture, and energy production for the city (WOHA, 2009).

WOHA Architects adopts systems thinking approach to address these challenges and create sustainable and iconic buildings that are also high amenity and provide a better quality of life for their users and the city. Some of their solutions are:

Vertical urbanism is a key design strategy for WOHA to create sustainable and iconic buildings in Singapore and beyond. They design buildings that are tall and deep, with multiple layers of functions, spaces, and greenery. This maximises land use, creates diverse and human-scaled environments, fosters community and social interaction, and reduces urban heat. Examples are the Parkroyal Collection Pickering, a hotel with lush green terraces and gardens; the SkyVille@Dawson, a public housing complex with 12 interconnected sky villages; and the Singapore 2050 Masterplan, a proposal for floating islands for housing, recreation, agriculture, and energy (WOHA, 2009). WOHA uses vertical urbanism to address high-density urban challenges in Singapore.

The biophilic design integrates nature into WOHA's buildings visually and functionally. They create green facades, roofs, terraces, and gardens with diverse plants and habitats, enhancing their buildings' appeal, comfort, quality, and performance while supporting biodiversity, carbon, and water. Examples are the Parkroyal Collection Pickering, a hotel with lush green terraces and gardens that harvest rainwater, use solar panels and natural ventilation (Whitewall, 2021); the Oasia Hotel Downtown, a vertical garden tower with 60 plant and 30 animal species within its red mesh facade and passive design strategies for thermal comfort without air-conditioning (*Financial Times*, 2021); and the School of the Arts Singapore, a school with green roofs for outdoor learning, recreation and socialisation, and heat gain and stormwater reduction (BBC, 2020). WOHA applies biophilic design to connect people with nature in Singapore and beyond.

Adaptive design is another strategy that WOHA uses to design flexible and adaptable buildings. They use modular systems, movable partitions, operable windows, and other elements that allow reconfiguration, expansion, or transformation. They also use passive design strategies such as natural ventilation, daylighting, shading, and insulation that reduce mechanical systems and energy consumption. Examples are the Enabling Village, a community hub for people with disabilities that features accessible ramps, pathways, and facilities (DesignSingapore Council, 2017); the SkyVille@Dawson, a public housing complex that offers buyers flexible floor plans with a column-free and beam-free main space (ArchDaily, 2012); and the Parkroyal Collection Pickering, a hotel that features a sky garden system that can be adapted for different uses.

In sum, WOHA Architects is a leading practice in designing sustainable and iconic buildings in Singapore and beyond. Their projects demonstrate how architecture can address the challenges of the 21st century such as climate change, population growth, and urbanisation while enhancing the quality of life, well-being, and resilience of their users and the city. Their projects also showcase their creativity, innovation, and vision in creating new forms of urban environments that are vibrant, engaging, and planned for long-term growth and sustainability.

References

ArchDaily (2012). *SkyVille @ Dawson / WOHA* [Online]. Available at: www.archdaily.com/215386/skyville-dawson-woha (Accessed: 19 April 2023).

BBC (2020). *How 'biophilic' design can create a better workspace* [Online]. Available at: www.bbc.com/worklife/article/20200929-how-biophilic-design-can-create-a-better-workspace (Accessed: 19 March 2023).

Department of Statistics Singapore (2020). *Population trends 2020* [Online]. Available at: www.singstat.gov.sg/-/media/files/publications/population/population2020.pdf (Accessed: 3 March 2023).

DesignSingapore Council (2017). *WOHA's enabling village is drawing communities* [Online]. Available at: https://designsingapore.org/stories/woha-enabling-village-is-drawing-communities/ (Accessed: 9 March 2023).

Financial Times (2021). *It's a jungle in here: the rise of the 'biophilic' home* [Online]. Available at: www.ft.com/content/3fb26ab2-a70c-4e3e-af01-ec907b5c2ba3 (Accessed: 12 March 2023).

Whitewall (2021). *WOHA designs biophilic buildings to nurture the city and its people* [Online]. Available at: https://whitewall.art/design/wohas-biophilic-buildings-that-nurture-the-city-and-its-people (Accessed: 19 March 2023).

WOHA (2009). *Singapore 2050 Masterplan / WOHA | ArchDaily* [Online]. Available at: www.archdaily.com/42777/singapore-2050-masterplan-woha (Accessed: 19 April 2023).

WOHA (2018). *Garden City Mega City: Rethinking Cities for the Age of Global Warming 2016.* Singapore: Pesaro Publishing.

16 Golden Agri-Resources' focus on sustainable palm oil production

Amin Hosseinian Far

Professor of Systems Thinking, University of Northampton, United Kingdom

The production of palm oil, a versatile and widely used vegetable oil, can have negative impacts on the environment and society. To address these impacts, Golden Agri-Resources (GAR), one of the world's largest palm oil companies, has been pursuing sustainable and responsible palm oil production. This paper examines how GAR has overcome the challenges and has embarked on a successful sustainability journey, which involves adopting various policies, practices, and innovations that comply with international standards and certifications.

Environmental impact: One of the major challenges of palm oil production is its environmental impact, which can include deforestation, greenhouse gas emissions, and loss of biodiversity (Murphy et al., 2021). GAR has taken proactive steps to mitigate these impacts and protect the environment. The company has adopted a zero-deforestation policy since 2011, which prohibits the development of high conservation value (HCV) and high carbon stock (HCS) areas, as well as peatlands of any depth (GAR, 2015). GAR has also implemented sustainable land use practices, such as the use of cover crops, intercropping, and integrated pest management, to enhance soil health and biodiversity. Moreover, GAR has aligned its practices with the principles and criteria of the Roundtable on Sustainable Palm Oil (RSPO), which is a multi-stakeholder initiative that promotes the production and use of certified sustainable palm oil (CSPO) (RSPO, 2018). By doing so, GAR has demonstrated its commitment and leadership in reducing the environmental footprint of palm oil production.

Labour practices: Labour practices are another challenge that the palm oil industry has faced, as it has been accused of violating the rights and welfare of workers, such as forced labour and child labour (ILO, 2018). GAR has taken decisive steps to tackle this challenge and ensure decent work for its employees and suppliers. The company has implemented a comprehensive labour policy that covers a zero-tolerance approach to forced and child labour, fair wages and working conditions, and community engagement. The company has also established a social and environmental risk assessment (SERA) system to identify and mitigate potential social risks in its operations

DOI: 10.4324/9781032660547-53

and supply chain. Moreover, GAR has partnered with various stakeholders, such as the International Labour Organization (ILO), the United Nations Children's Fund (UNICEF), and local NGOs, to improve the welfare and rights of workers and communities. Through these actions, GAR has shown its dedication to respecting human rights and labour standards in the palm oil sector.

Supply chain traceability: The global palm oil supply chain is complex, which can pose challenges in tracing the origin of products and ensuring they are produced sustainably (WWF, 2019). GAR has overcome this challenge by implementing a traceability system that allows it to track the origin of its palm oil products and ensure they meet relevant sustainability standards. GAR has also developed a Traceability Dashboard that provides transparent information on its suppliers and mills, such as their locations, certifications, and grievances. Furthermore, GAR has joined the Palm Oil Innovation Group (POIG), which is a platform that aims to support the implementation and verification of innovations in the palm oil sector, such as the use of satellite monitoring and blockchain technology. With these measures, GAR has shown its devotion to enhancing the transparency and accountability of its palm oil supply chain.

Stakeholder engagement: Palm oil production can have significant impacts on local communities, and it is important to engage with these stakeholders to ensure their interests are taken into account (FAO, 2015). GAR has implemented a comprehensive stakeholder engagement programme, which includes consultations with local communities, the establishment of grievance mechanisms, and partnerships with NGOs and other stakeholders. GAR has also adopted a Free Prior Informed Consent (FPIC) approach to respect the rights of indigenous peoples and local communities concerning land acquisition and development. Through this programme, GAR aims to foster trust, collaboration, and mutual benefit with its stakeholders, as well as to address any issues or concerns that may arise from its operations. Through this approach, GAR has manifested its adherence to elevating the social and community aspects of sustainable palm oil production.

GAR has demonstrated its leadership and commitment to sustainable palm oil production through its various efforts to address the environmental and social challenges of the sector. The company has not only implemented its own sustainability policy but has also aligned its operations with internationally recognised standards and certifications, such as the RSPO and the CDP. The company has also leveraged technology and innovation to improve the efficiency and transparency of its operations, such as the use of drones for land mapping and monitoring, and the achievement of 98% traceability to plantation (TTP) for its entire palm supply chain. By doing so, GAR has enhanced its reputation and performance, as well as contributing to the global goals of sustainable development. GAR's sustainability journey is an inspiring example of how palm oil companies can balance economic growth with environmental and social responsibility.

References

FAO (2015). *'Palm Oil', Strengthening Sector Policies for Better Food Security and Nutrition Results*. Rome: Food and Agriculture Organization of the United Nations. https://doi.org/10.4060/a-i5790e

GAR (2015). *Fighting climate change* [Online]. Available at: www.goldenagri.com.sg/sustainability/climate-change/ (Accessed: 26 May 2023).

ILO (2018). *World Employment and Social Outlook 2018: Greening with Jobs*. Geneva: International Labour Office. https://doi.org/10.1007/978-92-2-130928-4

Murphy, D.J., Goggin, K., & Paterson, R.R.M. (2021). Oil palm in the 2020s and beyond: challenges and solutions. *CABI Agriculture and Bioscience, 2*(39). https://doi.org/10.1186/s43170-021-00058-3

RSPO (2018). *Principles & criteria for sustainable palm oil production* [Online]. Available at: https://rspo.org/resources/certification/rspo-principles-and-criteria (Accessed: 30 June 2023).

WWF (2019). *Palm oil buyers scorecard: measuring the progress of palm oil buyers* [Online]. Available at: https://palmoilscorecard.panda.org/ (Accessed: 30 June 2023).

Part IV

Innovation and technology

1 Grab overcoming global adversities to become Southeast Asia's leading ride-hailing and delivery company

Teoh Teik Toe

Academic Director and Associate Director for AI Lab and IMARC Center/Nanyang Technological University, Singapore

What does it take to become the dominant player in the ride-hailing and delivery industry in Southeast Asia? Grab, the homegrown company that has achieved this feat knows the answer. But it was not easy. Grab had to face and overcome many obstacles along the way. In this article, we will explore some of the strategies and solutions that Grab used to rise above the competition and win the hearts of millions of customers.

Localising its services: Grab recognised the importance of localising its services to meet the needs of customers in each Southeast Asian country it operates in. This involved adapting to local payment systems, languages, and regulations. Grab also offers a range of services beyond ride-hailing, including food delivery, grocery delivery, and mobile payments. Grab made its services fit the needs and wants of customers in different Southeast Asian countries. For example, Grab had different kinds of vehicles and payment options in different places. Grab also used the local languages and cultures in its app (Stiltner, 2021). Uber did not do this. Uber only accepted credit cards, which many people did not have or use. Uber also had problems with the laws and customs of different places. In 2018, Uber gave up and sold its business in Southeast Asia to Grab for a part of Grab's company (Fallarme, 2021).

Strategic partnerships: Grab has established strategic alliances with other firms to broaden its service offerings and market reach. For instance, the company teamed up with Indonesian e-commerce platform Tokopedia to introduce a grocery delivery service, and with Mastercard to offer a prepaid debit card for users in the region (Grab, 2020). Grab also partnered with HEINEKEN to provide beer delivery and payment options across Southeast Asia (Grab, 2019). Furthermore, Grab entered a cloud partnership with Microsoft to harness its technology and know-how in big data, artificial intelligence, and mobility (Microsoft, 2018).

Innovative solutions: Grab has been inventive in solving the problems it encounters. For instance, the company created GrabPay, a mobile payment system that enables users to pay for goods and services through the app. Grab also introduced GrabExpress, a same-day courier service that lets users send packages and documents fast and easily. Moreover, Grab developed GrabMaps,

DOI: 10.4324/9781032660547-55

a full stack of mapping technology that offers a detailed and precise view of Southeast Asia built by and for the local community (Grab, 2023). GrabMaps supports Grab's services in all eight countries it operates in and acts as an enterprise service for other companies such as Amazon Web Services (Business Wire, 2023).

Continuous growth and expansion: Grab has been pursuing continuous growth and expansion, both within its current markets and into new ones. The company has reached more than 500 cities in 8 Southeast Asian countries and has plans to keep expanding into new markets and services (The Global VC, 2021). Grab has also increased its gross merchandise value (GMV) by 29% year-over-year to $16.1 billion in 2021, surpassing its guidance range (Grab, 2022).

Grab has also tried new opportunities in grocery delivery, advertising, and financial services, using its superapp model and large customer base (Reuters, 2023).

A customer-centric approach: Grab has always been committed to providing a great customer experience, which has helped to create customer loyalty and trust. The company has spent a lot on customer service, safety features, and driver training programmes to ensure a high-quality experience for all users (Association of MBAs, 2020). Grab has also followed a customer-centric, not customer-led, approach to innovation, which means predicting and meeting the needs and wants of customers, not just responding to their feedback (Forbes, 2020). Grab has also used data and analytics to learn about customer behaviour and preferences and to customise its services and offers (Sprinklr Blog, 2020).

Overall, Grab's success can be attributed to its ability to adapt to local markets, form strategic partnerships, innovate, focus on growth, and provide a great customer experience. By doing so, Grab has become a dominant player in the Southeast Asian ride-hailing and delivery market.

References

Association of MBAs (2020). *Customer experience lessons from Singapore superapp Grab* [Online]. Available at: www.associationofmbas.com/customer-experience-lessons-from-singapore-superapp-grab/ (Accessed: 8 May 2023).

Business Wire (2023). *Grab makes 'world's most innovative companies' by fast company for 2023* [Online]. Available at: www.businesswire.com/news/home/20230302005936/en/Grab-Makes-%E2%80%98World%E2%80%99s-Most-Innovative-Compan ies%E2%80%99-by-Fast-Company-for-2023 (Accessed: 8 May 2023).

Fallarme, D. (2021). *Hyperlocal: the strategy behind Grab's rise in Southeast Asia*. APAC Marketers [Online]. Available at: www.apacmarketers.com/grab-hyperlocal/ (Accessed: 8 May 2023).

Forbes (2020). *Guiding principles to rethink your approach to CX innovation* [Online]. Available at: www.forbes.com/sites/sap/2020/11/17/5-guiding-principles-to-rethink-your-approach-to-cx-innovation/ (Accessed: 8 May 2023).

Grab (2019). *HEINEKEN and Grab announce strategic collaboration in Southeast Asia* [Online]. Available at: www.grab.com/sg/press/business/heineken-and-grab-announce-strategic-collaboration-in-southeast-asia/ (Accessed: 8 May 2023).

Grab (2020). *Grab partners Tokopedia to launch grocery delivery service GrabMart* [Online]. Available at: www.grab.com/sg/press/others/grab-partners-tokopedia-to-launch-grocery-delivery-service-grabmart/ (Accessed: 8 May 2023).

Grab (2022). *Grab reports fourth quarter and full year 2021 results* [Online]. Available at: www.grab.com/sg/press/others/grab-reports-fourth-quarter-and-full-year-2021-results/ (Accessed: 8 May 2023).

Grab (2023). *Grab makes 'world's most innovative companies' by Fast Company for 2023* [Online]. Available at: www.grab.com/sg/press/others/grab-makes-worlds-most-innovative-companies-by-fast-company-for-2023/ (Accessed: 8 May 2023).

Microsoft (2018). *Grab forges strategic cloud partnership with Microsoft to drive innovation and adoption of digital services across Southeast Asia* [Online]. Available at: https://news.microsoft.com/apac/2018/10/08/grab-forges-strategic-cloud-partnership-with-microsoft-to-drive-innovation-and-adoption-of-digital-services-across-southeast-asia/ (Accessed: 8 May 2023).

Reuters (2023) *Singapore's Grab brings forward profitability goal, sees strong 2023* [Online]. Available at: www.reuters.com/business/grab-forecasts-2023-revenue-above-estimates-demand-boom-2023-02-23/ (Accessed: 8 May 2023).

Sprinklr Blog (2020). *Ways Grab is driving customer centricity with Sprinklr* [Online]. Available at: www.sprinklr.com/blog/customer-centricity/ (Accessed: 8 May 2023).

Stiltner, M. (2021). *How localization helped Grab beat Uber in Southeast Asia* [Online]. Available at: www.rapyd.net/blog/how-localization-helped-grab-beat-uber-in-southeast-asia/ (Accessed: 8 May 2023).

The Global VC (2021). *Understanding the rise of the Grab Superapp and its future* [Online]. Available at: https://500.co/theglobalvc/understanding-the-rise-of-the-grab-superapp-and-its-future/ (Accessed: 8 May 2023).

2 OCBC Bank's focus on digital banking services

Amin Hosseinian Far

Professor of Systems Thinking, University of Northampton,
United Kingdom

Digital transformations in the banking sector provide an opportunity to reimagining banking products and services (Lugovsky, 2021). OCBC Bank, one of the leading banks in Singapore, embarked on a digital transformation journey to enhance its banking services and customer experience. However, the bank encountered several challenges along the way, such as changing customer expectations, increasing competition, and evolving regulations. This case study explores how OCBC Bank overcame these challenges and achieved success in digital banking.

Customer adoption: The first challenge that OCBC Bank faced was customer adoption of digital banking services. Some customers were hesitant to adopt new technologies, while others were concerned about the security of digital transactions. Some of the common barriers to digital banking adoption include lack of awareness, trust, convenience, and personalisation (Deloitte, 2021). To address this challenge, OCBC Bank invested in education and its outreach efforts to help customers understand the benefits of digital banking services and the adopted security measures to protect their accounts. The bank invested in advanced technologies and systems to protect customer data and transactions from unauthorised access or fraud. Consequently, the bank achieved a 40% increase in digital customers and a 35% increase in mobile banking transactions in 2019. The bank also received several awards and recognition for its digital excellence and innovation (OCBC, 2020).

Technological infrastructure: The second challenge was the need for robust technological infrastructure to support digital banking services. This included investments in new platforms and systems, as well as incorporation of robust cybersecurity measures to protect against cyber threats and cyber-enabled crimes. Some of the common challenges for banks in developing a modern infrastructure for digital banking include legacy systems, data silos, regulatory compliance, skills gap, and vendor management (IDC, 2021). To address this challenge, OCBC Bank made significant investments in cybersecurity technologies and established partnerships with technology companies to develop and implement cutting-edge digital banking solutions. As a result, the bank

DOI: 10.4324/9781032660547-56

achieved a 99.9% uptime for its internet banking platform and a 99.8% uptime for its mobile banking platform in 2019.

Regulatory compliance: A third challenge was related to regulatory compliance, as digital banking services are subject to a range of regulatory requirements and standards. Some of the common challenges for banks in complying with digital banking regulations include data protection, consumer protection, anti-money laundering, financial inclusion, and competition (McKinsey, 2021). To address this challenge, OCBC Bank worked closely with regulators to ensure that its digital banking services complied with all relevant regulations and standards. Accordingly, the bank achieved a high level of compliance performance and received no material regulatory sanctions or penalties in 2019. The Monetary Authority of Singapore (MAS) is the main financial regulator and the Central Bank in Singapore oversees such regulatory compliance (MAS, n.d.).

Competition: The digital banking space is highly competitive, with several new entrants vying for market share. Some of the common sources of competition for banks in the digital era include FinTech firms, BigTech firms, and digital banks (OECD, 2020). To compete effectively, OCBC Bank focused on offering a differentiated value proposition, including the provision of a wide range of digital banking services, seamless user experiences, and exceptional customer service. Subsequently, the bank achieved a 40% increase in digital customers and a 35% increase in mobile banking transactions in 2019.

Through these efforts, OCBC Bank succeeded in establishing itself as a leading provider of digital banking services in Singapore and beyond. The bank has won numerous awards for its digital banking offerings and has expanded its business into other areas, such as wealth management and insurance, to broaden its revenue base and drive growth. As a result, OCBC Bank is well-positioned to maintain its continuing success in the rapidly evolving digital banking landscape in the years ahead.

References

Deloitte (2021). *Digitalization in banking: how banks could influence customer channel preferences* [Online]. Available at: www2.deloitte.com/xe/en/insights/industry/financial-services/digitalization-in-banking.html (Accessed: 15 April 2023).

IDC (2021). *A modern infrastructure for the digital bank: driven by agility, efficiency, and thanks to 2020 resiliency* [Online]. Available at: https://blogs.idc.com/2021/06/16/a-modern-infrastructure-for-the-digital-bank/ (Accessed: 15 April 2023).

Lugovsky, V. (2021). *Digital transformation in banking: how to make the change* [Online]. Available at: www.forbes.com/sites/forbesbusinesscouncil/2021/12/29/digital-transformation-in-banking-how-to-make-the-change/?sh=3b94f1086999 (Accessed: 15 April 2023).

MAS (n.d.). *Digital bank licence* [Online]. Available at: www.mas.gov.sg/regulation/Banking/digital-bank-licence (Accessed: 15 April 2023).

McKinsey (2021). *Lessons from the rapidly evolving regulation of digital banking* [Online]. Available at: www.mckinsey.com/industries/financial-services/our-insig hts/lessons-from-the-rapidly-evolving-regulation-of-digital-banking (Accessed: 15 April 2023).

OCBC Bank (2020). *Annual report 2019: leading change* [Online]. Available at: www.ocbc.com/group/who-we-are/pdf/2019-annual-report.pdf (Accessed: 15 April 2023).

OECD (2020). *Digital disruption in banking and its impact on competition* [Online]. Available at: www.oecd.org/daf/competition/digital-disruption-in-banking-and-its-impact-on-competition-2020.pdf (Accessed: 15 April 2023).

3 ST Engineering's diversification into cybersecurity

Leon Choong

Regional CEO (ASEAN), Amity Global Institute, Singapore

ST Engineering (2022) is a global leader in engineering and technology solutions that serves customers across various sectors, such as aerospace, electronics, and defence. The company has a strong track record of delivering innovative and reliable products and services that enhance the safety, security, and efficiency of its customers. In recent years, the company has also ventured into the cybersecurity industry, which is one of the fastest growing and most dynamic markets in the world (Statista, 2022). The company aims to provide comprehensive and integrated cybersecurity solutions that can protect its customers from ever-changing cyber threats and challenges. By leveraging its engineering and technology expertise, as well as its strategic partnerships and collaborations, the company has established itself as a trusted and respected player in the cybersecurity domain. Here are some of the challenges ST Engineering faced when diversifying into cybersecurity and how they succeeded:

Competition: The cybersecurity industry is a highly contested and competitive field, with many established players and new start-ups competing for market share. ST Engineering had to differentiate itself from the competition and carve out a niche in the market. To do this, the company followed a strategy of providing innovative solutions that were tailored to the specific needs of its clients (Kraus et al., 2021). By doing so, the company was able to provide value-added services that addressed the unique challenges and needs of its clients in the cybersecurity domain. Additionally, the company leveraged its expertise and experience in other domains, such as aerospace, electronics, and land systems, to offer integrated and holistic solutions that enhanced the security and resilience of its clients' systems and operations. This enabled the company to create a strong brand reputation and customer loyalty in the cybersecurity industry.

Talent acquisition: Hiring and retaining skilled cybersecurity professionals is a challenge that many companies face (ISACA, 2020). ST Engineering addressed this issue by investing in the development of its current employees and improving their cybersecurity skills and knowledge. The company also

DOI: 10.4324/9781032660547-57

collaborated with universities and other institutions to build pipelines of new talent and offer them training and mentorship opportunities. Furthermore, the company created a culture of innovation and excellence that attracted and motivated cybersecurity professionals who wanted to work on cutting-edge projects and solve complex problems. The company also offered competitive compensation and benefit packages that enhanced employee satisfaction and retention.

Cybersecurity landscape: The cybersecurity landscape is constantly evolving, with new threats appearing frequently (McGinty, 2023). ST Engineering had to cope with these threats and be able to adapt rapidly to new technologies and methods. To achieve this, the company dedicated substantial resources to research and development and maintained close contact with its clients to ensure that its solutions were meeting their needs. Moreover, the company adopted a proactive and preventive approach to cybersecurity, rather than a reactive and corrective one. The company used advanced tools and techniques, such as artificial intelligence, machine learning, and blockchain, to detect and prevent cyberattacks before they could cause damage. The company also conducted regular audits and assessments of its systems and processes to identify and eliminate any vulnerabilities or weaknesses.

Regulatory environment: The cybersecurity industry faces a complex regulatory environment, with different laws and regulations in different countries (Madnick, 2022). ST Engineering had to comply with these regulations and make sure that its solutions met the relevant laws and standards. To achieve this, the company set up a dedicated team to oversee and handle regulatory issues. The team's tasks included monitoring the evolving regulatory landscape, performing risk assessments and audits, applying best practices and policies, and communicating with regulators and clients. The team also offered training and advice to other employees on regulatory compliance matters. Additionally, the company sought to influence and shape the regulatory environment by participating in industry associations and forums, providing feedback and suggestions to regulators, and advocating for fair and balanced regulations that supported innovation and security.

In conclusion, ST Engineering has successfully diversified into the cybersecurity industry by leveraging its existing expertise and capabilities in other industries. The company has developed a portfolio of innovative cybersecurity solutions, such as threat intelligence, advanced analytics, and incident response services, which address the complex and evolving needs of its clients. ST Engineering has also established strategic partnerships with leading cybersecurity companies and organisations to enhance its capabilities and expand its reach. Through these efforts, ST Engineering has positioned itself as a key player in the cybersecurity industry and continues to innovate and adapt in this dynamic space.

References

ISACA (2020). *State of cybersecurity 2020: global update on workforce efforts, resources and cyberoperations* [Online]. Available at: www.isaca.org/resources/state-of-cybers ecurity (Accessed: 1 May 2023).

Kraus, S., Jones, P., Kailer, N., Weinmann, A., Chaparro-Banegas, N., & Roig-Tierno, N. (2021). Digital transformation: an overview of the current state of the art of research. *SAGE Open, 11*(3), 21582440211047576.

Madnick, S. (2022). *Cybersecurity trends: looking over the horizon*. McKinsey [Online]. Available at: www.mckinsey.com/capabilities/risk-and-resilience/our-insights/cybers ecurity/cybersecurity-trends-looking-over-the-horizon (Accessed: 1 May 2023).

McGinty, D. (2023). *Cybersecurity in today's rapidly changing threat landscape: a comprehensive look at emerging risks, data protection and privacy laws, and customer trust* [Online]. Available at: https://blogs.sap.com/2023/04/12/cybersecurity-in-tod ays-rapidly-changing-threat-landscape-a-comprehensive-look-at-emerging-risks-data-protection-and-privacy-laws-and-customer-trust/ (Accessed: 1 May 2023).

Statista (2022). *Cybersecurity – Worldwide | Statista Market Forecast* [Online]. Available at: www.statista.com/outlook/tmo/cybersecurity/worldwide (Accessed: 1 May 2023).

ST Engineering (2022). *ST Engineering and Microsoft launch cloud-based cybersecurity service platform* [Online]. Available at: www.stengg.com/en/newsroom/news-relea ses/st-engineering-and-microsoft-launch-cloud-based-cybersecurity-service-platf orm/ (Accessed: 1 May 2023).

4 ST Kinetics' diversification into robotics and autonomous systems

Saikat Gochhait

Assistant Professor, Symbiosis International University, India

ST Kinetics is a Singapore-based defence and engineering company that has diversified into the field of robotics and autonomous systems. The company has developed and deployed various robotic and autonomous solutions, such as unmanned ground vehicles, unmanned aerial vehicles, and autonomous logistics systems, for both military and civilian applications. However, diversifying into this field was not easy, as the company faced several challenges, such as technological complexity, regulatory uncertainty, and market competition. This case will examine some of these challenges and how ST Kinetics overcame them to succeed in the field of robotics and autonomous systems.

Developing expertise in new technology: ST Kinetics wanted to be good at making robots and machines that can work by themselves. These robots and machines can do many things, such as driving, carrying things, and helping people. But making and using these robots and machines was hard. ST Kinetics spent a lot of money and time on research and development and hired people who knew a lot about robots (*Singapore Business Review*, 2017). They also worked with other companies, universities, and research centres that were good at robots (Mui, 2017; Land Transport Authority, 2017; National Instruments Singapore, 2017). They bought a company in the United States that made robots that can carry things. These things helped ST Kinetics to improve their skills and products in making robots and machines that can work by themselves.

Meeting the needs of diverse industries: ST Kinetics also faced the challenge of catering to different industries that required robotics and autonomous systems. These industries involved manufacturing, logistics, and defence. The company tackled this challenge by developing a variety of robots and machines that could be customised to fit the needs of each industry, by engaging with customers to comprehend their demands. For instance, ST Kinetics collaborated with the Land Transport Authority to develop and trial autonomous buses (Land Transport Authority, 2017). They also partnered with National Instruments Singapore to evaluate the performance of their robots and machines in Singapore (Mui, 2017).

DOI: 10.4324/9781032660547-58

Ensuring safety and reliability: Safety and reliability are essential factors in developing and deploying robots and machines that can work by themselves. ST Kinetics addressed this challenge by conducting rigorous testing and quality control procedures, and by ensuring that they adhered to the standards for safety and reliability. For instance, ST Kinetics collaborated with National Instruments Singapore to evaluate the performance of their robots and machines in terms of braking distance, obstacle avoidance, and weather conditions (Mui, 2017). They also employed a novel modelling paradigm for their robots and machines that could verify if they were safe and reliable to operate in different scenarios (Ojha & Guan, 2021).

Overcoming regulatory and legal barriers: Robotics and autonomous systems are still developing fields, so they often encounter rules and laws that restrict their use. ST Kinetics tackled this challenge by collaborating with the regulators and authorities to ensure compliance with the applicable laws and regulations, and by informing customers and other stakeholders on the advantages and drawbacks of robotics and autonomous systems. For example, ST Kinetics followed some guidelines for addressing legal and ethical issues in robotics (Leenes et al., 2017). Furthermore, they investigated different levels of autonomy for their robots and machines and how they affect safety and reliability (Yang et al., 2017). Moreover, they examined how their robots and machines can interact with people in different situations (Lopes et al., 2019).

Through these efforts, ST Kinetics has succeeded in establishing itself as a leading provider of robotics and autonomous systems in Singapore and beyond. The company has developed a range of products and services that are used in a variety of industries and has established partnerships with leading companies and institutions to continue driving innovation in the field. By focusing on quality, safety, and customer needs, ST Kinetics has positioned itself for continued success in the future.

References

Land Transport Authority (2017). *LTA inks agreement with ST Kinetics to develop & trial autonomous buses* [Online]. Available at: www.smartnation.gov.sg/media-hub/press-releases/lta-inks-agreement-with-st-kinetics-to-develop-and-trial-autonomous-buses (Accessed: 16 May 2023).

Leenes, R., Palmerini, E., Koops, B.J., Bertolini, A., Salvini, P., & Lucivero, F. (2017). Regulatory challenges of robotics: some guidelines for addressing legal and ethical issues. *Law, Innovation and Technology, 9*(1), 1–44. www.tandfonline.com/doi/full/10.1080/17579961.2017.1304921

Lopes de Sousa Jabbour, A.B., Jabbour, C.J., Sarkis, J., & Filho, M.G. (2019). Unlocking the circular economy through new business models based on large-scale data: an integrative framework and research agenda. *Technological Forecasting and Social Change, 144*, 546–552. www.sciencedirect.com/science/article/pii/S0040162518312460

Mui, R. (2017). *ST Kinetics, National Instruments to test autonomous systems in Singapore* [Online]. Available at: www.straitstimes.com/business/companies-mark ets/st-kinetics-national-instruments-to-test-autonomous-systems-in-singapore (Accessed: 16 May 2023).

National Instruments Singapore (2017). *NI and ST Kinetics partner to test autono-mous vehicle systems in Singapore* [Online]. Available at: www.ni.com/en-sg/about-ni/newsroom/news-releases/ni-and-st-kinetics-partner-to-test-autonomous-vehi cle-systems-in-singapore.html (Accessed: 16 May 2023).

Ojha, A., & Guan, S. (2021). Reliability and safety of autonomous systems: a logic-based modelling paradigm for online diagnostics and prognostics. *Robotics, 10*(1), 10. www.mdpi.com/2218-6581/10/1/10

Singapore Business Review (2017). *ST Engineering acquires robotics firm Aethon* [Online]. Available at: https://sbr.com.sg/building-engineering/news/st-engineer ing-acquires-robotics-firm-aethon (Accessed: 16 May 2023).

Yang, G.Z., Cambias, J., Cleary, K., Daimler, E., Drake, J., Kiekens, C., & Taylor, R.H. (2017). Medical robotics - regulatory, ethical, and legal considerations for increasing levels of autonomy. *Science Robotics, 2*(4), eaam8638. www.science.org/doi/10.1126/scirobotics.aam8638

5 SATS innovates in-flight logistics with new technology

Lo Wai Meng Sally

Academic Director, Amity Global Institute, Singapore

SATS is a leading provider of in-flight logistics services, such as catering, ground handling, and cargo management. The company has to handle a large volume of goods every day while ensuring accuracy and timeliness in its operations. This is a daunting challenge, as any mistake or delay can have serious consequences for the company and its clients. To overcome this challenge, SATS introduced several technological innovations and process improvements, such as automated guided vehicles (AGVs), smart glasses, and digital twins. These innovations helped SATS to enhance its operational efficiency, quality, and safety (Changi Airport Group, 2021).

SATS has been innovating its logistics operations in several ways. One such innovation is the use of AGVs to move goods in warehouses and ports. These are electric vehicles without drivers that can find their way around by themselves. SATS works with Changi Airport to test these vehicles for carrying luggage on planes. This saves manpower and cuts down pollution. SATS also uses these vehicles for moving food in its kitchens. This makes the work faster and safer (SATS Ltd., 2019). AGVs help SATS to handle goods better and need fewer workers, which improves efficiency and accuracy. Additionally, AGVs can reduce human errors, accidents, and injuries, as well as increase the flexibility and scalability of operations. AGVs are widely used in logistics and manufacturing industries, as they can transport various types of goods, such as pallets, containers, rolls, and carts. AGVs are an example of how SATS leverages technology to enhance its logistics performance.

Additionally, SATS uses digital technologies to enhance its logistics operations. For example, it has a mobile app that tracks goods in real time with RFID tags and sensors (SATS Ltd., 2018). This improves response time and visibility for customers. It also has a digital platform that offers end-to-end logistics and food-service solutions in Asia (SATS Ltd., 2020). This platform serves as a one-stop, go-to-market platform for food-service solutions in Asia, connecting customers with a wide range of products and services. Moreover, SATS uses cloud computing technology to store and process data from various sources, such as IoT devices, sensors, and cameras. This enables SATS to analyse data and optimise its operations, such as route planning, inventory

DOI: 10.4324/9781032660547-59

management, and quality control (ShipBob, 2021). Cloud computing also allows SATS to access data and applications from anywhere and at any time, enhancing its flexibility and scalability (SIPMM Publications, 2021). Digital technologies help SATS to improve its logistics performance and customer satisfaction.

Furthermore, SATS uses data analytics to improve its logistics operations. The company has created tools and algorithms to analyse data on inventory, demand, and delivery. This helps the company to understand its operations better and make smarter decisions on how to use its resources. For example, the company has a mobile app that lets its staff track and monitor goods in real time with RFID tags and sensors. This makes response time and visibility better for customers. The company also uses AI and ML techniques to improve its forecasting and planning and to automate some processes like quality inspection and defect detection (SATS Ltd., 2020). This makes operational efficiency and accuracy better. Additionally, SATS uses data analytics to identify patterns and trends in customer behaviour and preferences. This helps the company to offer more personalised and customised solutions that meet customer needs and expectations. For instance, the company has a digital platform that connects customers with a wide range of food-service solutions in Asia, such as catering, delivery, and e-commerce (SATS Ltd., 2020). This platform allows customers to choose from different products and services based on their preferences and feedback. Data analytics helps SATS to enhance its logistics performance and customer satisfaction.

In conclusion, SATS has transformed its logistics operations with these innovations. The company has leveraged automation and data analytics to optimise its processes and use its resources more effectively. The company has also reduced costs and enhanced customer service by providing better visibility and traceability of goods, and by offering more customised and diverse solutions. SATS is well-positioned to grow its business and serve its customers excellently in the evolving and competitive market. SATS Ltd. (2020) reported a 10.5% increase in revenue in 2019/2020, despite the COVID-19 pandemic. The company also received many accolades for its service quality, innovation, and sustainability.

References

Changi Airport Group (2021). *Automating the transport of baggage in Changi Airport* [Online]. Available at: www.changiairport.com/corporate/media-centre/changijourneys/the-airport-never-sleeps/autonomous_tractor.html (Accessed: 26 April 2023).

SATS Ltd. (2018). *SATS launches new mobile app for cargo tracking* [Online]. Available at: www.sats.com.sg/Press%20Releases/SATS%20launches%20new%20mobile%20app%20for%20cargo%20tracking.pdf (Accessed: 26 April 2023).

SATS Ltd. (2019). *SATS harnesses automation to enhance productivity at its new eCommerce AirHub* [Online]. Available at: www.sats.com.sg/Press%20Releases/ SATS%20harnesses%20automation%20to%20enhance%20productivity%20at%20 its%20new%20eCommerce%20AirHub.pdf (Accessed: 26 April 2023).

SATS Ltd. (2020). *Food-service solutions and distribution* [Online]. Available at: www. sats.com.sg/services/details/food-products (Accessed: 26 April 2023).

ShipBob (2021). *Digital Logistics 101: definition, solutions, & top companies* [Online]. Available at: www.shipbob.com/blog/digital-logistics/ (Accessed: 26 April 2023).

SIPMM Publications (2021). *Key technologies for digital logistics* [Online]. Available at: https://publication.sipmm.edu.sg/key-technologies-digital-logistics/ (Accessed: 26 April 2023).

6 NetLink NBN Trust's response to changing telecommunications market conditions

Senthil Kumar Natarajan
Lecturer, University of Technology and Applied Sciences Salalah,
Sultanate of Oman

NetLink NBN Trust is a leading provider of fibre broadband services in Singapore. These are some of the challenges that the company faced in response to changing telecommunications market conditions, and how they succeeded in overcoming them:

Increased competition: As the sole owner of the nationwide fibre network that supports Singapore's Nationwide Broadband Network (NBN), NetLinkNBN Trust encountered growing competition from other telecom providers, especially in the mobile broadband sector (Yahoo Finance, 2022). The company's strategy to remain competitive was to provide broadband services that were fast, dependable, and suitable for both residential and commercial customers (Fenwick, 2022).

Changing customer demands: As mobile and cloud technologies have shaped new customer preferences for broadband services, such as on-demand access, mobility, and flexibility (O'Halloran, 2023; IBM Cloud, n.d.), NetLink NBN Trust, the sole owner and operator of Singapore's NBN, has responded to these evolving customers' needs by upgrading its network infrastructure and offering new products and services, such as managed network solutions and cloud-based storage. These efforts aim to improve customer satisfaction and experience, as well as to boost the company's revenue and market share.

Regulatory changes: The Infocomm Media Development Authority (IMDA) regulates the telecommunications industry in Singapore and establishes the licensing and regulatory framework for the telecoms sector (Infocomm Media Development Authority, n.d.). NetLink NBN Trust, the operator of the fibre network that supports Singapore's NBN, had to adhere to various regulatory requirements, such as those concerning quality of service, interconnection, competition, and security (Tan & Tan, 2020). The company reacted to these regulatory changes by collaborating with the IMDA and other regulatory bodies to ensure that its products and services fulfilled all the required standards. This helped the company to keep its licence valid, avoid sanctions, and improve its reputation and credibility in the market.

Investing in innovation: NetLink NBN Trust valued innovation in the telecommunications industry and spent a lot on research and development

DOI: 10.4324/9781032660547-60

to keep its edge. The company created new technologies and processes that enabled it to provide faster, more dependable broadband services, and collaborated with leading technology companies to keep up with industry developments. For instance, the company offered a promotion to help small and medium enterprises (SMEs) and foster digital transformation by charging lower prices for its non-residential connections. The company also backed the local gaming and sports industry by sponsoring the Singapore Esports Open 2021 and supplying high-speed fibre broadband connectivity for the event (NetLink NBN Trust, n.d.).

Through these efforts, NetLink NBN Trust succeeded in establishing itself as a leading provider of fibre broadband services in Singapore. The company has a strong reputation for quality and reliability and has won numerous awards and certifications, such as the ISO 9001 certification for quality management and the Frost & Sullivan Singapore Broadband Service Provider of the Year award. By focusing on customer needs, innovation, regulatory compliance, and network infrastructure investment, NetLink NBN Trust has positioned itself for continued success in the future.

References

Fenwick, S. (2022). *Singapore mobile network experience report June 2022* [Online]. Available at: www.opensignal.com/reports/2022/06/singapore/mobile-network-experience (Accessed: 3 May 2023).

IBM Cloud (n.d.). *What is mobile cloud computing?* [Online]. Available at: www.ibm.com/cloud/learn/what-is-mobile-cloud-computing (Accessed: 3 May 2023).

Infocomm Media Development Authority (n.d.). *Telecommunication and security standards* [Online]. Available at: www.imda.gov.sg/regulations-and-licensing-listing/ict-standards-and-quality-of-service/Telecommunication-and-Security-Standards (Accessed: 3 May 2023).

NetLink NBN Trust (n.d.). *NetLink NBN Trust – investor relations* [Online]. Available at: www.netlinknbn.com/ (Accessed: 3 May 2023).

O'Halloran, J. (2023). *Global fixed and mobile business broadband to flourish from 5G* [Online]. Available at: www.computerweekly.com/news/365532029/Global-fixed-and-mobile-business-broadband-to-flourish-from-5G (Accessed: 3 May 2023).

Tan, C.W., & Tan, B. (2020). *In brief: telecoms regulation in Singapore* [Online]. Available at: www.lexology.com/library/detail.aspx?g=d29f388d-15f1-428a-afc4-732b6e20823e (Accessed: 3 May 2023).

Yahoo Finance (2022). *Singapore telecoms industry report 2023–2030 with telco transaction database* [Online]. Available at: https://finance.yahoo.com/news/singapore-telecoms-industry-report-2023-090300366.html (Accessed: 3 May 2023).

7 Sembcorp Marine's innovation in offshore and marine engineering

Choy Murphy

Director, Alionova Education Pte Ltd, Singapore

Sembcorp Marine is a global leader in offshore and marine engineering, with expertise in ship repair, shipbuilding, and rig building. The company has delivered innovative and high-quality solutions to customers in the oil and gas, renewable energy, and naval sectors. However, the company has also faced several challenges in the industry, such as fierce competition, high operational costs, and a slump in demand due to the global economic downturn. In this report, we will examine how Sembcorp Marine has overcome these challenges and achieved success in the offshore and marine engineering industry.

Sembcorp Marine has tried to be more innovative in how it does engineering work and uses technology. The company has spent a lot of money on finding new ways to make and use things that can help it work better and greener. For example, Sembcorp Marine has made new solutions such as the Integrated Centre for Environmental Solutions (ICES), which can help it build ships and rigs faster and cheaper. The company has also used three ways to find and work on new ideas and solutions, using its people and other partners. The company has worked with schools on different projects to make things better for the environment and energy, as well as its work. The company has also developed leading-edge designs for rigs and drillships such as the Pacific Class 400 jack-up design and the Jurong Espadon drillship design (Sembcorp Marine Ltd, 2021).

Sembcorp Marine has also entered new markets, such as offshore renewables and gas processing, to make its revenue more diverse and less dependent on the unstable oil and gas industry. Besides that, the company has taken steps to cut costs and make its operations more efficient and profitable. For example, Sembcorp Marine has won a major offshore renewables project to build the largest and most advanced high voltage direct current (HVDC) electrical transmission system for TenneT, a Dutch grid operator. The project will have a total capacity of 6 GW and is part of TenneT's offshore grid development programme, which plans to install 40 GW of offshore wind energy in the German and Dutch North Seas (Sembcorp Marine Ltd, 2023). Sembcorp Marine has also finished two offshore wind farm substations for Ørsted Wind Power, a Danish renewable energy company (Sembcorp Marine Ltd, 2021).

DOI: 10.4324/9781032660547-61

These projects show Sembcorp Marine's skills and experience in the renewable and clean energy sector. Sembcorp Marine has also taken various cost-cutting measures, such as lowering manpower costs, using yard space better, and making operations more efficient. These measures have helped the company to reduce its operating costs and increase its margins.

Sembcorp Marine has tried to be more innovative, diverse, and cost-effective in its business. This has helped the company deal with the difficulties in the offshore and marine engineering industry and keep being a top player in the market. For example, Sembcorp Marine has won many new contracts in the offshore renewables sector, such as the Hornsea 2 offshore wind farm project in the United Kingdom, the Sofia offshore wind farm project in the North Sea, and the big HVDC electrical transmission system project for TenneT in the Netherlands. These projects show Sembcorp Marine's skills and experience in giving integrated solutions for the offshore, marine, and energy industries. Sembcorp Marine has also taken steps to cut costs, such as lowering manpower costs, using yard space better, and making operations more efficient. These steps have helped the company to reduce its operating costs and increase its margins. According to UOB Kay Hian, Sembcorp Marine has made positive EBITDA in 2H22 and a free cash flow of over S$1 billion for 2022. These financial indicators suggest that Sembcorp Marine has improved and is ready for 2023 (Kay Hian Research, 2023).

References

Kay Hian Research (2023). *Sembcorp Marine – FY22 losses as expected, but the focus is on a brighter future – UOB* [Online]. Available at: https://sginvestors.io/analysts/research/2023/03/sembcorp-marine-uob-kay-hian-research-2023-03-01 (Accessed: 9 April 2023).

Sembcorp Marine Ltd (2021). *Accelerating strategic business expansion: Sembcorp Marine completes two offshore wind farm substations for Ørsted Wind Power* [Online]. Available at: www.sembmarine.com/2021/08/15/accelerating-strategic-business-expansion-sembcorp-marine-completes-two-offshore-wind-farm-substations-for-orsted-wind-power (Accessed: 9 April 2023).

Sembcorp Marine Ltd (2023). *Sembcorp Marine and GE jointly secure landmark offshore renewables project to build biggest and most advanced HVDC electrical transmission system for TenneT* [Online]. Available at: www.sembmarine.com/stock-exchange-announcements/sembcorp-marine-and-ge-jointly-secure-landmark-offshore-renewables-project-to-build-biggest-and-most-advanced-hvdc-electrical-transmission-system-for-tennet (Accessed: 9 April 2023).

Sembcorp Marine Ltd (n.d.). *Innovation and sustainable solutions* [Online]. Available at: www.sembmarine.com/sustainability/innovation-and-solutions-development (Accessed: 9 April 2023).

8 BreadTalk's innovation in the bakery industry

Subhasis Chatterjee

Doctoral Research Scholar, University of Northampton, United Kingdom

BreadTalk is a Singapore-based bakery chain that has gained popularity for its innovative approach to traditional baked goods. Here are some of the challenges that the company faced in innovation in the bakery industry, and how they succeeded:

Maintaining quality while innovating: One of the biggest challenges that BreadTalk faced was how to maintain the quality of its products while introducing new and innovative flavours and textures. The company overcame this challenge by investing heavily in research and development, and by hiring expert bakers and pastry chefs who were able to create new recipes that met the high standards of quality that BreadTalk was known for (Break, 2023). Additionally, the company used digital technologies, such as cloud computing and data analytics, to monitor and improve its operations, such as inventory management, quality control, and customer feedback. The company also adopted a culture of continuous innovation and differentiation, by launching new products every six months in line with seasonal trends, social events, and festivals. The company also localised and customised its products to suit the preferences and tastes of different markets (Centre for Management Practice, 2015). By doing so, the company was able to maintain its quality while innovating its products.

Developing new products and concepts: Another challenge for BreadTalk was how to come up with new and innovative products and concepts that would set it apart from other bakery chains. It is notable for changing the way people consume bread in a culture where buying bread was unheard of. To overcome this challenge, the company invested in market research and trend analysis to identify new and emerging trends in the bakery industry and worked with chefs and designers to develop unique and eye-catching product designs that appealed to customers. Additionally, the company used its culture of "creative differentiation" to launch new products every six months in line with seasonal trends, social events, and festivals. The company also localised and customised its products to suit the preferences and tastes of different markets (Centre for Management Practice, 2015). By doing so, the company was able to create a distinctive brand identity and attract loyal customers who appreciated its

DOI: 10.4324/9781032660547-62

freshness and relevance. Furthermore, the company used its innovation capabilities to diversify into other food-related businesses, such as food courts, restaurants, and tea houses. The company also explored new product categories, such as cakes, pastries, and ice cream (Lee et al., 2016). By developing new products and concepts, the company was able to expand its customer base and increase its revenue streams.

Expanding into new markets: BreadTalk faced challenges when expanding into new markets, particularly in countries with different cultural and culinary traditions. To overcome this challenge, the company developed customised product offerings that considered local tastes and preferences and established partnerships with local suppliers and distributors to ensure a steady supply of high-quality ingredients. For example, BreadTalk adapted its product range in each market to suit local palates and partnered with established F&B companies to expand into geographies it was familiar with. Additionally, the company adopted a flexible franchising model that allowed it to enter new markets quickly and efficiently while maintaining control over its brand image and quality standards. The company also provided training and support to its franchisees to ensure consistent service delivery and customer satisfaction (Lee et al., 2016). Moreover, the company leveraged its strong brand reputation and recognition to attract customers in new markets. The company also used social media and online platforms to engage with customers and promote its products (Centre for Management Practice, 2015). By expanding into new markets, the company was able to increase its market share and enhance its global presence.

Maintaining brand reputation: BreadTalk made high-quality, new, and tasty bread and cakes. It wanted to keep doing this as it got bigger and made more things. The company checked its products, taught its workers, and talked to its customers. For example, BreadTalk used natural ingredients from different places and made them into stuff for its bread and cakes. Then, food experts checked them. The company also taught its workers to be clean, nice, and smart and gave them prizes. Also, BreadTalk talked to its customers on the internet and in real life. It told them about itself, what it sold, and how they could say what they liked or didn't like. Plus, the company kept its good name by changing its products and prices for different places. The company also worked with other people to enter new markets fast and well while keeping its brand image and quality (World Branding Awards, n.d.). Also, the company used its culture of "creative differentiation" to make new products for different times, events, and festivals. The company also made other food-related things, such as food courts, restaurants, and tea houses (*Singapore Business Review*, 2016). By doing this, the company made a special brand identity and got loyal customers who liked its freshness and relevance.

Through these efforts, BreadTalk has become a top bakery chain in Singapore and other places. The company has received many prizes and praises for its new and different breads and cakes and has expanded to more than 15 countries. By making good, new, and valuable products and talking to its customers well, BreadTalk has made itself ready for more success in the future. For example, BreadTalk was named the best bakery brand by the World Branding Awards for four years in a row from 2018 to 2021, and as the powerful brand by the Influential Brands Award for four years in a row from 2014 to 2017. The company has also gone to new places such as Myanmar, Cambodia, and Laos, and worked with famous brands such as Song Fa Bak Kut Teh, Nayuki, and Wu Pao Chun Bakery. Also, BreadTalk has spent money on its team that makes many recipes for its different brands.

References

Break, A. (2023). BreadTalk: a case study of strategic management. *International Journal of Business and Management, 18*(2), 45–56.

Centre for Management Practice (2015). *BreadTalk: continuous innovation to keep the brand fresh* [Online]. Available at: https://sbr.com.sg/food-beverage/comment ary/breadtalk-continuous-innovation-keep-brand-fresh (Accessed: 12 April 2023).

Lee, M., Lim, C., Zerrillo, P., & Mathur, S. (2016). *BreadTalk: Continuous Innovation to Keep the Brand Fresh*. Singapore: Singapore Management University.

Singapore Business Review (2016). *BreadTalk: continuous innovation to keep the brand fresh* [Online]. Available at: https://sbr.com.sg/food-beverage/commentary/breadtalk-continuous-innovation-keep-brand-fresh (Accessed: 14 April 2023).

World Branding Awards (n.d.). *BreadTalk* [Online]. Available at: https://awards.brandingforum.org/brands/breadtalk/ (Accessed: 4 April 2023).

9 SISTIC adaptation to the digitalisation of the entertainment industry

Lim Keai

Academic Director (Senior), Amity Global Institute, Singapore

SISTIC is a Singapore-based ticketing and live events company that has been in the business for over 40 years. However, in recent years, the company faced significant challenges due to the digitalisation of the entertainment industry (Kraus et al., 2021). With the rise of digital platforms and online ticketing systems, SISTIC had to adapt quickly to remain relevant and competitive in an increasingly crowded market. This case study will explore how SISTIC overcame these challenges and achieved success in the digital era.

One of the primary challenges that SISTIC faced was the need to upgrade its technology to keep up with the evolving digital landscape (Rêgo et al., 2022). The company realised that its existing systems and processes were outdated and inefficient and that it had to innovate and adapt to the changing customer preferences and expectations. To address this challenge, the company invested heavily in its digital infrastructure and developed new online ticketing platforms that provided a seamless and convenient experience for customers. The company also leveraged data analytics and artificial intelligence to enhance its customer service and marketing capabilities.

Another challenge that SISTIC faced was the need to diversify its offerings beyond traditional live events such as concerts and theatre shows (Chidekel, 2021). The company recognised that the demand for live events was affected by various factors such as the COVID-19 pandemic, travel restrictions, social distancing measures, and changing consumer preferences. To cope with these uncertainties and to cater to a wider range of customers, the company expanded into new areas such as virtual events and hybrid events that combine online and offline experiences. The company also partnered with other platforms and content providers to offer more choices and variety to its customers. For example, SISTIC launched a new streaming platform called SISTIC Live that allows customers to watch live or on-demand performances from local and international artists (SISTIC, n.d.).

SISTIC also faced competition from new players in the market, such as online ticketing platforms and social media platforms that allow users to buy tickets directly. These platforms offered lower prices, faster transactions, and more convenience to customers who preferred to shop online. They also

DOI: 10.4324/9781032660547-63

leveraged their large user base, data analytics, and marketing strategies to attract and retain customers. To deal with this threat, SISTIC focused on providing exceptional customer service and building strong relationships with event organisers and venues. SISTIC also differentiated itself by offering exclusive access to premium events and loyalty programmes for its customers (Lee et al., 2018).

Additionally, SISTIC faced challenges in managing the logistics of live events, such as coordinating ticket sales, seating arrangements, and security. These tasks required a lot of planning, communication, and coordination among various stakeholders, such as event organisers, venue owners, ticket agents, and customers. SISTIC had to ensure that the ticket sales were accurate and transparent, that the seating arrangements were fair and comfortable, and that the security measures were adequate and effective. To resolve this issue, the company invested in sophisticated event management software that helped streamline these processes and improve efficiency (Richards et al., 2019).

In conclusion, SISTIC has demonstrated its resilience and innovation in the face of the digitalisation of the entertainment industry. By investing in technology, diversifying its offerings, focusing on customer service, and improving logistical processes, SISTIC has not only overcome the challenges posed by the digital era but also created new opportunities for growth and expansion. SISTIC has proven itself to be a leader and a pioneer in the ticketing and live events industry, and a trusted partner for both customers and event organisers. The company has also led the way in innovation and adaptation, continually enhancing its technology and expanding its offerings to satisfy the evolving demands and tastes of its customers and event organisers.

References

Chidekel, S. (2021). *The future of live events: AR, VR, and advertising* [Online]. Available at: www.forbes.com/sites/legalentertainment/2021/02/09/the-future-of-live-events-ar-vr-and-advertising/?sh=29362dd72b65 (Accessed: 18 May 2023).

Kraus, S., Jones, P., Kailer, N., Weinmann, A., Chaparro-Banegas, N., & Roig-Tierno, N. (2021). Digital transformation: an overview of the current state of the art of research. *SAGE Open, 11*(3). https://doi.org/10.1177/21582440211047576.

Lee, D., Hosanagar, K., & Nair, H.S. (2018). Advertising content and consumer engagement on social media: evidence from Facebook. *Management Science, 64*(11), 5105–5131. https://doi.org/10.1287/mnsc.2017.2902.

Rêgo, B.S., Jayantilal, S., Ferreira, J.J., et al. (2022). Digital transformation and strategic management: a systematic review of the literature. *Journal of the Knowledge Economy, 13*, 3195–3222. https://doi.org/10.1007/s13132-021-00853-3.

Richards, G., Censon, D., Gračan, D., Haressy, M., Kiráľová, A., Marulc, E., & Zavratnik, V. (2019). Event management software: a comparative analysis. *Event Management, 23*(4–5), 609–623. https://doi.org/10.3727/152599519X155 06259856232

SISTIC Singapore (n.d.). *SISTIC Singapore* [Online]. Available at: www.sistic.com.sg/ (Accessed: 18 May 2023).

10 SingPost's focus on e-commerce logistics solutions

Teoh Teik Toe

Academic Director and Associate Director for AI Lab and IMARC Center/Nanyang Technological University, Singapore

As the COVID-19 pandemic accelerated the growth of online shopping, Singapore Post (SingPost) shifted its focus to e-commerce logistics solutions. However, this strategic move also brought about various challenges for the postal and courier service provider. SingPost had to contend with the fierce competition and fast-changing dynamics of the e-commerce market, which demanded continuous innovation and adaptation from the company. How did SingPost overcome these challenges and succeed in its e-commerce logistics venture?

The COVID-19 pandemic and the transition to online shopping boosted Singapore's e-commerce market by 87% in 2020, according to a report by CNBC. However, this also posed a challenge for SingPost, as it had to compete with other e-commerce platforms, payment services, and last-mile service providers that entered the market during the crisis. To stand out and satisfy the evolving customer needs, SingPost had to provide faster, cheaper, and more dependable delivery services, as well as broaden its product range and regional coverage (CNBC, 2021).

Another challenge that SingPost faced was the requirement to spend a lot on technology and infrastructure to facilitate e-commerce logistics operations. SingPost had to obtain or create new technologies, such as automated parcel sortation systems and last-mile delivery tracking systems, to increase efficiency and improve the customer experience (Risberg et al., 2022). For instance, SingPost inaugurated a new integrated logistics hub in Singapore in 2016, which boosted its parcel processing capacity from 100,000 to 300,000 parcels per day (SingPost, 2016). SingPost also invested in innovative technologies such as drones, robots, and artificial intelligence to experiment with new methods of delivering parcels (SingPost, 2019).

SingPost also encountered challenges associated with the high volume of parcels and packages that had to be processed and delivered during peak periods, such as the holiday season. This necessitated SingPost to implement complex planning and scheduling systems, as well as to recruit and train additional staff to cope with the increased workload. However, SingPost also faced some operational issues such as delays, misdeliveries, and customer complaints

DOI: 10.4324/9781032660547-64

during these periods, which impacted its reputation and profitability (Lim et al., 2019; *The Straits Times*, 2022).

Despite these challenges, SingPost was able to succeed in its focus on e-commerce logistics solutions by leveraging its extensive network and expertise in postal and courier services. SingPost expanded its e-commerce logistics capabilities through strategic partnerships with major e-commerce companies such as Alibaba, Lazada, and Shopify, and acquisitions of other logistics firms such as Quantium Solutions, CouriersPlease, and Freight Management Holdings. These moves enabled SingPost to offer end-to-end solutions across the e-commerce value chain, from warehousing and fulfilment to cross-border delivery and returns management (SingPost, 2018).

SingPost also invested in developing a new industry standard for last-mile delivery of parcels in partnership with the Singapore Standards Council and Enterprise Singapore. The standard aims to guide the e-commerce industry in areas such as packaging, labelling, data collection and transmission, communication content, and operational practices (Tan et al., 2018). The standard is expected to improve the overall e-commerce experience for customers, as well as raise operational efficiencies for all stakeholders across the value chain (SingPost, 2022).

To sum up, SingPost encountered various challenges while concentrating on e-commerce logistics solutions, such as the intense competition and fast-changing trends of the e-commerce market, the requirement to spend a lot on technology and infrastructure, and the large volume of parcels and packages during busy periods. However, SingPost managed to overcome these challenges by using its wide network and experience in postal and courier services, growing its e-commerce logistics capabilities through strategic alliances and acquisitions, and investing in innovative technologies and infrastructure. SingPost also created a new industry standard for last-mile delivery of parcels in partnership with the Singapore Standards Council and Enterprise Singapore. By doing so, SingPost was able to improve its competitiveness and customer satisfaction in the e-commerce logistics market.

References

CNBC (2021). *Singapore e-commerce players face challenges in logistics and delivery* [Online]. Available at: www.cnbc.com/2021/06/30/singapore-e-commerce-players-face-challenges-in-logistics-and-delivery.html (Accessed: 30 April 2023).

Lim, S.Y., Jin, X., Srai, J.S., & Gregory, M.J. (2019). Factors influencing consumers' satisfaction with last mile delivery services: a case study of Singapore. In: Srai J., Harrington T., Kumar M., Graham G., Tiwari M., Prakash A., Mishra N., Kumar V., Choudhary A., Singh R., Dwivedi Y., Madaan J., & Modi P. (eds). *Revisiting Supply Chain Risk. Lecture Notes in Management and Industrial Engineering*. Springer, Cham. https://doi.org/10.1007/978-3-030-25634-7_3.

Risberg, A., Hilletofth, P., & Eriksson, D. (2022). A systematic literature review on e-commerce logistics: towards an e-commerce and omni-channel decision framework.

The International Review of Retail, Distribution and Consumer Research, 33(1), 67–91. https://doi.org/10.1080/09593969.2022.2089903.

SingPost (2016). *SingPost launches new integrated logistics hub* [Online]. Available at: www.singpost.com/about-us/news-releases/singpost-launches-new-integrated-logistics-hub (Accessed: 30 April 2023).

SingPost (2018). *SingPost annual report 2018* [Online]. Available at: www.singpost.com/sites/default/files/Singpost_AR18.pdf (Accessed: 30 April 2023).

SingPost (2019). *SingPost Annual Report 2019* [Online]. Available at: www.singpost.com/sites/default/files/Singpost_AR19.pdf (Accessed: 30 April 2023).

SingPost (2022). *Singapore introduces a new industry standard for eCommerce and logistics players to boost customer satisfaction and operational efficiencies* [Online]. Available at: www.singpost.com/about-us/news-releases/singapore-introduces-new-industry-standard-ecommerce-and-logistics-players (Accessed: 30 April 2023).

Tan, Z., Lee, L.H., & Chew, E.P. (2018). Impact of urban logistics policies on e-commerce deliveries in Singapore. *Transportation Research Part E: Logistics and Transportation Review, 118*, 1–16. https://doi.org/10.1016/j.tre.2018.07.007.

The Straits Times (2022). *SingPost Q1 operating profit falls 47% on higher costs, post and parcel weakness* [Online]. Available at: www.straitstimes.com/business/companies-markets/singpost-q1-operating-profit-falls-47-on-higher-costs-post-and-parcel-weakness (Accessed: 21 April 2023).

11 Yangzijiang Shipbuilding's focus on innovation and automation

Samson Tan

Director of Regional Strategy and Operations (Singapore), Civica Asia Pacific, Australia

In the highly competitive and dynamic shipbuilding industry, innovation and automation are key drivers of success and sustainability. However, embracing new technologies and processes also entails various challenges and risks that require strategic management and adaptation (Brooks et al., 2016). This is the case study of Yangzijiang Shipbuilding, one of the largest private shipbuilders in China, listed in Singapore, and how it overcame the obstacles and seized the opportunities of innovation and automation. From technology adoption and workforce training to quality control and industry competition, this study will explore the challenges Yangzijiang Shipbuilding faced and how it succeeded in transforming its production processes and strengthening its position in the global shipbuilding market.

Technology adoption: One of the biggest challenges for Yangzijiang Shipbuilding was the need to adopt new technologies and tools to improve its production processes. To address this challenge, the company invested heavily in research and development and established partnerships with technology companies to develop and implement innovative solutions. For example, Yangzijiang Shipbuilding collaborated with Siemens to develop a digital ship-yard platform that integrates data from design, engineering, production, and quality control (Siemens, 2020). The platform enables the company to optimise its workflows, reduce errors, enhance efficiency, and improve product quality. Moreover, Yangzijiang Shipbuilding also adopted advanced technologies such as 3D printing, robotics, artificial intelligence, and clean energy to build more sophisticated and environmentally friendly vessels (Kim et al., 2020).

Workforce training: Adopting new technologies and processes also requires a highly skilled workforce capable of operating and maintaining these systems. To address this challenge, Yangzijiang Shipbuilding invested in employee training and development programmes and established a strong culture of innovation and continuous learning. The company provides various training courses for its employees to upgrade their skills and knowledge in areas such as digitalisation, automation, safety, quality, and management (Yangzijiang Shipbuilding Holdings Ltd., 2020). The company also encourages its employees to participate in innovation competitions and projects to foster creativity and

DOI: 10.4324/9781032660547-65

problem-solving abilities. Furthermore, Yangzijiang Shipbuilding also recruits talent from universities and research institutes to strengthen its research and development capabilities.

Quality control: Automation and innovation also require robust quality control processes to ensure that products meet the highest standards. To address this challenge, Yangzijiang Shipbuilding implemented advanced quality control systems and processes and established a culture of quality and excellence across its operations. The company uses various tools such as big data analytics, smart sensors, digital twins, and blockchain to monitor and improve the quality of its products and services (Yangzijiang Shipbuilding Holdings Ltd., 2020). The company also adheres to international quality standards and certifications such as ISO 9001, ISO 14001, OHSAS 18001, and IACS (Shipbuilding Industry Outlook, 2021). Additionally, Yangzijiang Shipbuilding also solicits feedback from its customers and stakeholders to continuously enhance its customer satisfaction and loyalty.

Industry competition: The shipbuilding industry is highly competitive, with several large players vying for business. To compete effectively, Yangzijiang Shipbuilding focused on offering high-quality products and services, competitive pricing, and exceptional customer service. The company has established a strong reputation for quality and reliability and has diversified its business into other areas, such as shipping and finance, to broaden its revenue base and drive growth. As a result of its innovation efforts, Yangzijiang Shipbuilding has secured new orders for 69 vessels worth US$5.6 billion in the first half of 2022 (Singapore Business Review Staff Reporter, 2022), exceeding its 2023 target of US$3 billion. It has also achieved its highest-ever total outstanding order book value of US$14.6 billion for 180 vessels (Rawson et al., 2019).

Yangzijiang Shipbuilding has demonstrated that innovation and automation are not only challenges but also opportunities for the shipbuilding industry. By investing in research and development, partnering with technology companies, training its workforce, implementing quality control systems, and offering high-quality products and services, the company has achieved remarkable results in terms of efficiency, productivity, profitability, and customer satisfaction. The company has also diversified its business portfolio to include shipping and finance, which provide additional sources of income and competitive advantage. Yangzijiang Shipbuilding has thus become a global leader in the shipbuilding industry, with a record-high order book and a solid reputation. The company is ready to face the future challenges and opportunities of the industry with confidence and vision.

References

Brooks, B., Coltman, T., & Yang, M. (2016). Technological innovation in the maritime industry: the case of remote pilotage and enhanced navigational assistance. *The Journal of Navigation*, 69(4), 777–793. https://doi.org/10.1017/S037346331 6000039

Kim, M., Joung, T.-H., Jeong, B., & Park, H.-S. (2020). Autonomous shipping and its impact on regulations, technologies, and industries. *Journal of International Maritime Safety, Environmental Affairs, and Shipping,* 4(2), 17–25. https://doi.org/10.1080/25725084.2020.1779427

Rawson, K.J., Wang, J., Day, A.H., Dai, S., Khoo, S., Ahmed, M.R., Smith, G.H., Akinturk, A., Aktas, B., Atlar, M., Harris, C.D., Abolfathi, S., Turan, O., Demirel, Y.K., Tezdogan, T., Incecik, A., Turan, G., Fangohr, S., Hudson, D.A., Temarel, P., Oguz, E., & Qian, W. (2019). Shipbuilding innovation: enabling technologies and economic drivers. *Journal of Ship Production and Design,* 34(2), 144–157. https://doi.org/10.5957/JSPD.34.2.170011

Shipbuilding Industry Outlook (2021). *States increasingly environmentally friendly options among market trends (2021).* GlobeNewswire [Online]. Available at: www.globenewswire.com/news-release/2021/07/22/2267543/0/en/Shipbuilding-Industry-Outlook-2021-States-Increasingly-Environmentally-Friendly-Options-Among-Market-Trends.html (Accessed: 11 May 2023).

Siemens (2020). *Siemens helps Yangzi Delta shipyard become one of China's most advanced shipyards with digitalization solutions – Press release* [Online]. Available at: https://press.siemens.com/cn/en/pressrelease/siemens-helps-yangzi-delta-shipyard-become-one-chinas-most-advanced-shipyards (Accessed: 11 May 2023).

Singapore Business Review Staff Reporter (2022). *Yangzijiang Shipbuilding secures new orders for 37 vessels.* Singapore Business Review [Online]. Available at: https://sbr.com.sg/shipping-marine/news/yangzijiang-shipbuilding-secures-new-orders-37-vessels (Accessed: 11 May 2023).

Yangzijiang Shipbuilding Holdings Ltd. (2020). *Annual report 2020* [Online]. Available at: https://links.sgx.com/FileOpen/YZJ_AR2020.ashx?App=Announcement&FileID=651053 (Accessed: 11 May 2023).

12 DSO National Laboratories developed advanced defence technologies for Singapore

Jakia Rajoana

Senior Lecturer, Teesside University, United Kingdom

Introduction

DSO National Laboratories is a research and development organisation that develops advanced defence technologies for the Singaporean military. DSO plays a vital role in enhancing Singapore's national security and defence capabilities, especially in a complex and uncertain regional and global environment. However, DSO also faces several challenges in developing these technologies, such as keeping up with rapid technological advancements, balancing research and development with practical applications, and ensuring the security of sensitive military information. This case study will examine how DSO had overcome these challenges and achieved success in developing cutting-edge defence technologies. It will explore some of the future directions and opportunities for DSO in the defence research landscape.

Operational challenges and organisational strategies

To overcome these challenges, DSO has invested heavily in its research and development capabilities, including hiring top talent and collaborating with leading research institutions worldwide. DSO also focuses on developing technologies that are relevant and practical for the Singaporean military, working closely with the military to understand their needs and requirements. To innovate and create value, organisations need top talent. Mahony (2022) suggests that a strong employee value proposition that aligns with the organisation's purpose, culture, and identity can attract top talent. DSO uses strategies like scholarships, internships, mentorships, awards, and career development to attract and retain top talent (DSO National Laboratories, n.d.). DSO also enhances its R&D capabilities by collaborating with leading research institutions worldwide. These partnerships give DSO access to cutting-edge research, scientific talent, and best practices for defence and security problems. Perkmann and Salter (2018) show that long-term collaborations between companies and universities can benefit both parties in terms of innovation, knowledge transfer, and trust. Hence, DSO has various local and international partners, such as NUS, NTU, A*STAR, MIT, and Dstl (DSO National Laboratories, n.d.).

DOI: 10.4324/9781032660547-66

Cybersecurity is key for the military, as it relies on cyberspace for various functions (Ho, 2016). Cyber-attacks can harm critical infrastructures and classified military information (Thales Group, n.d.). DSO also places a strong emphasis on cybersecurity to protect sensitive military information. It has implemented robust security measures to safeguard its networks, data, and research facilities. It has developed high-security products and solutions for military information, such as secure communications equipment (TEOREM), secure email messaging (XOmail), secure access to multiple security levels and domains (THEMIS), secure connection of critical information system networks (ELIPS-SD), and secure monitoring of internet attacks (CYBELS SENSOR) (Thales Group, n.d.). DSO also collaborates with other defence agencies and industry partners to enhance its cybersecurity capabilities and share best practices (RAND Corporation, 2021).

Another challenge DSO faced was developing technologies that are cost-effective and efficient, given Singapore's small size and limited resources. To address this, DSO focuses on developing technologies that are versatile and can be used for multiple purposes, as well as collaborating with industry partners to leverage their expertise and resources. Versatile technologies can do multiple functions or adapt to different situations. For example, DSO has developed a versatile UAV called the Black Kite, which can do various missions like reconnaissance, surveillance, target acquisition, and communications relay (MINDEF Singapore, n.d.). Versatile technologies can help the military to be more effective and efficient, as they can reduce the need for multiple specialised systems and platforms and allow for more flexibility and agility in responding to different scenarios and threats (NATO Review, 2021). Additionally, DSO collaborates with industry partners to develop cost-effective and efficient technologies. This gives DSO access to their expertise, resources, networks, innovation, and commercialisation capabilities. For example, DSO and ST Engineering developed a smart combat helmet for soldiers (SIPRI, n.d.). Collaborating with industry partners can also help DSO to transfer its technologies to the civilian market and generate economic value for Singapore.

Summary

In conclusion, DSO has shown its ability to overcome its challenges by investing in research and development, collaborating with industry partners, and prioritising practical applications and cybersecurity. These efforts have enabled DSO to develop advanced defence technologies that have not only enhanced Singapore's national security but also contributed to the country's economic growth through the creation of new technologies and industries. DSO's success story demonstrates that defence research can have positive spillover effects for society and the economy.

References

DSO National Laboratories (n.d.). *About us* [Online]. Available at: www.dso.org.sg/about (Accessed: 23 May 2023).

Ho, A.W.S. (2016). Cyber attacks and the roles the military can play to support the national cyber security efforts. *Pointer: Journal of the Singapore Armed Forces, 42*(3), 4–14.

Mahony, M. (2022). How to attract top talent in 2022. *Harvard Business Review.* Available at: https://hbr.org/sponsored/2022/01/how-to-attract-top-talent-in-2022

MINDEF Singapore (n.d.). *Defence science & technology* [Online]. Available at: www.mindef.gov.sg/web/portal/mindef/defence-matters/defence-topic/defence-topic-detail/defence-science-and-technology (Accessed: 21 May 2023).

NATO Review (2021). *Quantum technologies in defence & security* [Online]. Available at: www.nato.int/docu/review/articles/2021/06/03/quantum-technologies-in-defence-security/index.html (Accessed: 23 May 2023).

Perkmann, M., & Salter, A. (2018). Why companies and universities should forge long-term collaborations. *Harvard Business Review.* Available at: https://hbr.org/2018/01/why-companies-and-universities-should-forge-long-term-collaborations

RAND Corporation (2021). *How the military might expand its cyber skills* [Online]. Available at: www.rand.org/blog/2021/04/how-the-military-might-expand-its-cyber-skills.html (Accessed: 20 May 2023).

SIPRI (n.d.). *Emerging military and security technologies* [Online]. Available at: www.sipri.org/research/armament-and-disarmament/emerging-military-and-security-technologies (Accessed: 23 May 2023).

Thales Group (n.d.). *Military information security* [Online]. Available at: www.thalesgroup.com/en/markets/defence-and-security/cyberdefence-solutions/military-information-security (Accessed: 22 May 2023).

13 StarHub's focus on mobile and broadband services

Preethi Thankappan Nair

Lecturer – Business Strategy, Co-Founding Director – Business Advice Centre, University of East London, United Kingdom

In the competitive and fast-paced telecommunications industry, StarHub has established itself as one of the top players in Singapore, offering a wide range of communication services to both individual and corporate customers. Among its core services are mobile and broadband, which are essential for staying connected in the digital age. However, providing these services is not without challenges, such as increasing customer expectations, technological disruptions, and regulatory changes. This case study will examine how StarHub faced these challenges and overcame them with its strategic focus on quality, customer service, and innovation.

Intense competition: The telecommunications sector in Singapore experiences fierce rivalry among multiple major companies striving for market dominance. To maintain its competitive edge, StarHub must consistently introduce innovative offerings and services to attract and retain its customer base. According to Tan (2019), innovation plays a pivotal role in establishing a competitive advantage within the telecommunications industry by enabling companies to distinguish themselves from competitors and provide valuable solutions to customers. StarHub has embraced a strategic approach focused on enhancing operational efficiency and productivity, as well as investing in emerging sectors like cybersecurity, digitalisation, and information and communications technology solutions (StarHub, 2018). By pursuing this strategy, StarHub has successfully reduced costs, improved the customer experience, and diversified its revenue streams, thereby solidifying its position within the market.

Increasing demand for data: As the usage of mobile devices and streaming platforms surged, there was an escalating need from consumers for larger data allowances delivered at accelerated speeds. To tackle this challenge, StarHub undertook significant investments in its network infrastructure, aiming to provide faster and more dependable broadband and mobile services. According to Lee et al. (2019), the quality of a network plays a crucial role in influencing customer satisfaction and loyalty within the telecommunications sector, given its impact on service performance and functionality. Recognising this, StarHub secured a provisional 5G license from IMDA, enabling them to construct

DOI: 10.4324/9781032660547-67

and operate a standalone 5G network infrastructure. This advancement will empower customers to access swifter network speeds and embrace novel digital services such as augmented reality (StarHub, 2020). This strategic investment clearly showcases StarHub's dedication to meeting the evolving demands of its customers and staying ahead of the technological curve.

Changing customer needs: The ever-changing preferences and requirements of consumers necessitate adaptability from companies operating in the telecommunications sector. StarHub confronted this challenge by introducing a diverse array of flexible mobile and broadband plans, allowing for customisation to cater to the unique needs of individual customers. According to Kim et al. (2018), customer-centricity plays a crucial role in determining customer satisfaction and loyalty within the telecommunications industry, as it signifies the extent to which companies comprehend and fulfil customer expectations and desires. To embody this principle, StarHub embarked on a transformative endeavour known as the DARE+ initiative, aspiring to become a comprehensive "Connecting Your Digital World" platform, delivering personalised solutions and seamless experiences to customers across multiple domains such as entertainment, education, healthcare, and finance (StarHub, 2022). This initiative exemplifies StarHub's vision of evolving beyond a mere telecommunications provider, aiming to become a trusted digital lifestyle partner for its customers.

Regulatory changes: The telecommunications industry in Singapore is highly regulated, with strict rules and regulations governing everything from pricing to network security. StarHub addressed this challenge by working closely with regulators to ensure compliance with relevant laws and regulations, and by investing in network security and privacy measures to protect its customers. According to Tan et al. (2017), regulatory compliance is a key factor influencing customer trust and loyalty in the telecommunications industry, as it reflects the extent to which firms adhere to ethical standards and safeguard customer interests. StarHub implemented various network security and privacy measures such as encryption, authentication, firewall, anti-virus, anti-spam, anti-phishing, anti-malware, and intrusion detection and prevention systems (StarHub, 2019). These measures demonstrate StarHub's responsibility and commitment to ensuring the safety and security of its customers and their data.

StarHub has proven itself as a leader in the mobile and broadband industry in Singapore, thanks to its relentless efforts to improve its quality, customer service, and innovation. The company has not only maintained its market share but also expanded its offerings to include new and exciting products and services, such as mobile payment and content streaming services, that cater to the evolving preferences of its customers. StarHub has shown that it can adapt to the changing environment and anticipate the future needs of the industry, ensuring its long-term growth and success.

References

Kim, H.J., Kim, Y.J., Lee, J.H., Lee, Y.J., & Park, S.H. (2018). Customer-centricity culture moderates the relationship between service quality attributes and customer satisfaction. *International Journal of Quality & Reliability Management, 35*(10), 2154–2172. https://doi.org/10.1108/IJQRM-01-2017-0010

Lee, Y.S., Kim, Y.J., Kim, H.J., & Park, S.H. (2019). Network quality, perceived value, and customer satisfaction in the mobile telecommunication service industry. *Total Quality Management & Business Excellence, 30*(11–12), 1339–1356. https://doi.org/10.1080/14783363.2017.1372498

StarHub (2018). *StarHub announces strategic efficiency transformation initiatives,* StarHub Newsroom [Online]. Available at: www.starhub.com/about-us/newsroom/2018/october/starhub-announces-strategic-efficiency-transformation-initiative.html (Accessed: 12 May 2023).

StarHub (2019). *StarHub privacy policy* [Online]. Available at: www.starhub.com/about-us/legal-notices-and-terms/personal-data-protection.html   (Accessed: 12 May 2023).

StarHub (2020). *StarHub awarded provisional licence to build and operate 5G standalone network infrastructure* [Online]. Available at: www.starhub.com/about-us/newsroom/2020/april/starhub-awarded-provisional-licence-to-build-and-operate-5g-standalone-network-infrastructure.html (Accessed: 12 May 2023).

StarHub (2022). *StarHub reports 10.7% YoY increase in 1Q2022 service revenue to $416M,* StarHub Newsroom [Online]. Available at: www.starhub.com/about-us/newsroom/2022/april/starhub-reports-1Q2022-results.html   (Accessed: 12 May 2023).

Tan, C.H., Teo, H.H., Tan, B.C.Y., & Kwok-Kee, W. (2017). Trust in an environment of regulatory compliance: the case of mobile phone service providers in Singapore. *Information & Management, 54* (4), 411–425. https://doi.org/10.1016/j.im.2016.09.003

Tan, K.S. (2019). Innovation and competitive advantage in the telecommunications industry: a case study of Singtel. *Journal of Business Strategy, 40*(4), 25–33. https://doi.org/10.1108/JBS-01-2018-0011

14 CPG Corporation becoming one of Asia's leading engineering and development firms

George Kapaya

Deputy Head – Accounting and Finance, Faculty of Business and Law University of Northampton, United Kingdom

Emerging from its origins as the Public Works Department of Singapore in 1833, CPG Corporation has undergone remarkable growth to become a prominent engineering and development firm in Asia, boasting an illustrious history and a global presence. Today, CPG Corporation stands as a multifaceted conglomerate, offering a comprehensive range of services that encompass engineering, architecture, project management, urban planning, environmental management, and facilities management. With a wide-reaching presence across Asia, the Middle East, and Africa, CPG Corporation caters to a diverse clientele from both the public and private sectors, delivering cutting-edge and sustainable solutions for the built environment (CPG Corporation, n.d.b).

ChallengesOne of the significant challenges CPG Corporation faced was in the 1990s when Singapore's construction industry faced a severe downturn. This resulted in a significant reduction in the demand for the company's services, and it had to look for other markets to sustain its operations. This required the company to adopt a diversification strategy, which involves expanding into new markets or products to reduce risk and increase growth opportunities (Al-Ansaari et al., 2014). Additionally, as the company expanded globally, it faced various challenges in dealing with diverse cultures, legal systems, and regulations. These challenges posed risks and uncertainties for the company, as it had to adapt to different customer preferences, business practices, and regulatory frameworks. The company also had to manage the complexity and coordination of its global operations and projects.

Another challenge that CPG Corporation encountered was in 2017 when a viaduct that it was building near the Pan-Island Expressway (PIE) collapsed, killing 1 worker and injuring 10 others. The company was found guilty of failing to take necessary measures to ensure the safety of workers and was ordered to pay S$43.8 million to CPG Consultants, the design firm for the project, after arbitration proceedings (Ng, 2023). The incident damaged the company's reputation and resulted in the termination of its contract with the Land Transport Authority (LTA). This was a major setback for the company, as it lost a significant source of revenue and faced legal and regulatory

DOI: 10.4324/9781032660547-68

consequences. The company also had to deal with the negative publicity and public scrutiny that followed the incident, which could affect its future business opportunities and customer trust (Gallardo-Gallardo et al., 2020).

How CPG Corporation succeededCPG Corporation succeeded by diversifying its services and expanding into new markets. The company moved beyond traditional engineering and construction work, offering more specialised services such as project management and architectural design. CPG Corporation also expanded globally, with a particular focus on emerging markets such as China and India, where demand for infrastructure development was high. The company's global expansion was supported by strategic partnerships and acquisitions that helped it establish a presence in new markets quickly. For example, CPG Corporation acquired China-based architectural firm P&T Group in 2004 to strengthen its foothold in China (Al-Ansaari et al., 2014). This diversification strategy enabled the company to reduce its dependence on the domestic market and tap into new sources of revenue and growth. The company also gained access to new customers, resources, and technologies through its global network.

CPG Corporation's success can also be attributed to its commitment to innovation and technology. The company has invested heavily in research and development, creating new technologies that have improved the efficiency and sustainability of its projects. Innovation is the process of creating new or improved products, services, or processes that meet customer needs or create value (Chen et al., 2011). For example, CPG Corporation developed proprietary software that helps optimise building design, reducing energy consumption, and improving environmental sustainability. The company also leveraged external technology sources to enhance its innovation. For instance, CPG Corporation collaborated with Autodesk to use Building Information Modeling (BIM) software to improve its design and construction processes. These innovation and technology initiatives have enabled the company to differentiate itself from competitors and to deliver high-quality and sustainable solutions for the built environment. The company has also gained recognition and awards for its innovation and technology achievements, such as the BCA Green Mark Platinum Award and the BIM Awards (CPG Corporation, n.d.b).

Another key factor in CPG Corporation's success is its focus on talent development. The company has invested in its employees, providing them with training and development opportunities, and creating a culture of continuous learning and improvement. Talent development is a process of attracting, retaining, and developing employees who have the skills and competencies to perform well and achieve organisational goals. This has helped CPG Corporation attract and retain top talent, allowing it to deliver high-quality projects consistently. The company also fostered a culture of collaboration and knowledge sharing among its employees across different disciplines and regions (Gallardo-Gallardo et al., 2020). These talent development practices have enhanced the company's human capital and intellectual capital, which are crucial for its innovation and competitiveness. The company has also received accolades for its talent development efforts, such as the HR Excellence Awards and the Employer of Choice Awards (CPG Corporation, n.d.a).

ConclusionCPG Corporation has proven itself as a leader in the engineering and development industry, thanks to its agility and versatility in responding to changing market conditions. The company has not only diversified its services and markets but also invested in innovation, technology, and talent development to enhance its efficiency, sustainability, and quality. By doing so, CPG Corporation has created value for its customers and stakeholders and secured its competitive advantage in the industry.

References

Al-Ansaari, Y., Bederr, H., & Chen, C. (2014). Strategic diversification and firm performance: an empirical investigation through the lens of upper echelons theory. *Journal of Management and Organization, 20*(4), 433–454. https://doi.org/10.1017/jmo.2014.34.

Chen, J., Chen, Y., & Vanhaverbeke, W. (2011). The influence of scope, depth, and orientation of external technology sources on the innovative performance of Chinese firms. *Technovation, 31*(8), 362–373. https://doi.org/10.1016/j.technovation.2011.03.002

CPG Corporation (n.d.-a). *Pandemic resilience* [Online]. Available at: www.cpgcorp.com.sg/pandemic-resilience/ (Accessed: 8 May 2023).

CPG Corporation (n.d.-b). *The CPG story* [Online]. Available at: www.cpgcorp.com.sg/the-cpg-story (Accessed: 8 May 2023).

Gallardo-Gallardo, E., Thunnissen, M., & Scullion, H. (2020). Talent management: context matters. *International Journal of Human Resource Management, 31*(4), 457–473. https://doi.org/10.1080/09585192.2019.1642645

Ng, H.S. (2023). *Or Kim Peow Contractors awarded S$43.8 million after arbitration proceedings over 2017 PIE viaduct collapse. Channel News Asia* [Online]. Available at: www.channelnewsasia.com/singapore/pie-viaduct-collapse-or-kim-peow-contractors-arbitration-cpg-consultants-3329126 (Accessed: 8 May 2023).

15 ComfortDelGro's transformation journey in the face of disruptive innovation

Nishad Nawaz

Associate Professor, Kingdom University, Kingdom of Bahrain

Partnership with Uber: In 2016, ComfortDelGro partnered with Uber to provide taxi services through the Uber app. This allowed ComfortDelGro to tap into Uber's large customer base and technology platform while also allowing Uber to expand its offerings in Singapore. However, this partnership ended in 2018 when Uber sold its Southeast Asia operations to Grab.

This partnership was a strategic alliance, where firms cooperate to share resources and capabilities for a common goal (Hill et al., 2019). It helped ComfortDelGro and Uber access new markets, technologies, skills and customers, and lower costs and risks. They aimed to leverage Uber's technology and ComfortDelGro's fleet management and operational excellence (ComfortDelGro Corporation Limited, 2017). ComfortDelGro also bought 51% of Uber's car rental subsidiary in Singapore, Lion City Holdings, for $642 million (*Singapore Business Review*, 2017), gaining access to Uber's 14,000 private-hire vehicles. However, Uber sold its Southeast Asian operations to Grab for a 27.5% stake in 2018 (*The Straits Times*, 2018), ending the alliance and leaving ComfortDelGro to compete with Grab.

Launch of its ride-hailing app: In 2017, ComfortDelGro launched the "ComfortDelGro Taxi Booking App" to compete with other ride-hailing apps. The app let customers book a ComfortDelGro taxi from their smartphones, with features like real-time tracking, estimated time of arrival, and fare estimates. This was a product differentiation strategy, where firms create a unique or superior product or service. Product differentiation can help firms attract and retain customers, charge higher prices, and increase customer loyalty (Hill et al., 2019). ComfortDelGro launched its app to differentiate itself from other taxi operators and ride-hailing platforms. It offered customers convenience, transparency, and reliability through its app features, and aimed to enhance customer experience and satisfaction. ComfortDelGro's CEO said the app was part of the company's digital transformation initiative to meet customers' changing needs and preferences (ComfortDelGro Corporation Limited, 2017). The app also helped ComfortDelGro collect data on customer behaviour and preferences, which could improve service quality and

DOI: 10.4324/9781032660547-69

efficiency. Tan et al. (2015) show how ComfortDelGro uses big data analytics to enhance supply chain innovation through its app.

Diversification into other transportation services: ComfortDelGro has diversified into other transportation services, such as bus and rail services, car rental, and engineering and inspection services. This diversification has reduced its reliance on the taxi business and helped it stay relevant in the changing transportation industry. This is a corporate-level strategy that expands into new products or markets different from the core business. Diversification can reduce dependence on a single product or market, exploit core competencies in new areas, and create value through economies of scope or synergies (Hill et al., 2019). ComfortDelGro diversified into transportation services related or complementary to its taxi business. It operates bus and rail services in Singapore and overseas markets. These services serve customers who prefer public transport over taxis or private-hire vehicles. It also offers car rental services through Moove Media Pte Ltd (Moove Media Pte Ltd, n.d.). It has ventured into engineering and inspection services through Vicom Ltd. and Setsco Services Pte Ltd (ComfortDelGro Corporation Limited, 2020). These businesses provide new income and growth opportunities and diversify their risks and exposure to the transportation industry. Chua et al. (2012) discuss how Vicom Ltd. manages complex IT projects with clan control.

Focus on improving customer experience: ComfortDelGro has improved its customer experience to remain competitive. It has invested in training programmes for its drivers, improved its fleet management systems, and developed new services such as airport transfer services to meet customer needs. This is a customer-oriented strategy, which involves understanding and satisfying customer needs and wants. Customer-oriented strategies can help firms create value for customers, build long-term relationships, and gain a competitive advantage (Hill et al., 2019). ComfortDelGro has improved its customer experience by enhancing its service quality and reliability. It has trained its drivers to provide safe and courteous service. It has also ensured that its vehicles are well-maintained and comply with safety and environmental standards. It has developed airport transfer services to cater to customers who travel to or from the airport. These services offer convenience, comfort, and affordability (ComfortDelGro Corporation Limited, 2020). Lee et al. (2018) show how ComfortDelGro's bus operations create a positive organisational climate that fosters work passion and commitment among its bus captains.

International expansion: ComfortDelGro has expanded internationally to other markets beyond Singapore, such as China, Australia, and the United Kingdom. This has diversified its revenue streams and reduced its dependence on any one market. This is a global strategy, which involves operating in multiple countries and regions. Global strategies can help firms access new markets, customers, resources, and opportunities, and achieve economies of scale and scope. ComfortDelGro has expanded to other markets with potential growth and profitability for its transportation services. It operates in seven countries outside Singapore. These markets have different characteristics and challenges that require product and service adaptation. For example, in China, it operates bus services in cities with large populations and public transport demand. In Australia, it operates taxi services in cities that compete with other taxi operators and ride-hailing platforms. In the United Kingdom, it operates rail services in London through Metroline Ltd (ComfortDelGro Corporation Limited, 2020). These rail services are part of the London Underground network that serves millions of commuters.

Overall, ComfortDelGro's response to the rise of ride-hailing apps has been to diversify its offerings, improve its customer experience, and expand into new markets. While the traditional taxi business remains an important part of the company's operations, ComfortDelGro's willingness to adapt to new trends and technologies has helped it to stay relevant in the rapidly changing transportation industry.

References

Chua, C.K., Lim, Y.M., Soh, C., & Sia, S.K. (2012). Enacting clan control in complex IT projects: a social capital perspective. *MIS Quarterly, 36*(2), 577–600. https://doi.org/10.2307/41703474

ComfortDelGro Corporation Limited (2017). *ComfortDelgro and UBER join forces* [Online]. Available at: https://comfortdelgro.com/documents/20143/35547/ComfortDelGro+and+Uber+Join+Forces.pdf (Accessed: 9 June 2023).

ComfortDelGro Corporation Limited (2020). *Annual report 2020* [Online]. Available at: www.comfortdelgro.com/documents/20143/35547/CDG+AR+2020.pdf (Accessed: 9 June 2023).

Hill, C.W.L., Schilling, M.A., & Jones, G.R. (2019). *Strategic Management: Theory & Cases: An Integrated Approach* (13th edn). Boston: Cengage Learning.

Lee, D.H., Teo, A.C.K., Lim, W.S.W., & Looi, K.H. (2018). The impact of organisational climate on employee's work passion and organisational commitment. *Journal of Management Development, 37*(1), 14–34. https://doi.org/10.1108/JMD-01-2017-0019

Moove Media Pte Ltd (n.d.). *Car rental* [Online]. Available at: www.moovemedia.com.sg/ / (Accessed: 9 June 2023).

Singapore Business Review (2017). *ComfortDelGro and Uber enter joint venture deal for $642m* [Online]. Available at: https://sbr.com.sg/transport-logistics/news/comfortdelgro-and-uber-enter-joint-venture-deal-642m (Accessed: 9 June 2023).

Tan, K.H., Zhan, Y., Ji, G., Ye, F., & Chang, C.H. (2015). Harvesting big data to enhance supply chain innovation capabilities: an analytic infrastructure based on deduction graph. *International Journal of Production Economics, 165*, 223–233. https://doi.org/10.1016/j.ijpe.2014.12.034

The Straits Times (2018). *Uber-ComfortDelGro tie-up through UberFlash to start from 6 am on Friday* [Online]. Available at: www.straitstimes.com/singapore/transport/uber-comfortdelgro-tie-up-through-uberflash-to-start-from-6am-on-friday (Accessed: 9 June 2023).

16 ST Engineering's focus on autonomous vehicles and drones

Senthil Kumar Natarajan
Lecturer, University of Technology and Applied Sciences Salalah,
Sultanate of Oman

The transportation sector and beyond is transforming with the emergence of autonomous vehicles and drones. These technologies can provide various advantages such as improving safety, efficiency, convenience, and accessibility, as well as lowering environmental impacts, congestion, and costs. However, they also present significant challenges such as creating reliable and robust technologies, adhering to complex and diverse regulations, and earning public trust and acceptance. In this context, ST Engineering, a Singapore-based company, has been a pioneer in developing and deploying innovative solutions for autonomous vehicles and drones. This case study will examine the challenges and opportunities that ST Engineering has encountered and overcome in its focus on autonomous vehicles and drones, and how it has become a leader in this rapidly growing market.

One of the biggest challenges for ST Engineering was developing the necessary technology for autonomous vehicles and drones. These technologies include advanced sensors, artificial intelligence algorithms, and communication systems. To address this challenge, ST Engineering invested heavily in research and development and worked closely with its partners to develop innovative solutions. For example, ST Engineering developed DroNet, a drone network system that enables city-wide drone applications such as facility or perimeter security, site inspections, deliveries, and more (ST Engineering Aerospace Ltd., n.d.). The company also developed autonomous buses and trucks that can operate safely and efficiently in various environments (ST Engineering Land Systems Ltd., 2020). These solutions reflect the concept of technological innovation, which refers to the creation and adoption of new products, processes, or services that enhance the value proposition for customers or improve the efficiency and effectiveness of operations (Garcia & Calantone, 2002).

Another challenge for ST Engineering was navigating the complex regulatory landscape for autonomous vehicles and drones. Different countries have different regulations regarding the operation of these vehicles, which could slow down or even prevent the deployment of ST Engineering's solutions. To overcome this challenge, ST Engineering worked closely with regulatory

DOI: 10.4324/9781032660547-70

authorities and industry bodies to develop guidelines and standards that ensured the safe and efficient operation of its autonomous vehicles and drones. For example, ST Engineering received authorisation from the Civil Aviation Authority of Singapore (CAAS) to perform aircraft inspections using its drone solution, DroScan (ST Engineering Aerospace Ltd., 2020). The company also collaborated with the Home Team to conduct long-distance flights using its unmanned drone for security sweeps (Abdullah, 2020). These actions illustrate the concept of regulatory compliance, which refers to the adherence to laws, rules, and standards that govern the activities of a business or industry (Asadi Bagloee et al., 2016).

A third challenge for ST Engineering was gaining public acceptance for autonomous vehicles and drones. Many people were sceptical about the safety and reliability of these technologies and were concerned about the potential impact on employment. To address this challenge, ST Engineering engaged in public education and outreach programmes and worked closely with its partners to demonstrate the safety and reliability of its solutions. For example, ST Engineering participated in trials for autonomous bus services in Singapore, which allowed the public to experience the technology first-hand and provide feedback (ST Engineering Land Systems Ltd., 2020). The company also delivered food to seafarers using its drone solution, which showcased the benefits of drone delivery for hard-to-reach locations (Abdullah, 2020). These efforts exemplify the concept of social acceptance, which refers to the degree to which new technology or innovation is perceived as desirable or beneficial by society or a specific group of stakeholders (Bissell et al., 2020).

In conclusion, ST Engineering has demonstrated that autonomous vehicles and drones are not only challenges but also opportunities for the transportation sector and beyond. By adopting a user-centric approach and investing in research and development, the company has created innovative solutions that are not only cutting-edge but also safe and reliable. By collaborating with regulatory authorities and industry bodies, and engaging in public education and outreach programmes, the company has gained trust and acceptance for its autonomous vehicles and drones. ST Engineering has thus become a leader in the autonomous vehicles and drones market, with a strong reputation and a competitive edge.

References

Abdullah, A.Z. (2020). *Foodpanda collaborates with ST Engineering on drone food delivery trials* [Online]. Available at: www.channelnewsasia.com/singapore/foodpanda-collaborates-st-engineering-on-drone-food-deliveries-618476 (Accessed: 21 May 2023).

Asadi Bagloee, S., Tavana, M., Asadi, M., & Oliver, T. (2016). Autonomous vehicles: challenges, opportunities, and future implications for transportation policies. *Journal of Modern Transportation*, 24(4), 284–303. https://doi.org/10.1007/s40534-016-0117-3

Bissell, D., Birtchnell, T., Elliott, A., & Hsu, E.L. (2020). Autonomous automobilities: the social impacts of driverless vehicles. *Current Sociology, 68*(1), 60–77. https://doi.org/10.1177/0011392118816743

Garcia, R., & Calantone, R. (2002). A critical look at technological innovation typology and innovativeness terminology: a literature review. *Journal of Product Innovation Management, 19*(2), 110–132. https://doi.org/10.1111/1540-5885.1920110.

ST Engineering Aerospace Ltd. (2020). *ST Engineering receives first-ever authorisation from CAAS to perform aircraft inspection – press release* [Online]. Available at: www.stengg.com/en/newsroom/news-releases/st-engineering-receives-first-ever-authorisation-from-caas-to-perform-aircraft-inspection/ (Accessed: 21 May 2023).

ST Engineering Aerospace Ltd. (n.d.). *DroNet* [Online]. Available at: http://dronet.com.sg/ (Accessed: 21 May 2023).

ST Engineering Land Systems Ltd. (2020). *Autonomous vehicles* [Online]. Available at: www.stengg.com/en/land-systems/autonomous-vehicles/ (Accessed: 21 May 2023).

17 Koufu maintaining quality and consistency

Saikat Gochhait

Assistant Professor, Symbiosis International University, India

Koufu is a well-known food and beverage company in Singapore that operates a wide range of food outlets, including food courts, coffee shops, and restaurants. The company faced challenges in maintaining quality and consistency across its outlets, especially as it expanded its operations. Quality and consistency are essential in the food and beverage industry, as they affect customer satisfaction, loyalty, and reputation. Here are some ways that Koufu succeeded in overcoming these challenges:

Challenges

Maintaining quality: As Koufu expanded its operations, it became challenging to maintain the quality of its food and service consistently across all its outlets. Quality refers to the degree to which a product or service meets or exceeds customer expectations (Endress+Hauser, n.d.). Quality can be influenced by various factors, such as ingredients, preparation methods, hygiene standards, packaging, storage, and delivery.

Consistency: Consistency in food and service is essential in the food and beverage industry. Koufu faced challenges in ensuring that its outlets provided consistent food and service quality to its customers. Consistency means that every dish or product has the same taste, look, aroma, and texture (Nimbly, 2023). Consistency can be affected by variations in recipes, ingredients, equipment, staff skills, and customer preferences.

Training: To maintain quality and consistency in its operations, Koufu had to ensure that all its staff received proper training. Training is the process of equipping employees with the knowledge and skills they need to perform their tasks effectively and efficiently (EdApp, 2022). By providing training, Koufu can help to enhance staff competence, motivation, productivity, and performance in the food and beverage industry.

DOI: 10.4324/9781032660547-71

Successes

Standardisation of processes: Koufu has standardised its processes across all its outlets, from food preparation to customer service. This ensures that customers receive the same quality of food and service no matter which outlet they visit. Standardisation is the process of establishing and implementing uniform procedures and specifications for a product or service (NQA, n.d.). Standardisation can help to reduce errors, waste, costs, and risks.

Technology integration: Koufu has implemented technology solutions to help manage its operations and maintain consistency. For example, the company has implemented a central kitchen system that helps to ensure consistent food quality across all outlets. Technology integration is the use of various technologies to support and enhance business processes and functions (Tan et al., 2023). Technology integration can help to improve efficiency, accuracy, speed, and flexibility.

Staff training and development: Koufu places a strong emphasis on staff training and development. The company provides regular training to its staff to ensure that they are equipped with the necessary skills and knowledge to maintain quality and consistency. Staff training and development are activities that aim to improve the capabilities and performance of employees (SFA, 2023). Staff training and development can help to increase staff morale, retention, innovation, and customer satisfaction.

Quality control: Koufu has implemented quality control measures across its outlets to ensure that food and service meet its standards. Quality control is the process of monitoring and verifying the quality of a product or service through inspections, tests, audits, or feedback (BSI, n.d.). Quality control can help to identify and correct problems, prevent defects, ensure compliance, and enhance quality.

Customer feedback: Koufu actively seeks customer feedback to identify areas for improvement. The company takes customer feedback seriously and uses it to make improvements to its operations and processes. Customer feedback is the information that customers provide about their experiences with a product or service (BrandAcademy, n.d.). Customer feedback can help to measure customer satisfaction, loyalty, and expectations, as well as provide insights and suggestions for improvement.

In conclusion, Koufu has demonstrated its commitment to excellence in the food and beverage industry by ensuring quality and consistency across its outlets. By standardising its processes, integrating technology solutions, training and developing its staff, controlling quality, and seeking customer feedback, the company has not only met but exceeded customer expectations and industry standards. These strategies have enabled Koufu to establish a strong brand identity, a loyal customer base, and a competitive edge in the market. Koufu has proven itself as a leader in the food and beverage industry and has positioned itself for sustainable growth and success in the future.

References

BrandAcademy (n.d.). *Training for the food and beverage industry* [Online]. Available at: https://brandacademy.co/industries/food-beverages/ (Accessed: 11 May 2023).

BSI (n.d.). *Food standards – food and beverage industry standards* [Online]. Available at: www.bsigroup.com/en-US/Industries-and-sectors/food-and-drink/food-and-drink-standards/ (Accessed: 11 May 2023).

EdApp (2022). *12 Restaurant staff training topics* [Online]. Available at: www.edapp.com/blog/restaurant-staff-training-topics/ (Accessed: 11 May 2023).

Endress+Hauser (n.d.). *Food & beverage – Trust in quality* [Online]. Available at: www.endress.com/en/industry-expertise/food-beverage-productivity-quality-cost (Accessed: 11 May 2023).

Nimbly (2023). *Maintaining food consistency: best practices for foodservice operators* [Online]. Available at: https://hellonimbly.com/maintaining-food-consistency-best-practices-for-foodservice-operators/ (Accessed: 11 May 2023).

NQA (n.d.). *What standards apply to the food & beverage industry?* [Online]. Available at: www.nqa.com/en-gb/certification/sectors/food-beverage (Accessed: 11 May 2023).

SFA (2023). *Information for food handlers* [Online]. Available at: www.sfa.gov.sg/food-retail/information-for-food-handlers/information-for-food-handlers (Accessed: 11 May 2023).

Tan, W.K., Husin, Z., Yasruddin, M.L., & Ismail, M.A.H. (2023). Recent technology for food and beverage quality assessment: a review. *Journal of Food Science and Technology, 60*(3), 1681–1694. https://doi.org/10.1007/s13197-022-05439-8

Part V

Financial performance and risk management

1 SMRT's response to increased competition in the public transport sector

Nadeem Aftab

Senior Lecturer in Banking and Finance, University of Northampton, United Kingdom

SMRT is a Singapore-based public transport operator that faced significant challenges in responding to increased competition in the public transport sector.

The public transport sector in Singapore has become increasingly competitive in recent years, with the entry of new players such as Grab and Go-Jek. These ride-sharing companies have changed the face of transport in Singapore by offering convenient and affordable alternatives to taxis and buses (Lim, 2021). To respond to this challenge, SMRT focused on improving the quality of its services, investing in new technology and infrastructure, and enhancing its customer service (Lee, 2018).

SMRT is a leading public transport operator that manages complex and demanding operations. It faced challenges in ensuring operational efficiency and excellence. It invested in new technologies and systems to enhance its operations, such as a new rail operating centre that leverages advanced analytics and data management to optimise train operations. The rail operating centre, which commenced operations in April 2019, consolidates the operations control centres for three lines and provides real-time situational awareness and integrated command and control for SMRT's rail network. The rail operating centre also features a digital overview display system that monitors track and maintenance activities throughout the network, enabling faster detection and resolution of potential faults. The rail operating centre is part of SMRT's vision to achieve higher standards of safety and reliability for its customers (SMRT, 2023a).

As a public transport operator, SMRT prioritises maintenance and safety for its trains and buses. However, it encountered challenges in ensuring the optimal condition and safety of its vehicles. To overcome these challenges, SMRT adopted various measures to enhance its maintenance and safety standards, such as investing in new equipment and technology, conducting more frequent maintenance checks, and providing better training and development opportunities for its staff. In addition, SMRT embraced a safety-first culture and a kaizen philosophy to pursue continuous and incremental improvement in its safety performance (SMRT, 2023b).

DOI: 10.4324/9781032660547-73

As a public transport operator, SMRT recognises the importance of the customer experience for its success. However, it encountered challenges in meeting the expectations of its customers. To overcome these challenges, SMRT implemented various measures to enhance the customer experience, such as installing air-conditioned bus stops, introducing new payment methods, and setting up a customer feedback system. In addition, SMRT organised its first Customer Experience Innovation Conference in 2019 to demonstrate its commitment to innovation and excellence in customer experience (SMRT, 2023c).

Through these efforts, SMRT succeeded in improving the quality of its services, enhancing its operational efficiency, and delivering a better customer experience. Today, SMRT remains a leading public transport operator in Singapore, with a focus on innovation, technology, and sustainability. The company continues to invest in new technologies and initiatives to improve its services and respond to changing customer needs and preferences.

References

Lee, T. (2018). *How SMRT is reinventing itself in the age of Grab and Go-Jek – through a startup* [Online]. Available at: www.techinasia.com/smrt-reinventing-age-grab-gojek-startup (Accessed: 13 April 2023).

Lim, S. (2021). *How Singapore transport firm ComfortDelGro is planning to overtake Grab and Go-Jek* [Online]. Available at: www.thedrum.com/news/2021/03/24/how-singapore-transport-firm-comfortdelgro-planning-overtake-against-grab-and-go-jek (Accessed: 12 April 2023).

SMRT (2023a). *Rail operations centre envisions integration of SMRT's transport network operations* [Online]. Available at: www.smrt.com.sg/Announcements/articl eid/rail-operations-centre-envisions-integration-of-smrts-transport-network-operati ons (Accessed: 2 April 2023).

SMRT (2023b). *Kaizen for safety* [Online]. Available at: www.smrt.com.sg/Kaizen/Kaizen-For-Safety (Accessed: 3 April 2023).

SMRT (2023c). *SMRT boosts service excellence efforts with first Customer Experience Innovation Conference* [Online]. Available at: www.smrt.com.sg/News-Room/Announcements-News-Release/articled/733/ (Accessed: 12 April 2023).

2 Dairy Farm International's expansion into e-commerce

Guo Yongsheng

Senior Lecturer in Accounting and Finance, TUIBS Finance, Teesside University, United Kingdom

Purpose: This case study examines how Dairy Farm International developed its e-commerce capabilities and delivered a great customer experience. It highlights the company's utilisation of new technologies to navigate the challenges of the digital era.

Introduction: Dairy Farm International is a prominent retail group operating across Asia, offering a diverse range of high-quality products, competitive pricing, and convenient delivery options. However, the company encountered significant hurdles in expanding into the e-commerce market, competing against major players like Alibaba and JD.com (Lim et al., 2016). Logistics posed a key challenge as Dairy Farm needed to ensure fast and efficient delivery across large and diverse markets (Risberg, 2023). Additionally, successful e-commerce operations require exceptional customer experience, necessitating quality control measures and responsible sourcing (Dairy Farm Group, 2021).

Actions: To address logistics challenges, Dairy Farm made substantial investments in infrastructure and technology, including automated warehouses, advanced delivery systems, milk run services, RFID technology (Inbound Logistics, 2015), and advanced algorithms (Yu et al., 2016). Embracing an omnichannel approach, Dairy Farm's e-commerce logistics supported its social and environmental goals, reducing costs, enhancing quality, and improving customer convenience and satisfaction (PLOS, 2021).

Furthermore, Dairy Farm recognised the need for a shift in mindset, culture, and technology. The company invested in digital transformation through employee training, strategic partnerships, and system enhancements. Launching yuu, a digital rewards club, across its brands and channels (Salesforce News, 2020), Dairy Farm fostered innovation and collaboration among its employees (Dairy Farm Group, 2021) while actively collaborating with various stakeholders to explore new technologies and solutions (*Cornell Chronicle*, 2022; *e3zine*, 2021).

Delivering a superior customer experience was a critical focus for Dairy Farm. The company invested in user-friendly platforms, personalised recommendations and promotions, and fast and reliable delivery options.

DOI: 10.4324/9781032660547-74

Leveraging MuleSoft's Anypoint Platform, Dairy Farm connected its systems and launched yuu, enabling seamless rewards across its brands and channels (Salesforce News, 2020). The company employed Salesforce Marketing Cloud for tailored content and promotions, and Tableau for customer data analysis (Tableau, 2021). Dairy Farm offered a variety of delivery modes, including home delivery, click-and-collect, locker pick-up, and milk run services (MuleSoft, 2020).

In addition, Dairy Farm employed pricing strategies based on value for money, profitability, and competitiveness. Utilising various pricing techniques, data analytics, and customer feedback, the company optimised its pricing decisions and offerings (Farooq et al., 2019). Following an omnichannel approach, Dairy Farm's delivery options aligned with its social and environmental goals.

Conclusion: Retail companies face significant challenges in the digital era and must adopt e-commerce as a selling channel while integrating other marketing functions to enhance efficiency and improve customer experience. Dairy Farm International has successfully developed a robust e-commerce infrastructure, including an efficient logistics network and a user-friendly digital platform. By establishing a strong online presence across Asia, Dairy Farm is well-positioned to compete in the highly competitive e-commerce market and continue growing its business in the years ahead.

References

Cornell Chronicle (2022). *Researchers to explore effect of big data on dairy farms* [Online]. Available at: https://news.cornell.edu/stories/2022/09/researchers-explore-effect-big-data-dairy-farms (Accessed: 9 May 2023).

Dairy Farm Group (2021). *Annual report 2021* [Online]. Available at: https://ar2021.dairyfarmgroup.com/ (Accessed: 9 May 2023).

e3zine (2021). *Dairy farm group accelerates digital transformation* [Online]. Available at: https://e3zine.com/dairy-farm-group-accelerates-digital-transformation/ (Accessed: 9 May 2023).

Farooq Q., Fu P., Hao Y., Jonathan T., & Zhang Y. (2019). A review of management and importance of e-commerce implementation in service delivery of private express enterprises of China. *SAGE Open*. https://doi.org/10.1177/2158244018824194

Inbound Logistics (2015). *The dairy supply chain: from farm to fridge* [Online]. Available at: www.inboundlogistics.com/articles/the-dairy-supply-chain-from-farm-to-fridge/ (Accessed: 9 May 2023).

Lim, Y.J., Osman A., Salahuddin S.N., Romle A.R., & Abdullah S. (2016). Factors influencing online shopping behavior: the mediating role of purchase intention. *Procedia Economics and Finance*. https://doi.org/10.1016/S2212-5671(16)00050-2

MuleSoft (2020). *Dairy Farm Group accelerates digital transformation* [Online]. Available at: www.mulesoft.com/press-center/digital-transformation-dairy-farm-group (Accessed: 9 May 2023).

PLOS (2021). *Public attitudes toward dairy farm practices and technology* [Online]. Available at: https://journals.plos.org/plosone/article?id=10.1371/journal.pone.0250850 (Accessed: 9 May 2023).

Risberg, A. (2023). A systematic literature review on e-commerce logistics: towards an e-commerce and omni-channel decision framework. *The International Review of Retail, Distribution and Consumer Research, 33*(1), 67–91. https://doi.org/10.1080/09593969.2022.2089903

Salesforce News (2020). *Dairy Farm Group accelerates digital transformation, leveraging MuleSoft, Salesforce, and Tableau to connect customer experiences across 2,000 physical stores – salesforce news* [Online]. Available at: www.salesforce.com/news/press-releases/2020/11/17/dairy-farm-group-digital/ (Accessed: 9 May 2023).

Tableau (2021). *Dairy Farm Group accelerates digital transformation* [Online]. Available at: www.tableau.com/about/press-releases/2021/dairy-farm-group-accelerates-digital-transformation-leveraging-mulesoft (Accessed: 9 May 2023).

Yu, Y., Wang, X., Zhong, R.Y., & Huang, G.Q. (2016). E-commerce logistics in supply chain management: practice perspective. *Procedia CIRP, 52,* 179–185. https://doi.org/10.1016/j.procir.2016.08.002

3 Vicom overcoming the challenges of the automotive testing industry

Easwaramoorthy Rangaswamy

Principal and Provost, Amity Global Institute, Singapore

Vicom is a leading provider of technical testing and inspection services in Singapore, with a particular focus on the automotive industry. The company was established in 1981 as a subsidiary of the Land Transport Authority (LTA) and was listed on the Singapore Exchange in 1995. It has seven inspection centres across the island and offers a range of services for vehicles, such as safety inspection, emission testing, type approval, accident reporting, and evaluation. Vicom also provides engineering, testing, inspection, and certification services for various industries, such as aerospace, marine, oil and gas, construction, electronics, biomedical, environmental, and food safety. Despite operating in a challenging and competitive market, Vicom has managed to overcome the difficulties and achieve success. Here are some examples of the challenges faced by Vicom and how it has overcome them:

Challenges

Increasing competition: The automotive testing industry is a fast-growing and highly competitive market, driven by factors such as rising vehicle production, stringent safety and emission regulations, increasing demand for electric vehicles (EVs), and technological advancements in testing equipment and software (Deloitte, 2022). Vicom has to compete with both established players such as TÜV SÜD, DEKRA, and SGS, as well as new entrants such as Luxoft, LogiGear, and McKinsey. To differentiate itself and attract customers, Vicom has to offer high-quality, reliable, and cost-effective testing services across a range of industries.

Technological advancements: The automotive industry is undergoing rapid and disruptive changes due to technological innovations such as EVs, autonomous vehicles (AVs), and connected vehicles. These innovations pose new challenges for testing providers such as Vicom, as they require specific tests for battery safety, thermal management, electromagnetic compatibility, charging infrastructure compatibility, noise emissions, sensor performance, software algorithms, artificial intelligence, and cybersecurity (Fagnant & Kockelman, 2018). To keep up with these changes and remain competitive, Vicom has

DOI: 10.4324/9781032660547-75

to invest in new equipment and technology, as well as upgrade its skills and capabilities.

Regulatory compliance: The automotive industry is subject to strict regulations and standards at both national and international levels. Testing providers such as Vicom have to comply with these regulations and standards to ensure the safety, performance, and environmental impact of vehicles. For example, in Singapore, Vicom has to follow the Vehicle Inspection and Type Approval System (VITAS), which is a set of standards and procedures for vehicle inspection and certification administered by the Land Transport Authority (LTA) (Vicom, 2023). Additionally, Vicom also has to adhere to international standards such as ISO 26262 for the functional safety of road vehicles and ISO 21434 for the cybersecurity engineering of road vehicles. Compliance can be complex and time-consuming, adding to the operational challenges faced by the company.

Successes

Diversification of services: Vicom has diversified its services beyond automotive testing to include engineering, testing, inspection, and certification services across a range of industries. This has helped the company to expand its customer base and revenue streams, reducing its dependence on the automotive industry. According to its annual report 2022 (Vicom, 2023), Vicom's non-vehicle testing business accounted for 38% of its total revenue in 2022, up from 35% in 2021. The company provides non-vehicle testing services for industries such as aerospace, marine, oil and gas, construction, electronics, biomedical, environmental, and food safety.

Investment in technology and infrastructure: Vicom has made significant investments in technology and infrastructure to enhance its testing capabilities and efficiency. For example, the company has upgraded its testing equipment and introduced new technologies such as computerised testing systems. The company has also invested in building new facilities such as the VICOM Emission Test Laboratory (VETL), which is a state-of-the-art laboratory for testing vehicle emissions under various driving conditions (Tan et al., 2021). Furthermore, the company has also leveraged digital technologies such as online booking systems, mobile applications, and data analytics to improve its customer service and operational performance.

Customer focus and service quality: Vicom has a strong focus on customer service and quality, which has helped to differentiate it from its competitors. The company has implemented customer feedback mechanisms and quality control processes to ensure that its services meet the highest standards. The company also strives to provide convenience and value-added services to its customers, such as priority booking, online prepayment, road tax renewal, insurance, vehicle evaluation, and accident reporting. The company's efforts have been recognised by various awards and accolades, such as the Singapore

Quality Class, the Singapore Service Class, the Enterprise 50 Award, and the Customer Satisfaction Index of Singapore (Vicom, 2023).

To sum up, Vicom has overcome the challenges of the automotive testing industry by diversifying its services, investing in technology and infrastructure, and focusing on customer service and quality. These strategies have helped Vicom to stay competitive and grow its business in a dynamic and challenging market, as well as advance the testing and inspection services in Singapore and beyond.

References

Deloitte (2022). *Automotive testing market size, share & trends analysis report* [Online]. Available at: www2.deloitte.com/us/en/insights/industry/retail-distribution/ consumer-behavior-trends-state-of-the-consumer-tracker/auto-industry-challenges. html (Accessed: 19 May 2023).

Fagnant, D.J., & Kockelman, K. (2018). On the future of transportation in an era of automated and autonomous vehicles. *Proceedings of the National Academy of Sciences of the United States of America (PNAS), 115*(20), 4887–4892. https://doi.org/ 10.1073/pnas.1805770115

Tan, C.C., Lam, C.S.P., Matchar, D.B., Zee, Y.K., & Wong, J.E.L. (2021). Singapore's health-care system: key features, challenges, and shifts. *The Lancet, 398*(10305), 1091–1104. https://doi.org/10.1016/S0140-6736(21)00252-X

Vicom (2023). *Annual report 2022* [Online]. Available at: www.vicom.com.sg/Inves tor-Relations/Annual-Report (Accessed: 19 May 2023).

4 United Overseas Bank's response to the global financial crisis

R. Amudha

Professor, CMS Business School, Jain (Deemed to be University), India

The 2008–2009 global financial crisis was a devastating event that shook the world economy and triggered the worst recession in Singapore's history. It began with the collapse of Lehman Brothers, a prominent American investment bank, and soon spread to other countries and sectors. In the midst of this turmoil, United Overseas Bank (UOB), one of Singapore's top three banks along with DBS and OCBC, faced numerous challenges and threats to its income, credit, and operations. To survive and thrive in the crisis, UOB adopted several strategies and measures, such as:

UOB maintained a strong capital and liquidity position throughout the crisis, which enabled it to cope with the financial stress and lend to customers who needed help. Its annual report (2008) stated that UOB had a core capital adequacy ratio (CAR) of 10.9% and a total CAR of 15.1% at the end of 2008, which were well above the regulatory minimum of 6% and 10% respectively. These ratios indicated that UOB had sufficient capital to absorb potential losses and meet its obligations. UOB also had a healthy loan-to-deposit ratio (LDR) of 85.2%, showing its ability to fund its lending activities without relying too much on external sources. UOB's strong capital and liquidity position helped it to achieve a net profit of S$2 billion for 2008, which was a 13.1% decline from 2007 but still a commendable result given the unprecedented times (UOB, 2008).

UOB managed its credit risks effectively by monitoring the credit quality of its loan portfolio closely and tightening lending standards where needed. A report by the Senior Supervisors Group (2009), a group of financial regulators from various countries, said that UOB was one of the few banks that performed well in credit risk management during the crisis. UOB was prudent in lending, avoiding excessive exposure to US subprime mortgages and other risky assets that caused heavy losses for many banks. UOB also had sound processes for identifying, measuring, and controlling credit risks, such as stress testing, loan loss provisioning, and collateral valuation. These processes helped UOB to assess the impact of potential shocks and take appropriate actions to mitigate them. UOB's good credit risk management helped

DOI: 10.4324/9781032660547-76

it to maintain a low level of bad loans and write-offs compared with its peers (Senior Supervisors Group, 2009).

UOB supported the Singapore government's efforts to stabilise the financial system during the 2008 financial crisis by participating in the government's guarantee schemes for interbank lending and bond issuance. These schemes were part of the government's S$2.9 billion stimulus package announced in November 2008, which aimed to restore confidence and liquidity in the banking sector and support economic growth (Vergara, 2022). UOB was one of the first banks to issue bonds under the bond guarantee scheme, raising S$1.5 billion in December 2008. The scheme guaranteed all Singapore dollar and foreign currency bonds issued by participating banks in Singapore until December 2010. UOB also used the interbank guarantee scheme, which covered all interbank deposits and placements among participating banks in Singapore until December 2010 (RBA, 2016). UOB's participation in these schemes helped it to diversify its funding sources and lower its funding costs during the crisis, as well as to demonstrate its solidarity and cooperation with the government and other banks.

The global financial crisis was a difficult time for many people and businesses, but UOB demonstrated its dedication and care for its customers by providing them with various forms of assistance and support. UOB did not abandon its customers who were facing financial difficulties, but instead restructured their loans and offered them temporary relief measures such as longer repayment periods and lower interest rates. By doing so, UOB not only helped its customers to overcome their challenges but also strengthened its customer loyalty and trust. UOB's customer-centric approach proved to be a key factor in its success and resilience during the crisis and earned it a reputation as a dependable and ethical bank.

References

RBA (2016). *The Australian government guarantee scheme: 2008–15* [Online]. Available at: www.rba.gov.au/publications/bulletin/2016/mar/5.html (Accessed: 17 April 2023).

Senior Supervisors Group (2009). *Risk management lessons from the global banking crisis of 2008* [Online]. Available at: www.fsb.org/wp-content/uploads/r_0910a.pdf (Accessed: 17 April 2023).

UOB (2008). *Annual report 2008* [Online]. Available at: www.uob.com.sg/web-resources/uobgroup/pdf/investor-relations/annual-reports/2008/uob-annual-report-2008.pdf (Accessed: 17 April 2023).

Vergara, E. (2022). *Singapore: government guarantee on deposits* [Online]. Available at: https://elischolar.library.yale.edu/journal-of-financial-crises/vol4/iss2/24 (Accessed: 17 April 2023).

5   Jardine Matheson Holdings' response to changing market conditions

Krishnamoorthy Renganathan
Director, Wise Consulting, Singapore

Jardine Matheson Holdings is an Asian-based conglomerate with expanded interests spanning multiple sectors. Its portfolio encompasses various industries such as engineering, construction, insurance, property development, retail, and beyond.

Jardine Matheson is a diversified group that was founded in China in 1832 and has extensive experience in the Asian region. It has a wide range of businesses in different sectors, such as retail, property, hotels, transport, and finance. It operates mainly in China and Southeast Asia, where it has strong networks and relationships, as well as in the United Kingdom, where it owns several luxury hotels and other businesses. This geographic diversification helps the group to lower its exposure to any single market and to take advantage of the growth opportunities in different regions. The group also supports its businesses with financial and other resources to create value and achieve sustainable growth over the long term (Jardine Matheson, 2022; Royal Gazette, 2023).

In addition, it has a broad portfolio of market-leading businesses in Asia and the United Kingdom. In addition to its core businesses in motor vehicles, property, food retailing, and hotels, the company has diversified into new sectors such as healthcare, where it has a strong presence in hospitals and healthcare facilities in China and Southeast Asia. This diversification enables the company to mitigate risks and leverage growth opportunities in different sectors, aligned with the rising middle class and urbanisation of its key markets. It has various businesses in sectors such as motor vehicles, property, food retailing, hotels, and healthcare. It has hospitals and healthcare facilities in China and Southeast Asia. This diversification helps it mitigate risks and leverage growth opportunities in different sectors. It also invests in technology to enhance customer engagement and operational efficiencies in its retail and property businesses (Jardine Matheson, 2020; Jardine Matheson, 2021).

The company has also pursued strategic partnerships with other companies to support its growth and competitiveness. For example, the company has entered into joint ventures with other leading companies in its core sectors, such as insurance and property development, to leverage its expertise, resources, and

DOI: 10.4324/9781032660547-77

risks. The company has also built its reputation as a preferred partner for high-growth Asian businesses, collaborating with a wide range of partners including technology companies, start-ups, original engineering manufacturing (OEM), suppliers, and entrepreneurs. The company has also invested significant capital to acquire 100% of Jardine Strategic, which improved corporate governance and generated substantial value for its shareholders (Jardine Matheson, 2022).

Through these efforts, Jardine Matheson has established a formidable competitive stance and generated lasting value for its shareholders. It has effectively navigated shifting market dynamics and capitalise on growth prospects across diverse sectors and markets. Emphasising strategic alliances, innovation, and expansion into various regions and industries, the company is well-positioned for future success. Its actions and choices are guided by the core principles of integrity, resilience, collaboration, and entrepreneurial spirit. Additionally, the company actively contributes to meaningful causes in education, mental health, environmental conservation, and other areas, aiming to create a positive impact and leave a lasting legacy for its stakeholders and future generations.

References

Jardine Matheson (2020). *Annual report 2020* [Online]. Available at: https://ar.jardines.com/2020/index.html (Accessed: 17 April 2023).

Jardine Matheson (2021). *Annual report 2021* [Online]. Available at: https://ar.jardines.com/2021/index.html (Accessed: 17 April 2023).

Jardine Matheson (2022). *Creating value at Jardines* [Online]. Available at: https://ar.jardines.com/2022/CreatingValueMD.html (Accessed: 17 April 2023).

Royal Gazette (2023). *Jardine Matheson to benefit from economic recovery* [Online]. Available at: www.royalgazette.com/international-business/business/article/20230519/jardine-matheson/ (Accessed: 17 April 2023).

6 Parkway Pantai's challenges and opportunities of being a healthcare provider

Jakia Rajoana

Senior Lecturer, Teesside University, United Kingdom

Purpose: The key aim of this case study is to showcase the challenges and opportunities of Parkway Pantai, a leading healthcare provider. Parkway Pantai is a leading healthcare provider in Asia with a presence in Malaysia, Singapore, India, China, Brunei, and the United Arab Emirates. The company operates a network of hospitals, clinics, and medical centres that offer a wide range of medical services, including primary care, speciality care, and diagnostic services. Parkway Pantai faces several challenges and opportunities as a healthcare provider.

Challenges

Rising healthcare costs: As the demand for healthcare services continues to grow, the cost of providing quality care also increases. Parkway Pantai needs to balance the need for quality care with the need to keep healthcare costs affordable for patients. This is a challenge faced by many healthcare systems around the world, especially in the United States, which has one of the highest public healthcare expenditures but not the best health outcomes (Bush, 2018). Some of the factors that contribute to rising healthcare costs include ageing populations, chronic diseases, new technologies, drug prices, and social determinants of health (Cutler, 2017). To address these factors, Parkway Pantai can adopt strategies such as improving efficiency and quality of care delivery, implementing value-based payment models, engaging patients and communities in health promotion and prevention, and collaborating with other stakeholders to address the root causes of health inequities (Emanuel et al., 2020).

Increasing competition: The healthcare industry is very competitive, and there are always new entrants in the market. Parkway Pantai must keep up with the competition by providing new and better services and using new technologies. This is a problem that many healthcare providers have in different countries, especially in transition economies, where the market situation and the strength of competition have changed a lot over time (Lábaj et al., 2018). Some of the things that affect how much and how well healthcare providers

DOI: 10.4324/9781032660547-78

compete include how much regulation there is, how important insurers are, how much power doctors have, how much information is available, and what consumers want (Garattini & Padula, 2019). To deal with these things, Parkway Pantai can try to do things like make its services and products stand out, make its quality and name better, make its network and coverage bigger, and work with other partners to make patients happier (Lee et al., 2009).

Regulatory compliance: The healthcare industry is very regulated, and Parkway Pantai has to follow many rules and standards to make sure patients are safe and get good care. This is a problem that many healthcare providers have in different situations, as rules can change depending on the country, sector, and level of government (Levi-Faur, 2020). Some of the things that affect how rules are made and followed in healthcare include what regulators want and care about, what evidence and knowledge they have, what costs and benefits there are for following the rules, and what feedback and involvement they get from others (Dunbar et al., 2021). To follow the rules, Parkway Pantai can try to do things like making internal plans and processes, teaching and training staff, checking and measuring how well they do, telling and sharing information, and working with regulators and other partners (Walshe & Rundall, 2001).

Success

Parkway Pantai has become a top healthcare provider in Asia by putting patients first, using new technologies, and growing its network of hospitals and clinics. The company has also worked with other healthcare providers, technology companies, and insurers to give more complete services to patients. Besides that, Parkway Pantai has a good name for quality care and patient safety, which has made it stand out from its competitors. This can be seen by its successes in different parts of healthcare delivery, such as making cancer treatments more personal for patients with molecular tests (Biopharma Dealmakers, 2020), helping people live healthier and happier with Brunei's Ministry of Health (Mosaic, 2019a), giving medical help for sports events and crises (Mosaic, 2019b), starting new institutes and clinics to help patients with lung diseases and joint problems, and taking safety steps to keep patients, visitors, and staff safe from COVID-19.

References

Biopharma Dealmakers (2020). Angsana Molecular: personalizing cancer treatments for Parkway Pantai patients. *Angsana Molecular & Diagnostics Laboratory Pte Ltd, 2020*(1), S8–S9. doi:10.1038/d43747-020-00484-8

Bush, M. (2018). Addressing the root cause: rising health care costs and social determinants of health. *North Carolina Medical Journal, 79*(1), 26–29. doi:10.18043/ncm.79.1.26. PMID:29439099.

Cutler, D.M. (2017). Rising medical costs mean more rough times ahead. *JAMA*, *318*(12), 1109–1110. doi:10.1001/jama.2017.12034. PMID: 28973614.

Dunbar, P., Browne, J.P., & O'Connor, L. (2021). Recent research into healthcare professions regulation: a rapid evidence assessment. *BMC Health Service Research*, *21*(1), 934. doi:10.1186/s12913-021-06946-8

Emanuel, E.J., Glickman, A., & Johnson, D. (2020). Health costs and financing: challenges and strategies for a new administration and Congress. *Health Affairs (Millwood)*, *39*(12), 2149–2156. doi:10.1377/hlthaff.2020.01560. PMID: 33284680.

Garattini, L., & Padula, A. (2019). Competition in health markets: is something rotten? *Journal of the Royal Society of Medicine*, *112*(1), 4–6. doi:10.1177/0141076818816935

Lábaj, M., Silanič, P., Weiss, C., & Yontcheva, B. (2018). Market structure and competition in the healthcare industry: results from a transition economy. *European Journal of Health Economics*, *19*(8), 1087–1110. doi:10.1007/s10198-018-0959-1

Lee, S.Y.D., Alexander, J.A., & Wang, Y.R. (2009). Health care competition, strategic mission, and patient satisfaction: research model and propositions. *Journal of Health Organization and Management*, *23*(6), 639–660. doi:10.1108/14777260911001644

Levi-Faur, D. (2020). Legislation and regulation: three analytical distinctions. *Regulation and Governance*, *14*(1), 1–16. doi:10.1080/20508840.2019.1736369

Mosaic (2019a). *A Parkway Pantai publication: Apr-Jun 2019* [Online]. Available at: www.parkwaypantai.com/docs/librariesprovider6/default-document-library/mosaic-issue_april-june-2019_digital.pdf?sfvrsn=b1c58f1e_0 (Accessed: 5 May 2023).

Mosaic (2019b). *A Parkway Pantai publication. Jan-Mar 2019* [Online]. Available at: www.parkwaypantai.com/docs/librariesprovider6/default-document-library/mosaic-issue_jan-mar-2019_digital.pdf?sfvrsn=4c7f8f1e_0 (Accessed: 5 May 2023).

Walshe, K., & Rundall, T.G. (2001). Evidence-based management: from theory to practice in health care. *The Milbank Quarterly*, *79*(3), 429–457. doi:10.1111/1468-0009.00214

7 The UOL Group's case study challenges of being a real estate developer

Guo Yongsheng

Senior Lecturer in Accounting and Finance, TUIBS Finance,
Teesside University, United Kingdom

Purpose: This study examines how UOL Group Limited, a real estate company, has navigated economic challenges and regulatory changes, focusing on the role of risk management during volatile periods.

Introduction: Founded in 1963, UOL Group is a Singaporean property company that has emerged as a leading real estate developer in Asia. The company possesses a diverse portfolio of properties, including residential, commercial, and hospitality developments.

Economic challenges: UOL Group has encountered various economic challenges over time, such as the Asian Financial Crisis in 1997, the Global Financial Crisis in 2008, and the COVID-19 pandemic in 2020. These challenges have led to decreased demand for properties, impacting the company's revenue and profitability. In 2020, UOL Group's revenue declined by 25.9% due to reduced contributions from its property development and hotel operations segments.

Regulatory changes: The real estate industry is subject to government regulatory changes, including adjustments to zoning laws, stamp duty rates, and foreign ownership restrictions. In response to market moderation, the Singapore government implemented additional buyer's stamp duty (ABSD) and stricter loan-to-value (LTV) limits for residential property purchases in 2018 (Tan, 2023). UOL Group had to adapt to these regulatory changes and explore new revenue-generating avenues.

Strategies: UOL Group effectively mitigated economic influences through financial management practices. Despite the challenges posed by the COVID-19 pandemic, the company reported a net profit of S$ 323.8 million in 2020. This success was attributed to higher fair value gains from investment properties and a greater share of profit from associated companies (UOL, 2023b). UOL Group consistently maintained a higher return on equity and lower debt-to-equity ratio compared with industry peers (Asia Pacific Enterprise Awards, 2023).

To address regulatory changes, UOL Group pursued strategies such as acquiring residential sites in Singapore through joint ventures with Singapore Land Group. These acquisitions, including Watten Estate Condominium for

DOI: 10.4324/9781032660547-79

S$550.8 million, a government land sale site at Ang Mo Kio Avenue 1 for S$381.4 million, and a freehold site at Meyer Road for S$392.2 million in 2021 and 2022 respectively (Burgos, 2023), reflect the company's efforts to replenish its land bank and diversify its offerings. Furthermore, UOL Group offered discounts and rebates to buyers of some projects to mitigate the impact of ABSD and expanded its presence in other markets, such as Australia, Vietnam, and the United Kingdom.

The company's strong brand reputation and commitment to quality design have played a significant role in attracting customers. UOL Group has received numerous awards for its properties, including prestigious accolades like the World Architecture Festival Award, Green Mark Platinum Award, FIABCI Prix d'Excellence Award, Aga Khan Award for Architecture, Urban Land Institute Awards for Excellence, and President's Design Award (UOL, 2023a). These awards have bolstered the company's reputation and facilitated buyer engagement.

Conclusion: Effectively managing economic and regulatory risks is crucial for companies. UOL Group has demonstrated its ability to navigate these challenges through robust financial management practices, market expansion into other regions, and the cultivation of a strong brand reputation. The company's high return on equity, low financial leverage, diversified business operations, and commitment to innovation and sustainability have contributed to its success in overcoming economic and regulatory obstacles.

References

Asia Pacific Enterprise Awards (2023). *UOL Group Limited* [Online]. Available at: https://apea.asia/singapore/hall-of-fame-sg-2019/uol-group-limited/ (Accessed: 9 May 2023).

Burgos, J. (2023). *Billionaire Wee Cho Yaw's UOL buys Singapore suburban redevelopment property for $295 million* [Online]. Available at: www.forbes.com/sites/jonathanburgos/2023/02/10/billionaire-wee-cho-yaws-uol-buys-singapore-suburban-redevelopment-property-for-295-million/?sh=75d54fbc2b7f (Accessed: 9 May 2023).

Tan, F. (2023). *UOL Group and Singapore Land Group jointly purchase Watten Estate Condominium en bloc for $550.8 mil* [Online]. Available at: theedgesingapore.com (Accessed: 9 May 2023).

UOL (2023a). *About UOL: awards* [Online]. Available at: www.uol.com.sg/about-uol/awards/ (Accessed: 9 May 2023).

UOL (2023b). *Corporate profile* [Online]. Available at: www.uol.com.sg/about-uol/corporate-profile/ (Accessed: 9 May 2023).

8 GlobalRoam maintaining its financial sustainability and profitability

Jonny Munby

Principal Lecturer (International), Teesside University, United Kingdom

GlobalRoam, a Singapore-based provider of mobile data solutions for travellers, faced challenges in maintaining its financial sustainability and profitability due to intense competition in the travel industry and rising costs. However, the company was able to overcome these challenges and succeed by implementing several key strategies.

GlobalRoam maintained financial sustainability and profitability by focusing on innovative products and services that met evolving customer needs. They invested in R&D, collaborated closely with customers, and created unique, valuable offerings. For instance, GlobalRoam developed smart mapping, enabling the sharing of DDI numbers among many users without additional software or equipment. They also created communication and authentication microservices, facilitating hybrid connections via traditional telco infrastructures and digital networks. These cost-effective solutions catered to the telecommunications sector (GlobalRoam Pte Ltd, 2009).

Another key strategy that helped GlobalRoam succeed was its focus on operational efficiency and cost control. The company implemented lean processes and streamlined its operations to reduce costs and improve efficiency (Cheng et al., 2018). This allowed GlobalRoam to offer competitive prices while maintaining profitability, even in the face of intense competition. Operational efficiency can help businesses achieve optimal output and goals without compromising quality and maximise resource utilisation to improve profit margins (Hubstaff, 2022; Asana, n.d.). By measuring and improving its operational efficiency, GlobalRoam was able to enhance its performance and customer satisfaction.

GlobalRoam also succeeded by expanding its customer base beyond its core market of travellers. The company recognised that there was a growing demand for mobile data solutions among businesses and government agencies, and worked to develop products and services that meet the needs of these customers. This expansion into new markets helped GlobalRoam diversify its revenue streams and reduce its dependence on any one customer segment. For instance, GlobalRoam partnered with StarHub to provide inflight connectivity and international calling services to travellers using StarHub's network

DOI: 10.4324/9781032660547-80

(StarHub, 2019a). GlobalRoam also offered maritime connectivity and hybrid communication solutions to businesses and government agencies that required reliable and secure data access across different platforms and locations. By tapping into these new markets, GlobalRoam was able to increase its customer base and revenue potential.

Finally, GlobalRoam succeeded by building strong relationships with its partners and suppliers. The company worked closely with its suppliers to negotiate favourable pricing and terms and built strong relationships with its partners to create mutual value. These partnerships allowed GlobalRoam to access new markets and customers, and to offer a wider range of products and services. For example, GlobalRoam partnered with StarHub, a leading telecommunication company in Singapore, to provide inflight connectivity and international calling services to travellers using StarHub's network (StarHub, 2019b). GlobalRoam also partnered with other telecommunication companies and service providers around the world to expand its reach and offer more choices to its customers (Kompass, n.d.).

GlobalRoam's ability to maintain financial sustainability and profitability can be attributed to several key factors. First, the company's commitment to innovation and the development of cutting-edge products and services played a vital role. Additionally, GlobalRoam's emphasis on operational efficiency and cost control helped optimise its resources. The company's successful expansion into new markets also contributed to its overall success. Furthermore, GlobalRoam's establishment of strong relationships with partners and suppliers further bolstered its competitive advantage. Through the implementation of these strategies, GlobalRoam overcame industry challenges and achieved notable success in the highly competitive travel sector.

References

Asana (n.d.). *Operational efficiency: do more with less. Asana* [Online]. Available at: https://asana.com/resources/operational-efficiency (Accessed: 22 April 2023).

Cheng, Q., Goh, B.W., & Kim, J.B. (2018). Internal control and operational efficiency. *Contemporary Accounting Research, 35*(2), 1102–1139.

GlobalRoam Pte Ltd (2009). *GlobalRoam is the technology provider for StarHub's Advanced Multimedia Services' pfingoTALK* [Online]. Available at: www.starhub.com/personal/mobile/mobile-phones-plans/value-added-services/roaming/postpaid-roaming/globalroam-108.html (Accessed: 22 April 2023).

Hubstaff (2022, July 18). *What is operational efficiency and how to measure it: a guide* [Online]. Available at: https://blog.hubstaff.com/operational-efficiency/ (Accessed: 22 April 2023).

Kompass (n.d.). *GlobalRoam Group Ltd. Kompass* [Online]. Available at: https://sg.kompass.com/c/globalroam-group-ltd/sg048880/ (Accessed: 12 April 2023).

StarHub (2019a). *About GlobalRoam 108* [Online]. Available at: www.starhub.com/personal/mobile/mobile-phones-plans/value-added-services/roaming/postpaid-roaming/globalroam-108.html (Accessed: 12 April 2023).

StarHub (2019b). *Inflight connectivity* [Online]. Available at: www.starhub.com/personal/mobile/mobile-phones-plans/value-added-services/roaming/postpaid-roaming/data-plans/inflight-connectivity.html (Accessed: 22 April 2023).

9 Great Eastern Life faced challenges in attracting and retaining talent

Hala Mansour

Associate Professor, University of Northampton, United Kingdom

Great Eastern Life is one of the leading insurance companies in Singapore, but like many other companies, it faced challenges in attracting and retaining top talent. Here are some ways that Great Eastern succeeded in overcoming these challenges:

Challenges

Competition for talent: the talent race: Great Eastern encountered fierce competition from various firms, particularly within the financial services industry, in their quest to secure top-tier talent. A study conducted by PwC revealed that Singapore's insurance sector is projected to experience an annual growth rate of 6.6% between 2019 and 2024. This expansion is fuelled by rising demand for life and health insurance products (PwC, 2020), necessitating the presence of skilled professionals capable of delivering innovative solutions and customer-centric services. Nevertheless, Great Eastern faced additional challenges in attracting and retaining talent (Great Eastern, 2021a), as it had to contend not only with other insurance companies but also with sectors such as banking, technology, and e-commerce.

Talent retention: Retaining its talented workforce was a crucial priority for Great Eastern, especially considering the intensifying competition and dynamic nature of the business landscape. The COVID-19 pandemic acted as a catalyst for the insurance industry's digital transformation, compelling Great Eastern to embrace innovative technologies and streamline operations to better engage customers (Great Eastern, 2021b). Consequently, the company made substantial investments in upskilling and reskilling its employees, ensuring they possessed the necessary digital skills and capabilities. Additionally, Great Eastern actively fostered a culture of innovation, collaboration, and empowerment, seeking to motivate its workforce and cultivate their loyalty (Great Eastern, 2021a).

DOI: 10.4324/9781032660547-81

Successes

Attractive employee value proposition: Great Eastern created an attractive employee value proposition (EVP) that emphasised its commitment to employee development, work-life balance, and an inclusive and diverse work environment. This helped to attract top talent and retain existing employees (Mortensen & Edmondson, 2023).

Comprehensive training and development programmes: Great Eastern invested in comprehensive training and development programmes to help employees develop the skills they need to succeed. These programmes include leadership development, skills training, and job rotations (Noe et al., 2014).

Employee recognition and rewards: Great Eastern implemented a range of employee recognition and reward programmes to acknowledge the contributions of its employees. These programmes include bonuses, awards, and public recognition.

Emphasis on work-life balance: Great Eastern recognised the importance of work-life balance for its employees and implemented policies to support this. This includes flexible work arrangements, such as telecommuting and part-time work, as well as health and wellness programmes.

Diversity and inclusion: Great Eastern placed a strong emphasis on diversity and inclusion in its hiring and retention practices. The company actively sought to hire a diverse workforce and created an inclusive work environment where all employees feel valued and respected (Berdahl & Moore, 2021).

Talent management: Great Eastern implemented a talent management programme that identifies high-potential employees and provides them with development opportunities to help them reach their full potential.

In conclusion, Great Eastern's ability to attract and retain exceptional talent can be credited to its focus on employee growth, maintaining work-life balance, fostering diversity and inclusion, and implementing effective talent management practices. By prioritising these strategies, the company has cultivated a robust and motivated workforce, established its reputation as a preferred employer, and attained enduring success in a highly competitive industry.

References

Berdahl, J. L., & Moore, C. (2021). Workplace diversity and inclusion: a review and agenda for future research. *Annual Review of Organizational Psychology and Organizational Behavior*, 8, 1–28. https://doi.org/10.1146/annurev-orgpsych-012420-044714.

Great Eastern (2021a). *How Singapore insurer Great Eastern is embracing digitalisation* [Online]. Available at: www.greateasternlife.com/sg/en/about-us/media-cen tre/media-stories/how-singapore-insurer-great-eastern-is-embracing-digitalisation. html (Accessed: 17 April 2023).

Great Eastern (2021b). *#LIFEPROOF A REALITY – top achievers* [Online]. Available at: www.greateasternlife.com/content/dam/great-eastern/geachievers/pdf/2021/top-achievers.pdf (Accessed: 17 April 2023).

Mortensen, M., & Edmondson, A.C. (2023). Rethink your employee value proposition. *Harvard Business Review, 101*(1), 86–95. https://doi.org/10.2139/ssrn.3919159

Noe, R.A., Clarke, A.D.M., & Klein, H.J. (2014). Learning in the twenty-first-century workplace. *Annual Review of Organizational Psychology and Organizational Behavior, 1*(1), 245–275. https://doi.org/10.1146/annurev-orgpsych-031413-091321

PwC (2020). *Singapore insurance industry–market research report* [Online]. Available at: www.pwc.com/sg/en/publications/assets/singapore-insurance-industry-market-research-report.pdf (Accessed: 17 April 2023).

10 Dairy Farm Group's focus on retail and hospitality operations

Preethi Thankappan Nair

Lecturer – Business Strategy, Co-Founding Director – Business Advice Centre, University of East London, United Kingdom

Dairy Farm Group is a leading retail and hospitality company in Asia with a rich history and a diverse portfolio. Founded in 1886 as a dairy farm in Hong Kong, it expanded into various segments and markets across Asia. It operates over 9,997 outlets in 11 countries and regions, serving millions of customers every day. However, it also faced several challenges while expanding and growing its business, including:

Fierce competition: Dairy Farm Group faced intense competition in the retail and hospitality sectors from both local and global competitors, such as Carrefour, Tesco, Walmart, and Alibaba. To stay ahead of the competition, the company constantly innovated and adapted to the industry structure and profitability, as suggested by Porter (1980). It used a differentiation strategy to create a unique and personalised customer experience and loyalty programmes, which helped to increase customer retention and satisfaction (Ulvenblad & Cederholm Björklund, 2018). It also launched its e-commerce platforms, such as Cold Storage Online and Giant Online, to provide convenience and value to customers who preferred online shopping (DFI Retail Group, 2021).

Changing consumer behaviour: Dairy Farm Group developed an online presence and a seamless omnichannel experience to meet the rising demand for e-commerce from consumers. The company recognised that consumers in Asia were influenced by various factors, such as culture, health, and the environment when making purchasing decisions (Kotler et al., 2018). It used technology to improve its operational efficiency and customer satisfaction. It invested in digital technologies, such as e-commerce platforms, mobile apps, and data analytics, to enhance its product and service offerings and reach more customers online. It also partnered with Lazada and Shopee to expand its online reach and offer more choices to customers. It leveraged data analytics to understand customer preferences and personalise its marketing campaigns. Technology adoption can help dairy farmers improve their productivity and sustainability (Clay et al., 2020).

Operational efficiency: Dairy Farm Group had a vast network of stores and outlets, and operational efficiency was a challenge. The company streamlined

DOI: 10.4324/9781032660547-82

its processes and invested in technology to improve productivity and reduce costs. Operational efficiency is the ability to deliver products or services timely, cost-effectively, and quality-wise (Slack et al., 2019). Dairy Farm Group faced operational challenges, such as high labour costs, complex supply chains, inventory issues, and regulatory compliance. It implemented initiatives to optimise its operations and performance. For example, it introduced automation and robotics to reduce labour costs and improve accuracy. It adopted cloud-based solutions to streamline its supply chain and inventory control. It complied with the relevant laws and regulations in each market.

Despite these challenges, Dairy Farm Group has succeeded in growing its business by adopting several strategies, such as:

Focusing on customer experience: Dairy Farm Group put the customer at the centre of its business. The company invested in creating a unique and personalised customer experience to differentiate itself from its competitors. Customer experience is the sum of all the interactions that a customer has with a company over time (Pine II & Gilmore, 1999). Dairy Farm Group provided a superior customer experience across all its touchpoints, online and offline. For example, it enhanced its store formats and layouts to create a more appealing and comfortable shopping environment. It improved its product quality and assortment to cater to different customer segments and occasions. It offered various value-added services, such as home delivery, click-and-collect, self-checkout, and online payment options.

Diversification: Dairy Farm Group diversified its business by entering new markets and expanding its offerings. The company also formed partnerships with other businesses to leverage their expertise and resources. Diversification is a growth strategy (Ansoff, 1957) that involves entering new markets or offering new products or services that are different from the existing ones. Dairy Farm Group pursued diversification to capture new opportunities and reduce its dependence on a single market or product category. For example, it entered new markets, such as Vietnam and Cambodia, through acquisitions and joint ventures. It expanded its offerings, such as health and beauty, home furnishings, and restaurants, to cater to different customer needs and lifestyles. It partnered with other businesses, such as IKEA, Yonghui, and Robinsons, to leverage its expertise and resources.

Sustainability: Dairy Farm Group made sustainability a key focus of its business. The company reduced its environmental footprint, promoted responsible sourcing, and supported local communities. Sustainability is the ability of an organisation to balance the economic, environmental, and social aspects of its operations (Elkington, 1997). Dairy Farm Group recognised that sustainability was a moral obligation and a competitive advantage. For example, it reduced its energy consumption and emissions by adopting renewable energy and energy-efficient equipment. It promoted responsible sourcing by ensuring that its suppliers met high standards of quality, safety, and ethics. It supported local communities by donating food and funds, providing employment, and engaging in social initiatives.

In sum, Dairy Farm Group has excelled in the retail industry by being customer-centric, technology-savvy, diversified, and sustainable. It has used technology to improve its operations, customer service, and data analysis. It has also diversified its brands and formats to suit different markets and segments in Asia while adopting sustainable practices and initiatives across its value chain.

References

Ansoff, H.I. (1957). Strategies for diversification. *Harvard Business Review, 35*(5), 113–124.

Clay, N., Garnett, T., & Lorimer, J. (2020). Dairy intensification: drivers, impacts and alternatives. *Ambio, 49,* 35–48. https://doi.org/10.1007/s13280-019-01177-y

DFI Retail Group (2021). *Annual report 2021* [Online]. Available at: https://ar2021. dairyfarmgroup.com/pdf/ar2021.pdf (Accessed: 2 June 2023).

Elkington, J. (1997). *Cannibals with Forks: The Triple Bottom Line of 21st Century Business.* Oxford: Capstone.

Kotler, P., Keller, K.L., Ang, S.H., Leong, S.M., & Tan, C.T. (2018). *Marketing Management: An Asian Perspective* (7th edn). Singapore: Pearson.

Pine II, B.J., & Gilmore, J.H. (1999). *The Experience Economy: Work Is Theatre & Every Business a Stage.* Boston, MA: Harvard Business School Press.

Porter, M.E. (1980). *Competitive Strategy: Techniques for Analyzing Industries and Competitors.* New York, NY: Free Press.

Slack, N., Brandon-Jones, A., & Johnston, R. (2019). *Operations Management* (9th edn). Harlow: Pearson.

Ulvenblad, P., & Cederholm Björklund, J. (2018). A leadership development programme for agricultural entrepreneurs in Sweden. *The Journal of Agricultural Education and Extension, 24*(4), 327–343. https://doi.org/10.1080/13892 24X.2018.1473260

11 Certis CISCO faced a shrinking market in the security industry, which was increasingly commoditised and faced downward price pressures

Desti Kannaiah

Associate Lecturer, Newcastle University, Singapore

The security industry is a tough and dynamic sector that needs constant innovation and adaptation. However, it faces many challenges, such as market saturation, commoditisation, price erosion, and regulatory pressures. These challenges threaten the survival and growth of security solutions providers, especially in Singapore. Certis CISCO is a leading provider of security solutions in Singapore and the region. How did it overcome the difficulties and succeed in the shrinking and commoditised security industry? What strategies did it use to differentiate itself from its competitors and create value for its customers?

One of the ways Certis CISCO succeeded was by focusing on innovation and technology. The company invested heavily in research and development to create new and advanced security solutions that could differentiate itself from competitors. By introducing cutting-edge technology, such as artificial intelligence, robotics, biometrics, and data analytics, Certis CISCO was able to provide value-added services and increase its competitive advantage in the market. According to Porter (1985), innovation is one of the generic strategies that can help a firm achieve a sustainable competitive advantage by offering unique products or services that are superior to those of rivals. Innovation can also help a firm reduce costs, improve quality, enhance customer satisfaction, and create entry barriers for potential competitors. Certis CISCO exemplified this strategy by developing innovative solutions that met the changing needs and expectations of its customers in the security industry.

Another way Certis CISCO succeeded was by building a strong brand identity and reputation. The company focused on providing high-quality services and building lasting relationships with customers. This helped Certis CISCO establish itself as a trusted and reliable brand in the market. According to Aaker (1991), brand identity is a set of associations that a firm creates or maintains to differentiate itself from competitors and communicate its value proposition to customers. Brand identity can influence customer perceptions, preferences, loyalty, and willingness to pay. Certis CISCO leveraged its brand identity to create a positive image and reputation among its customers and stakeholders.

DOI: 10.4324/9781032660547-83

Furthermore, Certis CISCO also diversified its business by expanding into new markets and offering new services. The company expanded beyond traditional security services and ventured into areas such as cybersecurity, facility management, and integrated security solutions. By diversifying its business, Certis CISCO was able to tap into new markets and gain access to new customers. Diversification is one of the growth strategies (Kumar & Singh, 2021) that can help a firm increase its sales and profits by entering new product-market combinations that are different from its existing ones. Diversification can also help a firm reduce risks, exploit synergies, and leverage core competencies (Ansoff, 1957). Certis CISCO adopted this strategy by expanding its portfolio of products and services to cater to different market segments and regions.

In addition, Certis CISCO also developed a strong online presence by using digital marketing and e-commerce platforms. This enabled the company to attract a broader audience and grow its customer base beyond conventional channels. By using digital channels, Certis CISCO was able to interact with customers on a more personal level and offer a smooth user experience.

Digital marketing is the application of digital technologies to create, communicate, deliver, and exchange offerings that have value for customers and stakeholders. Digital marketing can help a firm improve its visibility, accessibility, engagement, personalisation, and responsiveness (Kotler et al., 2017). Certis CISCO adopted this method by designing an interactive website, an online store, and social media accounts to market its products and services online.

Furthermore, Certis CISCO placed a significant emphasis on optimising costs and enhancing operational efficiency to bolster its financial performance. The company undertook measures to streamline its supply chain and operational processes, effectively reducing expenses and augmenting profitability. Operations management, encompassing the design, planning, control, improvement, and coordination of processes that convert inputs into outputs meeting customer requirements, played a pivotal role in this endeavour (Sarkar & Sarkar, 2021). By leveraging operations management, firms can attain cost efficiency, improve quality, enhance flexibility, bolster dependability, and assume environmental responsibility (Slack et al., 2019). Certis CISCO applied this principle by optimising its resources, processes, systems, and technologies to provide top-notch services at competitive costs.

In summary, Certis CISCO succeeded in the shrinking and commoditised security industry by focusing on innovation and technology, building a strong brand identity, diversifying its business, building a strong online presence, and optimising costs and operations. These strategies helped Certis CISCO differentiate itself from competitors and build a sustainable competitive advantage in the market.

References

Aaker, D.A. (1991). *Managing Brand Equity: Capitalizing on the Value of a Brand Name.* New York: Free Press.

Ansoff, H.I. (1957). Strategies for diversification. *Harvard Business Review, 35*(5), 113–124.

Kotler, P., Keller, K.L., Ang, S.H., Leong, S.M., & Tan, C.T. (2017). *Marketing Management: An Asian Perspective* (7th edn). Singapore: Pearson.

Kumar, V., & Singh, R.K. (2021). Diversification strategy and firm performance: a review of literature and future research directions. *Journal of Strategy and Management, 14*(2), 315–337. https://doi.org/10.1108/JSMA-03-2020-0064.

Porter, M.E. (1985). *Competitive Advantage: Creating and Sustaining Superior Performance.* New York: Free Press.

Sarkar, S., & Sarkar, A. (2021). Operations management in the era of Industry 4.0: a review and research agenda. *International Journal of Production Research, 59*(16), 4958–4980. https://doi.org/10.1080/00207543.2021.1894318

Slack, N., Brandon-Jones, A., Johnston, R., & Betts, A., (2019). *Operations and Process Management: Principles and Practice for Strategic Impact* (5th edn). Harlow: Pearson.

12 HRnetGroup overcoming challenges in the human resources industry

Nadeem Aftab

Senior Lecturer in Banking and Finance, University of Northampton, United Kingdom

In the dynamic and competitive human resources industry, HRnetGroup stands out as a leading provider of comprehensive and customised solutions for clients across various sectors and regions. Based in Singapore, the company offers a wide range of services, including recruitment, payroll management, and consulting, to meet the diverse and evolving needs of employers and job seekers. Despite facing numerous challenges such as increasing competition, changing labour markets, and technological disruption, HRnetGroup has demonstrated resilience and innovation through its effective strategies. This case study will explore some of the challenges and successes that HRnetGroup has experienced in its journey to becoming one of the most reputable and trusted human resource service providers in Asia.

Challenges

Increasing competition: The human resources industry is highly competitive, with many established players competing for market share. HRnetGroup has had to differentiate itself from competitors and offer unique value propositions to clients. Its competitive advantage lies in its specialisation and niche focus, which allows it to offer customised solutions to clients in specific industries and sectors. This strategy enables HRnetGroup to cater to the unique needs and preferences of its clients, as well as to leverage its expertise and experience in these niche areas (Tan & Lim, 2022).

Changing labour markets: Labour markets are constantly changing, with new trends and demands emerging. HRnetGroup has had to keep up with these changes and adapt its services to meet the evolving needs of clients and job seekers. For instance, HRnetGroup has leveraged technology to enhance its online recruitment platforms and digital solutions, as well as to provide data-driven insights and analytics to clients (HRnetGroup, 2022). This approach helps HRnetGroup to improve its efficiency and effectiveness, as well as to offer innovative and value-added services to its clients and job seekers.

Technological disruption: Technology has disrupted the human resources industry, with the rise of online recruitment platforms and other digital

DOI: 10.4324/9781032660547-84

solutions. HRnetGroup has had to embrace technology and incorporate it into its operations to stay competitive. However, technology also poses challenges such as cyber risks, data privacy issues, and regulatory compliance (Seet et al., 2019). Therefore, HRnetGroup has invested in enhancing its cybersecurity measures, safeguarding its data assets, and adhering to the relevant laws and regulations in the countries where it operates.

Successes

Specialisation and niche focus: HRnetGroup has specialised in certain industries and niche areas such as technology, healthcare, and finance. This has allowed the company to differentiate itself from competitors and offer specialised services that meet the unique needs of clients in these industries. For example, HRnetGroup has established a strong presence in the technology sector, which is one of the fastest-growing and most lucrative sectors in Asia (CGS-CIMB Research, 2022). By focusing on these niche areas, HRnetGroup has been able to leverage its expertise and experience, as well as capture the growth opportunities and market potential in these sectors.

Emphasis on service quality and customer satisfaction: HRnetGroup has emphasised on service quality and customer satisfaction to build long-term relationships with clients. The company has implemented rigorous quality control measures and customer feedback mechanisms to continuously improve its services. For example, HRnetGroup has adopted the net promoter score (NPS) system to measure customer loyalty and satisfaction and has achieved an average NPS of 70% across its business segments (HRnetGroup, 2022). This indicates that HRnetGroup has a high level of customer retention and referral, which reflects its reputation and trustworthiness in the human resources industry.

Strategic partnerships and acquisitions: HRnetGroup has formed strategic partnerships and made strategic acquisitions to expand its service offerings and gain access to new markets. This has helped the company to stay competitive and grow its business. For example, HRnetGroup has acquired a stake in Octomate, a fintech start-up that provides payroll automation solutions, which enhances its value proposition to clients in the finance sector (Maybank Research, 2022). By partnering with and acquiring innovative and complementary businesses, HRnetGroup has been able to diversify its revenue streams and increase its market share in the human resources industry.

HRnetGroup has shown remarkable adaptability and foresight in the face of various challenges in the human resources industry. By focusing on its core competencies and niche areas, the company has been able to offer specialised and tailored solutions to its clients in different industries and sectors. By prioritising service quality and customer satisfaction, the company has built long-lasting and loyal relationships with its clients and job seekers. By forming strategic partnerships and acquisitions, the company has expanded its service offerings and market reach, as well as enhanced its value proposition. These strategies have enabled HRnetGroup to stand out from the crowd, maintain its competitive edge, and prepare for future opportunities and challenges in a fast-paced and dynamic industry.

References

CGS-CIMB Research (2022). *HRnetGroup – labour shortage a boon* [Online]. Available at: https://sginvestors.io/analysts/research/2022/07/hrnetgroup-cgs-cimb-research-2022-07-06 (Accessed: 14 June 2023).

HRnetGroup (2022). *Annual report 2021* [Online]. Available at: www.hrnetgroup.com/annual-reports (Accessed: 14 June 2023).

Maybank Research (2022). *HRnetGroup – acquires stake in fintech start-up Octomate; adding an external wing* [Online]. Available at: https://sginvestors.io/analysts/research/2022/10/hrnetgroup-maybank-research-2022-10-10 (Accessed: 14 June 2023).

Seet, R., Jones, J., Spoehr, J., Hordacre, A.L., O'Neil, M., & Barnett, K. (2019). The impact of digitalisation on work: Australian perspectives. *Journal of Industrial Relations, 61*(4), 502–524. https://doi.org/10.1177/0022185619852278.

Tan, K.H., & Lim, S.K. (2022). *HRnetGroup: the best is yet to come, CGS-CIMB Research Report* [Online]. Available at: www.itradecimb.com.sg/ (Accessed: 14 June 2023).

13 Manulife Singapore challenges of being a financial services provider

Teoh Teik Toe

Academic Director and Associate Director for AI Lab and IMARC Center/Nanyang Technological University, Singapore

In the dynamic and competitive financial services industry, how does a company stand out from the crowd and thrive in the face of challenges? This is the story of Manulife Singapore, a leading provider of insurance, investment, and retirement solutions that has been serving customers for over 130 years. Despite facing various obstacles such as increasing competition, regulatory changes, and low-interest rates, Manulife Singapore has not only survived but also succeeded by adopting a range of strategies that have enabled it to create value for its customers, partners, and shareholders. In this paper, we will explore some of these strategies and how they have contributed to Manulife Singapore's success.

Challenges

Increasing competition: The financial services industry is highly competitive, with many established players competing for market share. Manulife Singapore has had to differentiate itself from its competitors and offer unique value propositions to its clients. Competitive advantage can be achieved by either offering lower costs or higher differentiation than rivals (Porter, 1980). Manulife Singapore has chosen to pursue the latter strategy by focusing on customer-centricity, innovation, and digitalisation. These factors have enabled the company to create a strong brand identity, deliver superior customer service, and offer innovative products and solutions that cater to the diverse needs of its customers.

Regulatory changes: The financial services industry is heavily regulated, with frequent changes in regulations and compliance requirements. Manulife Singapore has had to stay up-to-date with these changes and adapt its operations accordingly. Regulation can have both positive and negative effects on financial institutions, such as enhancing stability, efficiency, and consumer protection while also imposing costs, constraints, and risks (Llewellyn, 1999). Manulife Singapore has tried to balance these effects by complying with the regulatory standards while also seeking opportunities to leverage them for competitive advantage.

DOI: 10.4324/9781032660547-85

Low-interest rates: Low-interest rates can impact the profitability of insurance products, which are a significant part of Manulife Singapore's business. The company has had to find ways to mitigate the impact of low-interest rates on its business. According to Cummins and Weiss (2014), low-interest rates can affect insurers' profitability by reducing investment income, increasing liability values, and creating asset-liability mismatches. Manulife Singapore has responded to these challenges by diversifying its product portfolio, optimising its asset allocation, and enhancing its risk management.

Successes

Digital transformation: Manulife Singapore has embraced digital transformation to improve its customer experience and streamline its operations. The company has implemented digital solutions such as online portals and mobile apps to make it easier for clients to access its services and manage their accounts. Digital transformation can help insurers enhance customer engagement, operational efficiency, and innovation capabilities (Deloitte, 2019). Manulife Singapore has demonstrated its digital leadership by partnering with fintech companies, launching digital insurance products, and investing in digital platforms.

Product innovation: Manulife Singapore has been innovative in developing new products and solutions to meet the evolving needs of clients. The company has launched new products such as retirement income solutions and digital insurance products that leverage technology to provide unique value propositions. Product innovation can help firms create new markets, satisfy customer needs, and gain a competitive advantage (Tidd & Bessant, 2018). Manulife Singapore has shown its product innovation by addressing the retirement needs of an ageing population, offering flexible and customisable insurance solutions, and creating healthy ecosystems for customers.

Strategic partnerships: Manulife Singapore has formed strategic partnerships with other companies to expand its service offerings and gain access to new markets. The company has partnered with financial technology companies to provide innovative solutions and improve its competitiveness. According to Dyer et al. (2009), strategic partnerships can help firms access complementary resources, capabilities, and knowledge that can enhance their performance and create value for customers. Manulife Singapore has exemplified its strategic partnerships by collaborating with DBS Bank, Jewel Changi Airport, and Haodf.com.

Overall, Manulife Singapore has successfully navigated the challenges of being a financial services provider through digital transformation, product innovation, and strategic partnerships. These strategies have helped the company to differentiate itself from its competitors, improve its customer experience, and position itself for long-term growth in a rapidly changing industry.

References

Cummins J.D., & Weiss M.A. (2014). Systemic risk and regulation of the U.S. insurance industry. *Journal of Risk and Insurance, 81*(3), 489–528. https://doi.org/10.1111/jori.12032

Deloitte (2019). *Digital transformation in insurance: a roadmap for success* [Online]. Available at: www2.deloitte.com/content/dam/Deloitte/sg/Documents/financial-services/sea-fsi-digital-transformation-in-insurance.pdf (Accessed: 23 May 2023).

Dyer J.H., Singh H., & Kale P. (2009). Splitting the pie: pent distribution in alliances and networks. *Managerial and Decision Economics, 30*(2–3), 137–148. https://doi.org/10.1002/mde.1436

Llewellyn D.T. (1999). *The economic rationale for financial regulation* [Online]. Available at: www.fca.org.uk/publication/occasional-papers/fsa-op-rationale-for-regulation.pdf (Accessed: 23 May 2023).

Porter M.E. (1980). *Competitive Strategy: Techniques for Analyzing Industries and Competitors.* New York: Free Press.

Tidd J., & Bessant J. (2018). *Managing Innovation: Integrating Technological, Market and Organizational Change* (6th edn). Chichester: John Wiley & Sons.

14 Prabal Gurung challenges of being a fashion designer

Choy Murphy
Director, Alionova Education Pte Ltd, Singapore

From Singapore to New York, Prabal Gurung has carved a niche for himself as a luxury fashion designer with a soul. His designs are not only beautiful and elegant but also reflect his values of diversity, inclusion, and social justice. However, his journey to success was not smooth or easy. He had to overcome many challenges along the way, especially as an immigrant in a highly competitive and exclusive industry. He faced barriers to entry, a lack of resources, and prejudice because of his ethnic background. But he did not let these obstacles stop him from pursuing his passion and achieving his dream.

Gurung faced many challenges in his journey to becoming a successful fashion designer, but he never gave up on his love for fashion and his ambition to succeed. He began his career as an intern at Donna Karan, where he gained valuable experience and skills in the industry. He learned how to design, produce, and market clothes for a global audience. He then moved on to work for several other renowned designers, such as Cynthia Rowley and Bill Blass, where he honed his craft and style. He developed his aesthetic and signature, which combined elegance, sophistication, and femininity. After years of hard work and learning, he finally realised his dream of launching his own label in 2009, which showcased his unique vision and voice (Gurung, 2014). His debut collection was well-received by critics and buyers, who praised his use of colours, prints, and textures. He also attracted the attention of celebrities and influencers, who wore his designs on red carpets and events.

One of the challenges that Gurung encountered was how to create a distinctive and memorable brand identity that would stand out in a competitive and saturated marketplace. To overcome this challenge, Gurung drew inspiration from his Nepalese roots and blended them with contemporary Western influences. He created designs that reflected his cultural heritage and his modern sensibility. He also leveraged the power of social media to display his designs and connect with a broader audience. Kaur (2020) reported that Gurung utilised Instagram as a strategic tool to convey his brand values, such as diversity, inclusion, and social justice. He also interacted with his followers by posting behind-the-scenes stories, personal reflections, and motivational messages. He used hashtags, captions, and images to communicate his brand

DOI: 10.4324/9781032660547-86

story and vision. Gurung's communication strategy on Instagram boosted his brand image and reputation as a global fashion leader. He also gained loyal fans and customers who admired his designs and his values.

Another challenge that Gurung had to deal with was the financial aspect of starting a fashion brand. He needed a significant amount of capital to produce, market, and distribute his collections. He overcame this by finding investors who shared his vision and were willing to provide the necessary funding. He also collaborated with other brands, such as Target and Lane Bryant, to create affordable and inclusive lines that reached a wider and more diverse customer base and generated more revenue. Thornquist (2018) suggested that fashion designers need to balance their creative expression with their business acumen and that they can learn from the everyday practices of fashion consumers, such as looking, wearing, choosing, discarding, and producing fashion. Additionally, they should rethink fashion from its emotional condition and inconstant state of mind, rather than from its systemic structure and logic. By doing so, they can create more meaningful and authentic fashion experiences for themselves and their consumers.

In conclusion, Prabal Gurung's success as a fashion designer was not easy. He faced numerous challenges, including discrimination, lack of resources, and financial constraints. However, his passion for fashion, determination to succeed, and willingness to learn helped him overcome these obstacles and establish himself as a respected designer in the industry. His story is an example of how immigrants can contribute to the American culture and economy through their creativity and innovation. Lee and Workman (2015) examined the phenomenon of compulsive buying and branding in relation to fashion consumption. They found that compulsive buyers tend to have higher levels of brand consciousness, brand loyalty, and brand attachment than non-compulsive buyers. They also suggested that compulsive buyers may use brands as a way of coping with their emotional distress or enhancing their self-esteem. Some notable lessons that can be learned or applied from Prabal Gurung's story are:

- The importance of having a clear and compelling brand vision and values that resonate with the target audience and differentiate the brand from the competitors
- The use of social media as a powerful tool to communicate the brand story, engage with the customers, and build a loyal fan base
- The benefits of collaborating with other brands or partners that share the same vision and values, and can help the brand reach new markets and customers
- The need to balance creativity and innovation with financial and operational management, and to adapt to the changing needs and preferences of the customers
- The role of emotions and psychology in influencing consumer behaviour and decision-making, especially concerning fashion consumption

References

Gurung, P. (2014). *Prabal Gurung bio*. Article Bio [Online]. Available at: https://art iclebio.com/prabal-gurung (Accessed: 7 May 2023).

Kaur, J. (2020). Prabal Gurung: a case study of a global fashion brand's communication strategy on Instagram. *International Journal of Fashion Design, Technology and Education, 13*(2), 232–242. https://doi.org/10.1080/17543266.2019.1700777

Lee, J., & Workman, J.E. (2015). Compulsive buying and branding phenomena. *Journal of Open Innovation: Technology, Market, and Complexity, 1*(3), 1–12. https://doi.org/10.1186/s40852-015-0003-z

Thornquist, C. (2018). The fashion condition: rethinking fashion from its everyday practices. *Fashion Practice, 10*(3), 289–310. https://doi.org/10.1080/17569 370.2018.1507147

15 SGAG monetisation and revenue generation

Nadeem Aftab

Senior Lecturer in Banking and Finance, University of Northampton, United Kingdom

What do you get when you combine local humour, viral memes, and social media? The answer is SGAG, a digital media company that has been making Singaporeans laugh since 2012. SGAG produces and distributes various types of content, such as videos, podcasts, articles, and web series, that cater to the tastes and interests of millennials and Gen Z. However, behind the scenes, SGAG has also faced some serious challenges in turning its content into cash. How did SGAG manage to monetise its content and generate revenue in a competitive and dynamic digital media landscape? This case study will explore some of the strategies that SGAG has adopted to overcome its challenges and achieve success.

Challenges

Limited advertising revenue: As a digital media company, SGAG primarily relies on advertising revenue to generate income. However, the company faced challenges in attracting advertisers due to the perceived risk of associating with humour-based content. This is a common concern for comedy platforms, as advertisers often worry about brand safety, content quality, and audience relevance (Hepmil Media Group, 2020).

Limited monetisation opportunities: SGAG's content is primarily distributed through social media platforms, such as Facebook, Instagram, and YouTube, which limits the company's ability to monetise its content. The platforms often take a significant portion of the revenue generated from ads or sponsorships. For instance, Facebook takes 45% of the revenue from video ads shown on its platform (Constine, 2017). Moreover, social media platforms are constantly changing their algorithms and policies, which can affect the visibility and reach of SGAG's content. This makes it challenging for SGAG to predict and optimise its revenue streams.

Limited resources: SGAG began its journey as a small startup with scarce resources, which posed a challenge for the company to afford costly production equipment or recruit more personnel (Ki & Kim, 2021). The company had to depend on its creative and innovative abilities to produce captivating

DOI: 10.4324/9781032660547-87

and viral content with low costs. The company also had to overcome various obstacles and risks associated with running a startup in a competitive and uncertain market.

Successes

Diversified revenue streams: SGAG has diversified its revenue streams beyond just advertising to include e-commerce, events, and merchandise sales. This has helped the company to reduce its reliance on advertising revenue and expand its revenue streams. For example, SGAG launched its online store in 2018, selling products such as T-shirts, mugs, stickers, and masks featuring its popular memes and slogans. The company also organises live events such as comedy shows, workshops, and festivals to connect with its fans and generate ticket sales. E-commerce is an effective business strategy for rural and small-town businesses to overcome geographic disadvantages and increase sales (Liang & Choi, 2019).

Strong social media presence: SGAG has a strong presence on social media, with millions of followers on various platforms. This has helped the company to attract advertisers and sponsorships, as well as promote its e-commerce and merchandise sales. According to Hepmil Media Group (2020), SGAG reaches over 2 million Singaporeans weekly through its 8 platforms. The company also leverages its social media data and insights to create targeted and customised content for different audiences and platforms. Social media platform type can have a significant impact on consumer purchase intention in social commerce, as different platforms offer different levels of social presence, usefulness, enjoyment, and trust (Lee & Lee, 2018).

Unique content: SGAG has focused on creating unique and relatable content that resonates with its target audience. This has helped the company to build a loyal fanbase and attract advertisers and sponsors looking to target millennials and Gen Z. The company produces various types of content such as memes, videos, podcasts, articles, and web series that cover topics such as current affairs, lifestyle, culture, entertainment, and education. The company also uses humour as a tool to raise awareness and spark conversations about social issues such as mental health, cyberbullying, racism, and gender equality. Digital media platforms enable binge-watching and video-on-demand (VOD) usage by providing convenient access, personalised recommendations, and social interactions. TV content preferences and viewing motivations vary depending on the type of VOD service (subscription-based or transaction-based) and the genre of TV content (drama or comedy) (Kim & Kim, 2019).

Strategic partnerships: SGAG has formed strategic partnerships with other companies and organisations to create sponsored content or co-branded merchandise. This has helped the company to generate additional revenue while promoting its brand and products. For example, SGAG collaborated with Netflix to create a parody video series called Stranger Things SG that promoted the streaming service's original show Stranger Things (SGAG,

2019). The company also partnered with Singtel to create a rap video that educated the public about the non-emergency hotline 995 (SGAG, 2020a). The company also worked with government agencies such as the Ministry of Education (MOE) and the National Environment Agency (NEA) to create humorous yet informative content that encouraged civic-mindedness and social responsibility (SGAG, 2020b).

Overall, SGAG has successfully overcome its monetisation and revenue generation challenges by diversifying its revenue streams, building a strong social media presence, creating unique content, and forming strategic partnerships. These strategies have helped the company to generate revenue, attract advertisers and sponsors, and position itself for long-term growth in a competitive digital media landscape.

References

Constine, J. (2017). *Facebook will split revenue with creators for shows it funds but not News Feed videos*. TechCrunch [Online]. Available at: https://techcrunch.com/2017/06/08/facebook-video-revenue-share/ (Accessed: 30 May 2023).

Hepmil Media Group (2020). *How consumer behaviour patterns have changed post-pandemic – White paper* [Online]. Available at: www.sgag.sg/whitepaper (Accessed: 30 May 2023).

Ki, C.-W., & Kim, Y. (2021). SGAG: how a Singaporean digital media company monetized its content and generated revenue. *International Journal of Electronic Commerce Studies, 12*(1), 1–22. https://doi.org/10.7903/ijecs.2119

Kim, Y., & Kim, Y. (2019). Digital media platforms and the use of TV content: binge watching and video-on-demand in Germany. *Media Culture and Society, 41*(5), 745–761. https://doi.org/10.1177/0163443719831612

Lee, J., & Lee, H. (2018). The effect of social media platform type on consumer purchase intention in social commerce. *Telematics and Informatics, 35*(8), 2248–2260. https://doi.org/10.1016/j.tele.2018.07.015

Liang, L., & Choi, H.C. (2019). E-commerce as a business strategy: lessons learned from case studies of rural and small town businesses. *International Journal of Electronic Commerce Studies, 10*(1), 25–42. https://doi.org/10.7903/ijecs.1784

16 Pacific Century Regional Developments Limited

The dot-com crash

Nishad Nawaz

Associate Professor, Kingdom University, Kingdom of Bahrain

Pacific Century Regional Developments Limited (PCRD) is a holding company that faced significant challenges during the dot-com crash in the early 2000s. The dot-com crash was a period of rapid decline in the stock prices of internet-based companies, which resulted in many bankruptcies, layoffs, and losses for investors (Chen et al., 2009). To succeed, PCRD had to overcome several challenges and develop strategies to weather the storm and emerge as a successful company.

One of the ways PCRD succeeded was by diversifying its portfolio and reducing its exposure to the technology sector. Diversification is a strategy that involves expanding a company's operations into different industries or markets to reduce risk and increase growth potential (Ansoff, 1957). The company shifted its focus to more stable and established businesses, such as property development, infrastructure, and telecommunications. This helped PCRD reduce its risk profile and maintain a more stable revenue stream during the dot-com crash. For example, PCRD acquired a 75% stake in Singapore-based property developer SingHaiyi Group Ltd in 2003, which gave PCRD access to SingHaiyi's residential and commercial projects in Singapore, Malaysia, and China (PCRD, 2020). Diversification can also have positive effects on a company's stock price crash risk, as it can reduce the volatility of earnings and cash flows and increase the transparency of information (Wang et al., 2023).

Another way PCRD succeeded was by restructuring its business to improve efficiency and reduce costs. Restructuring is a strategy that involves changing the organisational structure, processes, or systems of a company to enhance its performance or competitiveness (Deloitte US, n.d.). The company streamlined its operations and consolidated its business units to eliminate redundancies and improve coordination. This helped PCRD reduce overhead costs and improve profitability during a challenging economic environment. For example, PCRD merged its internet service provider Pacific Internet Ltd with another internet service provider Asia Netcom Corp Ltd in 2007, which created synergies and economies of scale for both companies (PCRD, 2007). Restructuring can also help a company adapt to changing market conditions, customer preferences, or technological innovations (Deloitte US, n.d).

DOI: 10.4324/9781032660547-88

Furthermore, PCRD also took advantage of distressed assets and investment opportunities during the dot-com crash. Distressed assets are assets that have lost their value due to financial or operational difficulties or market downturns (Altman et al., 2010). Investment opportunities are situations where a company can invest in new projects or ventures that have positive net present values or expected returns (Ross et al., 2019). The company acquired distressed assets at discounted prices and invested in companies that showed potential for long-term growth. This helped PCRD position itself for future growth and take advantage of opportunities that emerged after the market downturn. For example, PCRD acquired a 22.4% stake in Hong Kong-based telecommunications company PCCW Ltd in 2005, which gave PCRD access to PCCW's broadband, mobile, media, and IT solutions businesses in Hong Kong and other regions (PCRD, 2005). Distressed asset investment can also generate high returns for investors who can identify undervalued assets and exploit market inefficiencies (Altman et al., 2010).

Moreover, PCRD also focused on building a strong balance sheet to weather the storm during the dot-com crash. A balance sheet is a financial statement that shows a company's assets, liabilities, and equity at a given point in time (Berk et al., 2017). A strong balance sheet has high liquidity, low debt, and high equity. The company reduced debt levels and improved liquidity to ensure it had the financial resources to weather the downturn. This helped PCRD maintain its financial stability and emerge as a strong company after the market recovered. For example, PCRD reduced its total debt from S$1.2 billion in 2002 to S$0.4 billion in 2006, while increasing its cash and cash equivalents from S$0.2 billion in 2002 to S$0.6 billion in 2006 (PCRD, 2006). A strong balance sheet can also enhance a company's creditworthiness, solvency, and resilience to external shocks (Ross et al., 2019).

Finally, PCRD also leveraged its extensive network and relationships to identify new opportunities and partnerships. A network is a set of connections or interactions among individuals or organisations that share common interests or goals (Granovetter, 1973). A relationship is a bond or association between individuals or organisations that involves mutual trust or cooperation (Morgan & Hunt, 1994). The company had strong relationships with business and government leaders in Asia and used these relationships to identify new investment opportunities and partnerships that could drive growth. This helped PCRD expand its market presence and influence in the Asia-Pacific region. For example, PCRD partnered with the Singapore government to develop the Singapore Sports Hub, a state-of-the-art sports, entertainment, and lifestyle complex that opened in 2014 (PCRD, 2014). A network and relationship can also provide a company with access to valuable information, resources, or capabilities that can enhance its competitive advantage or innovation potential (Granovetter, 1973; Morgan & Hunt, 1994).

In summary, PCRD succeeded in overcoming the challenges of the dot-com crash by diversifying its portfolio, restructuring its business, taking advantage of distressed assets and investment opportunities, building a strong balance sheet, and leveraging its extensive network and relationships. These strategies helped PCRD weather the storm and emerge as a successful company that continues to drive growth and innovation in the Asia-Pacific region.

References

Altman, E.I., Resti, A., & Sironi, A. (2010). Distressed debt investing: principles and technique. *Journal of Applied Corporate Finance, 22*(2), 72–83. https://doi.org/10.1111/j.1745-6622.2010.00267.x.

Ansoff, H.I. (1957). Strategies for diversification. *Harvard Business Review, 35*(5), 113–124.

Berk, J., DeMarzo, P., Harford, J., Ford, G., & Mollica, V. (2017). *Fundamentals of Corporate Finance* (4th edn). Melbourne: Pearson Australia. https://doi.org/10.1016/B978-0-13-350767-6.00001-8

Chen, H., De, P., Hu, Y.J., & Hwang, B.H. (2009). Wisdom of crowds: the value of stock opinions transmitted through social media. *Review of Financial Studies, 27*(5), 1367–1403. doi: https://doi.org/10.1093/rfs/hht090.

Deloitte US (n.d.). *Corporate restructuring strategies in postpandemic recovery* [Online]. Available at: www2.deloitte.com/us/en/pages/consulting/articles/corporate-restructuring-post-pandemic.html (Accessed: 30 October 2021).

Granovetter, M.S. (1973). The strength of weak ties. *American Journal of Sociology, 78*(6), 1360–1380.

Morgan, R.M., & Hunt, S.D. (1994). The commitment-trust theory of relationship marketing. *Journal of Marketing, 58*(3), 20–38.

PCRD (2005). *Annual report 2005* [Online]. Available at: www.pcrd.com.sg/wp-content/uploads/2019/12/PCRD-Annual-Report-2005.pdf (Accessed: 30 May 2023).

PCRD (2006). *Annual report 2006* [Online]. Available at: www.pcrd.com.sg/wp-content/uploads/2019/12/PCRD-Annual-Report-2006.pdf (Accessed: 30 May 2023).

PCRD (2007). *Annual report 2007* [Online]. Available at: www.pcrd.com.sg/wp-content/uploads/2019/12/PCRD-Annual-Report-2007.pdf (Accessed: 30 May 2023).

PCRD (2014). *Annual report 2014* [Online]. Available at: www.pcrd.com.sg/wp-content/uploads/2019/12/PCRD-Annual-Report-2014.pdf (Accessed: 30 May 2023).

PCRD (2020). *Annual report 2020* [Online]. Available at: www.pcrd.com.sg/wp-content/uploads/2021/04/PCRD_Annual_Report_2020.pdf (Accessed: 30 May 2023).

Ross, S.A., Westerfield, R.W., & Jaffe, J.F. (2019) *Corporate Finance*. 12th ed. New York: McGraw-Hill Education

Wang Q., Shen, J., & Ngai E.W.T. (2023). Does corporate diversification strategy affect stock price crash risk?. *International Journal of Production Economics, 258*(108794). https://doi.org/10.1016/j.ijpe.2023.108794

17 Scoot faced challenges in building brand awareness and loyalty

Matthew Sullivan

Distinguished Global Educator and Former Head of School at NPS International School, Singapore

In the competitive and dynamic airline industry, building a strong brand image and attracting loyal customers is crucial for success. However, this is not an easy task, especially for low-cost airlines that have to balance between offering affordable prices and delivering quality services. Scoot, a Singapore-based low-cost carrier, faced several challenges in establishing its brand identity and reputation in the market. Despite these difficulties, the company has managed to overcome them and achieve remarkable results through various innovative and effective strategies. This case study will examine some of the challenges that Scoot faced and the strategies that it adopted to overcome them and enhance its brand awareness and loyalty.

Competition: One of the major challenges that Scoot faced was the intense competition in the airline industry, where many well-known and established airlines were vying for the same customers. To stand out from the crowd, Scoot had to offer something different and valuable to its target market. Scoot did this by adopting a low-cost business model that enabled it to offer affordable airfares while also providing a unique and enjoyable in-flight experience. Scoot's in-flight experience included a fun and quirky branding that reflected its personality, comfortable seating that offered more legroom and recline options, and a wide range of entertainment options such as movies, music, games, and Wi-Fi. Scoot also offered a flexible booking system that allowed customers to customise their travel preferences and add-ons. These features gave Scoot a competitive edge and a unique value proposition to its customers (Scoot, n.d.). Scoot's strategy can be seen as an example of differentiation, which is one of the generic strategies proposed by Michael Porter Differentiation involves creating a product or service that is perceived as unique and superior by the customers and appealing to a specific market segment that values these attributes (Porter, 1980).

Limited budget: Another challenge that Scoot faced was the limited budget for marketing and advertising, which constrained its ability to reach and attract potential customers. As a low-cost airline, Scoot had to be more resourceful and innovative in its marketing strategies, and rely on social media as a powerful tool to communicate and interact with its customers. Scoot used various social

DOI: 10.4324/9781032660547-89

media platforms, such as Facebook, Instagram, and Twitter, to showcase its brand personality, share its latest promotions and offers, and solicit feedback and suggestions from its customers. Scoot also launched creative and memorable marketing campaigns, which often used catchy slogans, such as "Scoot to where the action is" or "Scoot off to your next adventure," and eye-catching visuals, such as colourful graphics or humorous videos. Furthermore, Scoot employed unconventional marketing tactics, such as collaborating with popular influencers who endorsed its brand or shared their travel experiences with Scoot, and hosting social media contests that encouraged customers to participate and win prizes. These methods helped Scoot to build brand awareness and engagement among its target audience, as well as to generate word-of-mouth and viral effects (Scoot, 2022). These methods can be classified as guerrilla marketing, which is a form of marketing that uses low-cost, unconventional, and creative ways of reaching customers and creating a buzz around a brand or product (Levinson & Rubin, 1998).

A final challenge that Scoot faced was the negative perception of low-cost airlines as low-quality or unreliable. Some customers may have doubts about the safety, comfort, or convenience of flying with a low-cost carrier. To overcome this challenge, Scoot has had to provide high-quality services that exceed customer expectations and enhance customer satisfaction. Scoot has done this by offering affordable airfares that provide value for money, unique and enjoyable in-flight experiences that cater to different customer needs and preferences, and hassle-free booking processes that allow customers to customise their travel plans and options. Scoot has also focused on improving the customer experience by implementing various initiatives, such as offering free Wi-Fi on board to keep customers connected and entertained, and providing a dedicated customer service hotline to address customer queries and complaints. These actions are consistent with the service quality model (SERVQUAL), which proposes that customers evaluate service quality based on five dimensions: reliability (the ability to perform the service dependably and accurately), responsiveness (the willingness to help customers and provide prompt service), assurance (the knowledge and courtesy of employees and their ability to convey trust and confidence), empathy (the caring and individualised attention given to customers), and tangibles (the appearance of physical facilities, equipment, personnel, and communication materials) (Parasuraman et al., 1988).

In conclusion, Scoot has demonstrated how a low-cost airline can overcome various challenges and succeed in building a strong brand image and loyalty in the market. Scoot has done this by adopting a differentiation strategy that offers unique value propositions to its customers, such as affordable prices, enjoyable in-flight experience, a flexible booking system, and high-quality services. Scoot has also leveraged social media and guerrilla marketing to create brand awareness and engagement among its target audience, as well as to generate word-of-mouth and viral effects. Furthermore, Scoot has developed a distinctive brand identity and personality through its Scootitude – a daring attitude to be positive, uncompromising on safety and efficiency, spreading fun and humanity wherever they fly (Scoot, n.d.). This has helped the company to create an emotional bond with customers and foster brand loyalty (Aaker & Joachimsthaler, 2000). Scoot's success story shows how a low-cost airline can achieve competitive advantage and customer satisfaction by delivering value, quality, and fun to its customers.

References

Aaker D.A., & Joachimsthaler E. (2000). *Brand Leadership*. New York: Free Press.

Levinson J.C., & Rubin P. (1998). *Guerrilla Marketing: Secrets for Making Big Profits from Your Small Business*. Boston: Houghton Mifflin.

Parasuraman A., Zeithaml V.A., & Berry L.L. (1988). SERVQUAL: a multiple-item scale for measuring consumer perceptions of service quality. *Journal of Retailing* 64(1), 12–40. https://doi.org/10.1016/S0022-4359(88)80019-3

Porter M.E. (1980). *Competitive Strategy: Techniques for Analyzing Industries and competitors*. New York: Free Press.

Scoot (2022). *Media centre & press release | Scoot* [online]. Available at: www.flyscoot.com/en/the-scoot-family/media-centre (Accessed 2 June 2023).

Scoot (n.d.). *Scootitude | About Scoot* [online]. Available at: www.flyscoot.com/en/discover/about-scoot/scootitude (Accessed 2 June 2023).

Part VI

Industry-specific challenges and opportunities

1 SMU challenges of being an education provider

Jonny Munby

Principal Lecturer (International), Teesside University, United Kingdom

Singapore Management University (SMU) is a public university in Singapore that was founded in 2000 with the vision of becoming a premier university for management education and research in Asia. As a young and ambitious university, SMU encountered several challenges in its early years, such as establishing its identity, attracting talent, and building its reputation.

One of the biggest challenges was establishing its brand and reputation as a credible institution of higher learning (Pang & Lim, 2018). SMU was competing with well-established universities in Singapore such as the National University of Singapore and Nanyang Technological University, which had been around for much longer. To overcome this challenge, SMU focused on providing a unique educational experience that differentiated it from its competitors (Tan & Tan, 2004). SMU's curriculum emphasises a strong foundation in business, as well as the development of critical thinking, communication, and leadership skills. SMU also established partnerships with renowned universities worldwide to offer exchange programmes and internships for students, giving them exposure to different cultures and business environments (Tan & Tan, 2005).

Another challenge SMU faced was attracting top talent to its faculty and student body, as it had to compete with other established universities in the region and globally. To address this, SMU implemented a rigorous hiring process for faculty members and offered competitive salaries and benefits packages that matched or exceeded international standards. The university also established scholarship programmes to attract top students from around the world, especially those who demonstrated academic excellence, leadership potential, and social responsibility. SMU's efforts paid off, as the university is now widely recognised as a top business school in Asia, ranking among the best in various indicators such as teaching quality, research output, and employability (QS World University Rankings, 2023).

SMU faced another challenge in enhancing its research capabilities and reputation, as it had to balance its focus on teaching excellence and applied research. To overcome this, SMU adopted a stringent selection process for faculty members and provided attractive salaries and benefits packages (Careers@ SMU, 2023) that encouraged them to pursue high-quality research and

DOI: 10.4324/9781032660547-91

publications. The university also offered scholarship programmes to draw top students from around the world (College of Graduate Research Studies, n.d.) who were interested in pursuing doctoral studies and research careers. SMU's efforts were rewarded, as the university is now widely regarded as a top business school in Asia (Tan & Tan, 2004) and has received international recognition and awards for its research achievements. SMU has also achieved success in creating interdisciplinary research clusters that concentrate on emerging areas such as technology-enhanced immersive learning, data sciences, earth hazards, and national security. These clusters aim to enhance SMU's research impact and collaboration with other institutions and industry partners, as well as to address real-world problems and challenges.

In conclusion, SMU overcame its challenges by offering a unique education experience, recruiting high-quality faculty and students, and enhancing its infrastructure and facilities. As a result, SMU has earned a high reputation as an institution of higher learning and a key player in Singapore's knowledge economy. SMU has adopted a distinctive interactive pedagogy that sharpens the student's critical thinking and communication skills. SMU has also forged partnerships with prestigious universities worldwide to provide exchange programmes and internships for students, giving them opportunities to learn from different cultures and business environments. SMU has also improved its infrastructure and facilities, such as its city campus which consists of six buildings, and its Growing Infrastructure programme which develops leadership skills within the infrastructure sector across the region.

References

Careers@SMU (2023). *Working in Singapore Management University* [Online]. Available at: https://careers.smu.edu.sg/ (Accessed: 21 May 2023).

College of Graduate Research Studies (n.d.). *Academic research PhD programmes* [Online]. Available at: https://graduatestudies.smu.edu.sg/phd (Accessed: 18 May 2023).

Pang, L., & Lim, S.L. (2018). Brand Singapore: capturing the spirit of a nation. *Asian Journal of Business Research, 8*(2), 1–18. https://doi.org/10.14707/ajbr.180049

QS World University Rankings. (2023). *Top universities in the world* 2023 [Online]. Available at: www.topuniversities.com/university-rankings-articles/world-university-rankings/top-universities-world-2023#:~:text=QS%20World%20University%20Rankings%202023%3A%20Top%20global%20universities,%20United%20States%20%2018%20more%20rows%20 (Accessed: 18 May 2023).

Tan, C.T., & Tan, T.M. (2004). The Singapore Management University: a new model for a new Asia. *International Higher Education, 36*, 20–21. https://doi.org/10.6017/ihe.2004.36.7399

Tan, T.M., & Tan, C.T. (2005). The Singapore Management University: a successful start-up experience in higher education. *Higher Education Policy, 18*(1), 69–88.

2 YCH Group challenges and opportunities of being a logistics provider

Samson Tan

Director of Regional Strategy and Operations (Singapore), Civica Asia Pacific, Australia

YCH Group is a Singapore-based logistics and supply chain management company that offers a range of services, including warehousing, transportation, and freight management. Since its inception in 1955, the company has expanded to over 100 cities across Asia Pacific.

In a fiercely competitive and technologically evolving logistics industry, traditional supply chain logistics has been exposed for its deficiencies during the COVID-19 pandemic. These shortcomings include limited visibility, inadequate demand management, vulnerability to disruptions, and insufficient automation (HCLTech, 2022). To stand out in this landscape, YCH Group must embrace innovation, leverage technology, and offer customised solutions. Overcoming challenges such as soaring inconsistent tracking (Eurosender, 2021), transportation costs, inaccurate predictions, and a shortage of drivers (Endava, 2022) will be crucial. By adopting digital technology solutions, YCH Group can optimise its supply chain and logistics management, enabling it to effectively compete in the industry.

To stay ahead of the curve, it is imperative for YCH Group to leverage automation, robotics, and artificial intelligence to enhance operations. Technologies like these can reduce errors, boost efficiency, and speed up logistics delivery (*MIT Technology Review*, 2021; DHL, 2022; RTInsights, 2021). It is equally important for YCH Group to be agile and adapt to changes in cost and demand. For this purpose, networked technology and machine learning are needed to predict demand and plan routes (KNAPP, n.d.).

YCH Group has made significant investments in technology to enhance its operations and maintain its competitive edge in the logistics industry. The company has deployed automation and robotics in its warehouses to increase efficiency and accuracy, as well as to reduce labour costs and human errors. Additionally, it uses advanced technology systems and proprietary solutions, such as its award-winning Supply Chain City® and Y3PL platforms, to serve its customers across the electronics, chemical, pharmaceutical, and FMCG supply chain. These systems enable YCH Group to optimise its processes, improve its visibility, and offer value-added services to its customers.

DOI: 10.4324/9781032660547-92

YCH Group also delivers customised logistics solutions to meet the specific needs and preferences of its clients. This enables the company to distinguish itself from competitors and establish long-term relationships with clients based on trust and satisfaction. A case study by DHL (2019) shows that YCH Group offers customised solutions for Dell Technologies, one of its major clients, such as postponement services, reverse logistics, and inventory management. These solutions help Dell Technologies to reduce its inventory holding costs, improve its customer service, and enhance its environmental sustainability.

YCH Group also capitalises on its network of facilities across the Asia Pacific to provide end-to-end solutions to clients and secure a larger market share in the region. The company operates four facilities in Singapore, which function as its regional headquarters and innovation hub. It also has a presence in Australia, China, Hong Kong, Macau, India, Indonesia, Korea, Malaysia, Philippines, Thailand, and Vietnam. These facilities allow YCH Group to offer seamless and integrated logistics services to its clients across different markets and sectors.

In conclusion, YCH Group has demonstrated its commitment and leadership in sustainability by implementing various initiatives to minimise its environmental footprint. These initiatives include reducing its energy consumption, carbon emissions, and waste generation, as well as promoting green practices among its employees, partners, and customers. By doing so, the company has not only differentiated itself from competitors but also attracted clients who value and prioritise sustainability. YCH Group's sustainability efforts have also earned recognition and awards from various organisations and stakeholders.

References

DHL (2019). *YCH Group: customized solutions for Dell Technologies* [Online]. Available at: www.dhl.com/content/dam/dhl/global/core/documents/pdf/glo-core-ych-group-case-study.pdf (Accessed: 11 May 2023).

DHL (2022). *AI in logistics & supply chains* [Online]. Available at: www.dhl.com/global-en/delivered/digitalization/ai-in-logistics.html (Accessed: 12 May 2023).

Endava (2022). *Current challenges in the transportation & logistics industry* [Online]. Available at: www.endava.com/en/blog/Business/2022/Current-Challenges-in-the-Transportation-Logistics-Industry (Accessed: 15 May 2023).

Eurosender (2021). *Key logistics issues and challenges for 2023* [Online]. Available at: www.eurosender.com/blog/en/logistics-challenges/ (Accessed: 11 May 2023).

HCLTech (2022). *The central challenges for logistics in 2023 – and how to solve them with the right tools* [Online]. Available at: www.hcltech.com/blogs/central-challenges-logistics-2023-and-how-solve-them-right-tools (Accessed: 15 May 2023).

KNAPP (n.d.). *Robotics and artificial intelligence in logistics* [Online]. Available at: www.knapp.com/en/solutions/technologies/robotics-and-artificial-intelligence-in-logistics/ (Accessed: 21 May 2023).

MIT Technology Review (2021). *A new generation of AI-powered robots is taking over warehouses* [Online]. Available at: www.technologyreview.com/2021/08/06/1030 802/ai-robots-take-over-warehouses/ (Accessed: 21 May 2023).

RTInsights (2021). *Artificial intelligence is changing logistics automation* [Online]. Available at: www.rtinsights.com/artificial-intelligence-is-changing-logistics-aut omation/ (Accessed: 3 May 2023).

3 PSA Corporation managed the growth of Singapore's port to become a global hub

Easwaramoorthy Rangaswamy
Principal and Provost, Amity Global Institute, Singapore

PSA Corporation is one of the world's leading port operators, managing the ports of Singapore, Dalian, and Halifax. The corporation's growth can be attributed to various factors, including its ability to adapt to changing market conditions, implement innovative technologies and services, and attract global talent. However, there were also significant challenges along the way.

One of the key challenges that PSA Corporation faced was the need to keep up with the rapid growth of the shipping industry. In the 1990s, global trade grew at an unprecedented pace, and this put immense pressure on ports around the world to increase their capacity and efficiency. PSA Corporation responded to this challenge by investing in new technologies and expanding its operations. For example, it implemented automated container handling systems, enabling efficient cargo handling with fewer workers. This significant investment in new technologies and infrastructure greatly enhanced productivity and competitiveness. A key innovation was the utilisation of automated guided vehicles (AGVs) to seamlessly transport containers between quay cranes and yard cranes (AStar, 2022). Another strategy that PSA Corporation adopted was to expand its operations both locally and internationally across Asia, Europe, America, and Africa. By expanding its network, PSA Corporation was able to diversify its revenue sources, tap into new markets, and leverage synergies and economies of scale (PSA Singapore, 2023a).

PSA Corporation operates in a highly competitive port industry, where it faces rivalry from other ports in the region that offer similar or lower costs, higher efficiency, or better connectivity. For instance, China has been developing its ports along its coastline, such as Shanghai, Shenzhen, and Ningbo-Zhoushan, which have become some of the busiest and largest ports in the world (UNCTAD, 2019). Malaysia has also been expanding its ports, such as Port Klang and Tanjung Pelepas, which are strategically located near Singapore and offer lower tariffs and incentives to shipping lines (PKA, 2019; PTP, 2019).

To cope with this challenge, PSA Corporation had to continue investing in new technologies and services to differentiate itself from its competitors and

DOI: 10.4324/9781032660547-93

add value to its customers. One of the ways that PSA Corporation did this was by developing a range of value-added services that catered to the diverse and changing needs of cargo owners. These services included cold storage facilities for perishable goods, logistics solutions for e-commerce and distribution, and digital platforms for cargo visibility and management (PSA International, 2021). By offering these services, PSA Corporation was able to provide more convenience, efficiency, and security to its customers and enhance its competitive edge in the port industry.

Despite these challenges, PSA Corporation has been highly successful in managing the growth of Singapore's port. Today, the port is one of the busiest in the world, handling millions of containers every year. Its success has been driven by a culture of innovation, a focus on customer service, and a commitment to sustainability. For example, PSA Corporation has implemented green technologies such as electric cranes and AGVs (PSA Singapore, 2023b), and it has also launched initiatives to reduce carbon emissions and improve the efficiency of its operations (EMA, 2022).

In conclusion, PSA Corporation faced significant challenges in managing the growth of Singapore's port, but it was able to overcome them through innovation, investment, and a focus on customer service and sustainability. Its success has made it a model for other port operators around the world, and it continues to play a crucial role in driving Singapore's economy.

References

AStar (2022). *Developing solutions with PSA to manage AGV fleets at Tuas Port* [Online]. Available at: www.a-star.edu.sg/News/astarNews/news/press-releases/developing-solutions-with-psa-to-manage-agv-fleets-at-tuas-port (Accessed: 8 March 2023).

EMA (2022). *Singapore's first energy storage system at PSA's Pasir Panjang Terminal* [Online]. Available at: www.ema.gov.sg/media_release.aspx?news_sid=20220713RokuoGsvMaqz (Accessed: 28 March 2023).

PKA (2019). *Port Klang Authority annual report 2019* [Online]. Available at: www.pka.gov.my/wp-content/uploads/2020/08/PKA-Annual-Report-2019.pdf (Accessed: 8 March 2023).

PSA International (2021). *News release* [Online]. Available at: www.globalpsa.com/wp-content/uploads/nr210303.pdf (Accessed: 28 April 2023).

PSA Singapore (2023a). *Our story* [Online]. Available at: www.singaporepsa.com/about-us/our-story/ (Accessed: 28 April 2023).

PSA Singapore (2023b). *Sustainability* [Online]. Available at: www.singaporepsa.com/our-commitment/Sustainability/ (Accessed: 28 April 2023).

PTP (2019). *Pelabuhan Tanjung Pelepas annual report 2019* [Online]. Available at: www.ptp.com.my/wp-content/uploads/2020/06/PTP-Annual-Report-2019.pdf (Accessed: 30 April 2023).

UNCTAD (2019). *Review of maritime transport 2019* [Online]. Available at: https://unctad.org/system/files/official-document/rmt2019_en.pdf (Accessed: 30 April 2023).

4 Jurong Shipyard overcame the challenges of the oil and gas industry

Matthew Sullivan

Distinguished Global Educator and Former Head of School at NPS International School, Singapore

Jurong Shipyard is a leading provider of rig-building, ship-repair, and conversion services, and is a subsidiary of Sembcorp Marine, one of the world's largest offshore and marine engineering companies. The company faced several challenges in the oil and gas industry, which it successfully overcame through its strong focus on innovation, quality, and safety.

The decline in oil prices has led to a slowdown in the oil and gas industry, which has affected the business of Jurong Shipyard, a leading shipbuilding and repair company in Singapore. In response to this challenge, Jurong Shipyard has shifted its focus towards refurbishing and upgrading existing rigs and diversifying into other areas of the marine and offshore industry such as floating production storage and offloading (FPSO) vessels. This strategy has enabled Jurong Shipyard to secure new contracts and maintain its competitiveness in the global market.

Furthermore, the company faced the challenge of keeping pace with the rapid technological advancements in the offshore and marine industry. In response, Jurong Shipyard made substantial investments in research and development while initiating collaborations with partners and customers to foster innovation. As part of its initiatives, the company designed and constructed a series of 2600 TEU container vessels known for their exceptional speed, high container intake, and extensive reefer capacity (Jurong Shipyard, 2003). Additionally, Jurong Shipyard undertook the consolidation of its five Singapore yards into a mega-shipyard located in Tuas, aimed at bolstering operational efficiency and strengthening capabilities to serve the global oil and gas and marine sectors (Sembcorp Marine, 2014). A notable achievement resulting from these efforts was the successful development of the world's first new-build dual-fuel drillship, capable of utilising both LNG and diesel as fuel. This ground-breaking drillship, named Deepwater Atlas, was delivered to Transocean in 2022, marking a significant milestone for Jurong Shipyard (Sembcorp Marine, 2022). With its advanced drilling capabilities and exceptional environmental performance, the Deepwater Atlas became the world's first eighth-generation drillship, positioning Jurong Shipyard as a frontrunner in the offshore and marine industry (Offshore Energy, 2022).

DOI: 10.4324/9781032660547-94

Lastly, the shipyard encountered the vital challenge of upholding exemplary standards of safety and quality throughout its operations. To overcome this challenge, Jurong Shipyard implemented rigorous safety and quality management systems while making substantial investments in training and development programmes for its workforce. These systems were established following internationally recognised standards such as ISO 9001, ISO 14001, and OHSAS 18001, ensuring compliance with customer requirements, environmental regulations, and occupational health and safety practices (Jurong Shipyard, 2003). The training and development programmes were designed to enhance the skills and competencies of employees, fostering a culture of safety awareness and individual responsibility (Sembcorp Marine, 2003). As a testament to its commitment, Jurong Shipyard earned numerous accolades and awards for its exemplary safety and quality performance. Notably, the company was honoured with the prestigious Sword of Honour award from the British Safety Council, recognising its achievement in attaining the highest standards of health and safety management (MOM, 2009). Through these endeavours, Jurong Shipyard established itself as a prominent industry leader in safety and quality within the offshore and marine sectors (Sembcorp Marine, 2003).

In conclusion, Jurong Shipyard demonstrated its resilience and competitiveness in the oil and gas industry by adopting various strategies to cope with the challenges it faced. By investing in research and development, diversifying its products and services, and implementing high standards of quality and safety, Jurong Shipyard enhanced its capabilities and reputation as a leading provider of rig-building, ship-repair, and conversion services. Jurong Shipyard also contributed to the growth and success of its parent company, Sembcorp Marine, in the global offshore and marine engineering market.

References

Jurong Shipyard (2003). *SembCorp Marine's subsidiary, Jurong Shipyard secures two shipbuilding contracts worth S$110 million* [Online]. Available at: www.sembmar ine.com/stock-exchange-announcements/sembcorp-marines-subsidiary-jurong-shipyard-secures-two-shipbuilding-contracts-worth-s110-million (Accessed: 18 May 2023).

Jurong Shipyard (2016). *Jurong Shipyard secures contract for modification and upgrading of FPSO Fluminense* [Online]. Available at: www.sembmarine.com/wp-content/uploads/2016/08/JSPL-secures-contract-for-modification-and-upgrad ing-of-FPSO-Fluminense.pdf (Accessed: 18 May 2023).

MOM (2009). *Annex fact sheet about the Workplace Safety and Health (WSH) Awards* [Online]. Available at: www.mom.gov.sg/-/media/mom/documents/speeches/ 2009/annex-and-factsheet–wsh-awards-2009-%28240709%29.pdf (Accessed: 7 May 2023).

Offshore Energy (2022). *Deepwater titan ultra-deepwater dual-activity drillship* [Online]. Available at: www.deepwater.com/documents/RigSpecs/Deepwater%20 Titan.pdf (Accessed: 8 May 2023).

Sembcorp Marine (2003). *Shipyards operation review* [Online]. Available at: www.sem
    bmarine.com/scm2016/wp-content/uploads/2016/03/Operation-Review.pdf
    (Accessed: 16 May 2023).
Sembcorp Marine (2014). *Sembcorp to integrate Singapore yards at new 'mega' ship-
    yard* [Online]. Available at: www.offshore-mag.com/rigs-vessels/article/16757
    318/sembcorp-to-integrate-singapore-yards-at-new-mega-shipyard (Accessed: 13
    May 2023).
Sembcorp Marine (2022). *Sembcorp Marine delivers giant world's first 8th generation
    drillship to transocean* [Online]. Available at: www.offshore-energy.biz/sembc
    orp-marine-delivers-giant-worlds-first-8th-generation-drillship-to-transocean/
    (Accessed: 11 May 2023).

5 Razer's transition from gaming peripherals to mobile gaming

Choy Murphy

Director, Alionova Education Pte Ltd, Singapore

Razer is a Singapore-based company that started as a provider of gaming peripherals and has since transitioned to mobile gaming. Here are some of the challenges the company faced in its transition and how it overcame them to succeed.

Competitive landscape: Razer faced significant competition in the mobile gaming market from both established players like Tencent and Activision Blizzard, as well as newer entrants such as Niantic and Supercell (Clement, 2023). To tackle this challenge, Razer pursued several strategies: (1) *Innovation*: Razer prioritised innovation to create advanced mobile gaming devices with exceptional performance, display quality, and audio experience. (2) *Partnership*: Razer established partnerships with various game developers, publishers, and platforms to offer exclusive content, unique features, and benefits to their mobile gaming customers. (3) *Community*: Leveraging its strong brand recognition and dedicated fan base within the gaming industry, Razer fostered a vibrant community of mobile gamers. By pursuing these strategies, Razer aimed to differentiate itself in the competitive mobile gaming market, offering high-quality and immersive experiences (Stein, 2023) that resonated with its target audience.

Technical challenges: Razer faced a series of technical hurdles in the realm of mobile gaming, necessitating specialised knowledge and expertise in software development, user interface design, and mobile device optimisation. To tackle these challenges head-on, Razer made substantial investments in research and development (Statista, 2021) while collaborating with partners to develop ground-breaking solutions for mobile gaming. Here are some of the strategies employed by Razer to overcome these challenges: (1) *Research and development*: Razer allocated a significant portion of its resources to research and development, with an expenditure of US$61.1 million in 2021, equivalent to 9.0% of its total revenue (Razer, 2021). The company boasted a dedicated team of over 500 engineers and designers focused on creating new technologies, products, and features specifically tailored for mobile gaming. (2) *Collaboration*: Razer forged partnerships with various technology companies and platforms, leveraging their expertise and resources to enhance mobile

DOI: 10.4324/9781032660547-95

gaming. (3) *Innovation*: Razer introduced a range of innovative products and solutions that showcased their technical prowess and set them apart in the mobile gaming industry. Through these concerted efforts, Razer successfully navigated the intricate technical landscape of mobile gaming, cementing its position as a leading provider of cutting-edge gaming experiences on mobile devices.

Brand recognition: Razer faced a significant challenge in establishing brand recognition within the mobile gaming market, despite its existing reputation in the gaming peripherals industry. To overcome this obstacle, Razer capitalised on its well-established brand identity associated with quality and innovation (Baker, 2021). The company made substantial investments in targeted marketing and advertising campaigns aimed at the mobile gaming audience. Here are some strategies employed by Razer to address this challenge: (1) *Product launch*: Razer strategically launched its mobile gaming products and solutions through high-profile events and announcements, generating substantial media coverage and piquing consumer interest. (2) *Brand awareness*: Razer actively increased its brand awareness and visibility in the mobile gaming market by sponsoring and participating in events and platforms specifically tailored to the mobile gaming audience. (3) *Brand loyalty*: Razer nurtured brand loyalty and customer retention among mobile gaming enthusiasts by implementing a rewards and incentives programme. Through these concerted efforts, Razer effectively tackled the challenge of building brand recognition within the mobile gaming market. By leveraging its established reputation, implementing strategic product launches, increasing brand awareness through sponsorships, and fostering customer loyalty via rewards programmes, Razer successfully established itself as a prominent player in the mobile gaming industry.

Despite these challenges, Razer has succeeded in its transition from gaming peripherals to mobile gaming by taking a user-centric approach and investing in research and development. The company has built a reputation for delivering high-quality, immersive mobile gaming experiences that resonate with its target audience. By focusing on differentiation, investing in technical expertise, and leveraging its existing brand recognition, Razer has established itself as a leader in the mobile gaming market.

References

Baker, T. (2021). *Razer Edge will take on the mobile gaming market on January 26* [Online]. Available at: www.gamesradar.com/razer-edge-will-take-on-the-mobile-gaming-market-on-january-26/ (Accessed: 22 May 2023).

Clement, J. (2023). *Mobile gaming market share worldwide 2014–2022* [Online]. Available at: www.statista.com/statistics/1105448/mobile-gaming-market-share-worldwide (Accessed: 21 May 2023).

Razer (2021). *Razer delivers record high revenue and net profit of US\$31 million for the first half of 2021* [Online]. Available at: https://press.razer.com/company-news/razer-delivers-record-high-revenue-and-net-profit-of-us31-million-for-the-first-half-of-2021/ (Accessed: 24 May 2023).

Statista (2021). *Research and development expenses of Razer 2016–2021* [Online]. Available at: www.statista.com/statistics/1177699/razer-research-development-expenses/ (Accessed: 22 May 2023).

Stein, S. (2023). *Razer's Android gaming handheld is part mobile, part console. Here's what to know* [Online]. Available at: www.cnet.com/tech/gaming/razer-edge-game-handheld-arrives-what-to-know/ (Accessed: 19 May 2023).

6 City Energy adapted to the liberalisation of Singapore's gas market

Samson Tan

Director of Regional Strategy and Operations (Singapore), Civica Asia Pacific, Australia

For decades, City Energy enjoyed a dominant position as the sole provider of piped town gas in Singapore, supplying gas to households and businesses for cooking and heating purposes. However, in 2018, the company faced a major disruption when the Singapore government fully liberalised the gas market, opening it up to competition from other gas retailers. This was part of the government's efforts to foster a more competitive and efficient energy sector, as well as to diversify the sources of natural gas for the country (EMA, 2021). How did City Energy cope with this radical change in the market environment? How did it adapt its strategies and operations to survive and thrive in the face of new rivals? This case examines the challenges and opportunities that City Energy encountered in the aftermath of the gas market liberalisation, and how it leveraged its strengths and resources to maintain its market share and leadership.

Facing the challenge of market liberalization, City Energy adopted a differentiation strategy to stand out from its competitors. The company focused on providing superior customer service and leveraging its expertise of knowledge to offer innovative green energy solutions that catered to the needs of a growing Singapore and a changing planet (City Energy, 2021a). Moreover, the company made significant investments in developing new technologies that gave it a strategic competitive advantage in terms of improving its operations and efficiency. For instance, the company implemented smart gas meters and adopted digital platforms to enhance customer engagement and experience (City Energy, 2021b). Porter (1985) defined strategic competitive advantage as the ability of a firm to create more value for its customers than the cost of producing that value, and to do so better than its rivals. By investing in new technologies, City Energy aimed to increase its value proposition and reduce its cost structure, thus gaining an edge over its competitors.

In addition to differentiating itself from its competitors, City Energy also collaborated with other industry players to promote the benefits of piped-town gas to consumers and businesses. The company highlighted the safety, reliability, and environmental sustainability of its product, which could reduce carbon emissions and improve air quality. The company also expanded its

DOI: 10.4324/9781032660547-96

product offerings, such as introducing compressed natural gas for vehicles and liquefied petroleum gas for industrial applications. The company saw a potential opportunity in the passenger vehicle segment, as well as the possibility of extending its product to the commercial vehicle segment (City Energy, 2021c). These product diversification strategies are consistent with Ansoff's (1957) growth matrix, which suggests that firms can grow by offering new products to existing markets or existing products to new markets. By doing so, the company aimed to increase its market penetration and market development.

As the gas market became more competitive, City Energy faced the challenge of maintaining its market share and profitability. To address this, the company adopted a proactive pricing strategy that offered competitive prices and promotions to attract new customers and retain existing ones. The company also focused on increasing its operational efficiency and reducing costs to remain competitive (Tan et al., 2019). However, the company also faced the risk of external shocks from natural gas supply disruptions, which could affect its production costs and reliability (Wong & Chang, 2016). To mitigate this risk, the company diversified its sources of natural gas by importing liquefied natural gas (LNG) from various countries, thus enhancing its energy security and resilience (EMA, 2021). By doing so, the company reduced its dependence on a single source of natural gas and increased its flexibility to respond to market fluctuations.

In conclusion, this case has shown that City Energy successfully navigated the challenges of market liberalisation by adopting a proactive and dynamic approach to its business. The company did not rest on its laurels as the sole provider of piped town gas, but instead sought to differentiate itself from its competitors by enhancing its customer service, investing in technological innovation, and diversifying its product offerings. These strategies enabled the company to create value for its customers, improve its operational efficiency, and reduce its costs. As a result, the company has been able to retain its loyal customer base, attract new customers, and sustain its market share and leadership in Singapore's gas market. Moving forward, City Energy should continue to leverage its strengths and resources to explore new opportunities and overcome future challenges in the evolving energy sector.

References

Ansoff, H.I. (1957). Strategies for diversification. *Harvard Business Review*, 35(5), 113–124.

City Energy (2021a). *Sustainable energy solutions* | City Energy [Online]. Available at: www.cityenergy.com.sg/ (Accessed: 26 May 2023).

City Energy (2021b). *Consumer* – City Energy [Online]. Available at: www.cityenergy.com.sg/consumer (Accessed: 26 May 2023).

City Energy (2021c). *General enquiry* – City Energy [Online]. Available at: www.cityenergy.com.sg/contact-us/general-enquiry (Accessed: 24 May 2023).

EMA (2021). *Overview of gas market* – Energy Market Authority [Online]. Available at: www.ema.gov.sg/Gas_Market_Overview.aspx (Accessed: 26 May 2023).

Porter, M.E. (1985). *Competitive Advantage: Creating and Sustaining Superior Performance.* New York: Free Press.

Tan, K., Tan, C., & Tan, Y. (2019). *What went wrong with Singapore's energy market liberalisation?* [Online]. Available at: www.ntu.edu.sg/erian/news-events/news/det ail/what-went-wrong-with-singapore-s-energy-market-liberalisation (Accessed: 26 May 2023).

Wong, S.L., & Chang, Y. (2016). The effects of natural gas supply disruptions on macroeconomic performance in ASEAN-4 countries. *Energy Policy, 88,* 305–314. https://doi.org/10.1016/j.enpol.2015.10.035

7 NTUC FairPrice's challenges to becoming Singapore's largest supermarket chain

Melvin Goh Kim Ho
Associate Dean, Amity Global Institute, Singapore

For many Singaporeans, NTUC FairPrice is a household name that they trust and rely on for their daily grocery needs. As the largest supermarket chain in Singapore, NTUC FairPrice operates over 200 outlets across the country, serving millions of customers every year. However, behind this success story lies a series of challenges that the company had to overcome in its journey to becoming Singapore's leading supermarket chain. These challenges include intense competition from other supermarket chains and convenience stores, changing consumer preferences towards healthier and more sustainable products, and increasing operational costs due to rising wages and rents. How did NTUC FairPrice cope with these challenges? How did it adapt its strategies and operations to survive and thrive in the dynamic and competitive retail market? This case examines the challenges and opportunities that NTUC FairPrice encountered in the past decade, and how it leveraged its strengths and resources to maintain its market share and leadership.

One of the primary challenges faced by NTUC FairPrice was intense competition from other supermarket chains and convenience stores in Singapore. Lee and Tan (2006) conducted an empirical study on the competitive strategies of supermarket chains in Singapore and found that price competition was the most important factor influencing consumer choice. To overcome this, NTUC FairPrice adopted a competitive pricing strategy, offering lower prices on essential items to attract customers. However, this strategy also harmed the small stores and traditional markets that could not compete with the low prices of NTUC FairPrice. Lim and Lim (2017) analysed the impact of supermarket entry on the exit of small stores in Singapore and found that supermarket entry increased the exit hazard of small stores by 17%. Therefore, NTUC FairPrice's competitive pricing strategy not only affected its direct competitors but also the small and local retailers in Singapore. Additionally, NTUC FairPrice focused on building customer loyalty by providing a wide range of products and services, including online shopping and home delivery, to meet the needs of its diverse customer base. Chua and Wong (2019) analysed the impact of online grocery shopping on the demand for private car usage in Singapore and found that online grocery shopping could reduce car trips and emissions by replacing

DOI: 10.4324/9781032660547-97

physical trips to supermarkets. Therefore, by providing online shopping and home delivery services, NTUC FairPrice aimed to enhance customer convenience and satisfaction, as well as contribute to environmental sustainability.

Another challenge faced by NTUC FairPrice was changing consumer preferences, particularly towards healthier and more sustainable products. To address this, the company invested in expanding its range of fresh produce, organic products, and healthier food options. It also implemented sustainable practices, such as reducing plastic waste and promoting eco-friendly products, to align with consumer preferences and promote sustainability. Rangaswamy et al. (2021) found that Singaporean consumers are becoming more health-conscious and environmentally aware, and are willing to pay more for products that are healthy and sustainable. The authors also suggest that digital technology can help retailers communicate the benefits of such products to consumers and increase their awareness and trust. Therefore, by expanding its range of healthy and sustainable products and using digital technology to market them, NTUC FairPrice aimed to cater to the changing consumer preferences and increase its market share.

Finally, increasing operational costs posed a significant challenge for NTUC FairPrice. The company responded by streamlining its supply chain and adopting cost-saving measures, such as implementing energy-efficient technologies and reducing packaging waste. It also invested in training its employees to improve productivity and reduce operating costs. Rangaswamy et al. (2019) analysed the environmental footprint of plastic grocery bags and their alternatives in Singapore and found that plastic bags have lower environmental impacts than paper or cotton bags due to their lower weight and volume, which reduce transportation emissions and waste disposal costs. The authors also suggest that reducing plastic bag consumption or increasing recycling rates can further reduce the environmental impacts of supermarkets. Therefore, by implementing energy-efficient technologies and reducing packaging waste, NTUC FairPrice aimed to reduce its environmental footprint and operational costs.

In conclusion, this paper has shown that NTUC FairPrice has demonstrated remarkable resilience and adaptability in the face of various challenges in the retail market. The company has been able to adapt to changing market conditions and consumer preferences by offering affordable and quality products that cater to the needs and wants of its customers. The company has also adopted a customer-centric approach and leveraged technology and innovation to enhance its customer service, operational efficiency, and environmental sustainability. These strategies have enabled the company to create value for its customers, reduce its costs, and differentiate itself from its competitors. As a result, the company has been able to retain its loyal customer base, attract new customers, and sustain its market share and leadership in Singapore's supermarket industry. The paper also suggests that NTUC FairPrice can continue to leverage its strengths and resources to explore new opportunities and overcome future challenges in the evolving retail sector.

References

Chua, S. L., & Wong, C. Y. (2019). The impact of online grocery shopping on the demand for private car usage: the case of Singapore. *Transportation Research Part A: Policy and Practice, 130*, 1–13. https://doi.org/10.1016/j.tra.2019.09.016

Lee, J., & Tan, C.W. (2006). Competitive strategies of supermarket chains in Singapore: an empirical study. *International Journal of Retail & Distribution Management, 34*(8), 617–633. https://doi.org/10.1108/09590550610675926

Lim, K., & Lim, J. (2017). The impact of supermarket entry on the exit of small stores in Singapore: a duration analysis approach. *International Journal of Industrial Organization, 50*, 285–310. https://doi.org/10.1016/j.ijindorg.2016.08.004

Rangaswamy, A., Nawaz, N., Shivaiyer, N., Veksha, A., Bobacka, J., & Lisak G. (2022). The impact of digital technology on changing consumer behaviours with special reference to the home furnishing sector in Singapore. *Humanities and Social Sciences Communications, 9*(83). https://doi.org/10.1038/s41599-022-01102-x

Rangaswamy A., Veksha A., Bobacka J., & Lisak G. (2019). Location preemption by oligopolists: evidence from the Singapore supermarket industry. *International Journal of Retail & Distribution Management, 46*(1), 4 20. https://doi.org/10.1108/IJRDM-01-2017-0004

Rangaswamy A., Veksha A., Bobacka J., & Lisak G. (2021). Life cycle assessment of plastic grocery bags and their alternatives in cities with confined waste management structure: a Singapore case study. *Journal of Cleaner Production, 278*(123956). https://doi.org/10.1016/j.jclepro.2020.123956

8 Changi Airport Group's challenges in managing the growth of Singapore's award-winning airport

Matthew Sullivan

Distinguished Global Educator and Former Head of School at NPS International School, Singapore

For millions of travellers around the world, Changi Airport is more than just a place to catch a flight. It is a destination in itself, offering a range of services and amenities that make the journey as enjoyable as the destination. Changi Airport is managed by Changi Airport Group (CAG), a company that strives to deliver world-class service and excellence to its customers. However, behind this success story lies a series of challenges that CAG had to overcome in its journey to becoming one of the world's best airports. These challenges include limited physical space for expansion, increasing passenger traffic, and intense competition from other airports in the region such as Hong Kong International Airport, Incheon International Airport in South Korea, and Narita International Airport in Japan. This case examines the challenges and opportunities that CAG encountered in the past decade, and how it leveraged its strengths and resources to maintain its market share and leadership.

One of the primary challenges faced by CAG was limited physical space for expansion. To overcome this challenge, the company adopted an innovative approach, implementing smart solutions and leveraging technology to optimise the use of existing infrastructure. For example, CAG introduced automated check-in kiosks, self-bag drop systems, and biometric-based boarding procedures to enhance efficiency and streamline the passenger experience. Chutiphongdech et al. (2020) examined the business operations of Changi Airport and found that it has developed as a destination, offering various value propositions to its customers, such as convenience, comfort, entertainment, and shopping. The authors also suggest that CAG's digital transformation strategy is driven by its customer-centric culture and its vision to be a world-class airport. Ducksu (2021) analysed the design of Changi Airport T3 and found that it integrates natural performance and system into the building through horizontal and vertical integration of landscape and technology. The author also suggests that this design approach creates a sustainable airport environment that enhances the passenger experience and reduces the environmental footprint. Lee, Miller, et al. (2019) explored how CAG uses artificial intelligence (AI) to improve its operations and services, such as baggage handling, security screening, and customer feedback. The authors

DOI: 10.4324/9781032660547-98

also suggest that CAG's AI projects are guided by its SMART Airport Vision, which aims to leverage sensors, data fusion, data analytics, and AI to create a seamless and hassle-free journey for passengers.

Another challenge faced by CAG was managing the increasing passenger traffic at Changi Airport. To address this, the company invested in expanding the airport's capacity through the construction of new terminals and runways. It also implemented crowd management strategies, such as staggered flight schedules and automated immigration clearance, to ensure a smooth and efficient flow of passengers. Ducksu (2021) analysed the design of Changi Airport T3 and found that it integrates natural performance and system into the building through horizontal and vertical integration of landscape and technology. The author also suggests that this design approach creates a sustainable airport environment that enhances the passenger experience and reduces the environmental footprint. Tan (2021) uncovered fascinating facts behind the decision to build Changi Airport and how it eventually took shape. The author also suggests that Changi Airport's success is attributed to its continuous innovation and improvement of its products and services. Lee, et al. (2019) modelled and simulated the runway capacity of Changi Airport and found that it can handle up to 80 aircraft movements per hour under optimal conditions. The authors also suggest that runway capacity can be further improved by reducing aircraft separation distances and optimising runway configurations.

Finally, intense competition from other airports in the region posed a significant challenge for CAG. The company responded by focusing on enhancing the passenger experience through personalised services and amenities, new state-of-the-art terminals like Jewel, Changi reward Schemes, luxury lounges, entertainment options, and gourmet dining. It also invested in marketing and branding efforts to promote Changi Airport as a world-class destination and attract more passengers to choose Singapore as its transit hub. Tan (2021) uncovered fascinating facts behind the decision to build Changi Airport and how it eventually took shape. The author also suggests that Changi Airport's success is attributed to its continuous innovation and improvement of its products and services. Chutiphongdech et al. (2020) examined the business operations of Changi Airport and found that it has developed as a destination, offering various value propositions to its customers, such as convenience, comfort, entertainment, and shopping. The authors also suggest that CAG's digital transformation strategy is driven by its customer-centric culture and its vision to be a world-class airport. Wilson et al. (2019) assessed the impact of airport service quality on passenger satisfaction and found that airport facilities and servicescape make a unique contribution to passenger satisfaction. The authors also suggest that airport service quality can be enhanced by improving the reliability, responsiveness, and assurance of airport staff.

In conclusion, this case has shown that CAG has demonstrated remarkable resilience and adaptability in the face of various challenges in the aviation market. The company has been able to overcome the limited physical space for expansion by implementing smart solutions and leveraging technology to optimise the use of existing infrastructure. The company has also been able to manage the increasing passenger traffic by investing in expanding the airport's capacity and implementing crowd management strategies.

By focusing on enhancing the passenger experience with customized services and amenities, cutting-edge terminals, reward schemes, luxury lounges, entertainment options, and gourmet dining, the company has also managed to overcome the stiff competition from other airports. Moreover, the company has invested in marketing and branding strategies to showcase Changi Airport as a world-class destination and persuade more passengers to choose Singapore as their transit hub.

These strategies have enabled the company to create value for its customers, reduce its costs, and differentiate itself from its competitors. As a result, the company has been able to retain its loyal customer base, attract new customers, and sustain its market share and leadership in the global aviation industry. The case also suggests that CAG can continue to leverage its strengths and resources to explore new opportunities and overcome future challenges in the evolving aviation sector.

References

Chutiphongdech, T., & Vongsaroj, R. (2020). The success behind the world's best airport: the rise of the Changi. *SSRN Electronic Journal*. https://doi.org/10.48048/asi.2022.250905

Ducksu (2021). Articulate design thinking for sustainable airport environment: a case study of Singapore Changi Airport T3. *Transportation Research Procedia, 56,* 136–142. https://doi.org/10.1016/j.trpro.2021.09.016

Lee, M.D., Criss, A.H., Devezer, B., Donkin, C., Etz, A., Leite, F.P., & Vandekerckhove, J. (2019). Robust modeling in cognitive science. *Computational Brain and Behavior, 2*(3–4), 141–153. https://doi.org/10.1007/s42113-019-00029-y

Lee, S.M., Miller, S.J., Lee, J.H., & Park, J.H. (2019). Modelling and simulation studies of the runway capacity of Changi Airport. *The Aeronautical Journal, 123*(1266), 1327–1345. https://doi.org/10.1017/aer.2019.69

Tan, R.B.H. (2021). How Changi Airport came to be. *BiblioAsia, 17*(3). https://biblioasia.nlb.gov.sg/vol-17/issue-3/oct-dec-2021/changi-airport/

Wilson, J., Lee, M., Kim, H., & Choi, S. (2019). The impact of airport service quality on passenger satisfaction: the mediating role of perceived value. *Journal of Air Transport Management, 75,* 12–19. https://doi.org/10.1016/j.jairtraman.2019.01.008

9 Singapore Tourism Board promoting Singapore as a global tourist destination

Guo Yongsheng

Senior Lecturer in Accounting and Finance, TUIBS, Teesside University, United Kingdom

Singapore is a small island nation that has a lot to offer to visitors who are looking for a diverse and memorable travel experience. From its rich cultural heritage and stunning natural beauty to its modern skyscrapers and world-class attractions, Singapore has something for everyone. However, developing and marketing Singapore as a global tourist destination was not an easy task. The Singapore Tourism Board (STB) had to overcome various obstacles and challenges to showcase Singapore's unique appeal and value proposition to the world. Consequently, the key challenges faced by the STB and how it managed to overcome them with innovative strategies and solutions will be examined.

Singapore has to contend with strong competition from neighbouring countries such as Thailand, Malaysia, and Indonesia, which also boast a rich cultural and natural heritage that appeal to tourists. To stand out from the crowd, the STB emphasised Singapore's unique selling points, such as its multicultural heritage, modern cityscape, and safety. Singapore's competitive advantage stems from its ability to offer a diverse range of attractions and experiences that cater to different market segments and preferences. Moreover, the STB also adopted a market segmentation strategy to target different types of travellers, such as business travellers, families, millennials, and luxury seekers, and tailored its marketing campaigns accordingly (Chang et al., 2019).

Singapore faces the challenge of limited space for new tourism developments, as it is a small island nation with a high population density. The STB tackled this challenge by promoting sustainable tourism practices and highlighting its green spaces and parks, which offer visitors a respite from the urban environment. As part of the Singapore Green Plan 2030, the STB aims to transform Sentosa into a carbon-neutral destination by 2030 and to position Singapore as an exemplary sustainable tourism destination that balances economic, social, and environmental goals (Chan, 2021). Furthermore, the STB also leverages technology to create immersive and innovative experiences that transcend physical limitations, such as virtual reality tours and augmented reality trails, that showcase Singapore's culture, history, and nature (STB & Visa, 2020).

DOI: 10.4324/9781032660547-99

Singapore has a high cost of living, which can be a deterrent for budget-conscious travellers who are looking for more affordable destinations. To overcome this challenge, the STB worked to diversify Singapore's tourism offerings, promoting more affordable options such as food tours, heritage trails, and local experiences that showcase Singapore's culture and diversity. The STB also partnered with various stakeholders to offer attractive promotions and discounts to entice visitors to spend more on tourism-related activities, such as tourist attractions, hotels, and dining (STB & Visa, 2020). In addition, the STB tapped into the growing demand for wellness tourism, which is a high-value segment that can generate more revenue for the tourism sector. The STB launched the SingapoReimagine MICE Virtual Show in 2021, which showcased Singapore's wellness offerings such as yoga sessions, spa treatments, and healthy cuisine, as well as its capabilities in hosting safe and innovative events (STB, 2021).

Changing traveller preferences: As travellers become more discerning, the STB needed to constantly adapt and innovate to meet changing needs. The STB responded by promoting experiential tourism, showcasing unique events and festivals, and leveraging digital technologies to enhance the visitor experience. For example, the STB launched the SingapoRediscovers campaign in 2020, which encouraged locals to rediscover Singapore's hidden gems and support local businesses amid the COVID-19 pandemic. The STB also collaborated with various platforms such as Airbnb Experiences, Klook, and Tripadvisor to offer curated and personalised experiences for travellers. Additionally, the STB adopted a data-driven approach to understand traveller behaviour and preferences, and to provide customised recommendations and solutions (STB & Visa, 2020).

In conclusion, The STB has faced many challenges in developing and marketing Singapore as a global tourist destination, such as competing with other destinations, overcoming negative perceptions, and adapting to changing consumer preferences. However, the STB has also demonstrated its resilience and creativity in overcoming these challenges, by leveraging Singapore's strengths, creating distinctive experiences, and engaging with various stakeholders. As a result, the STB has successfully established Singapore as one of the leading tourist destinations in Asia, attracting millions of visitors each year who are drawn to Singapore's vibrant culture, scenic landscapes, and advanced urban infrastructure. The STB's efforts have not only contributed to Singapore's economic growth and social development but also enhanced Singapore's image and reputation as a must-visit destination that offers a unique blend of culture, nature, and modernity.

References

Chan, C.S. (2021). *Shifts in technology, sustainability present opportunities for tourism sector in the long run: Chan Chun Sing* [Online]. Available at: www.channelnewsasia.com/singapore/shifts-in-technology-sustainability-present-opportunities-for-tourism-sector-in-the-long-run-chan-chun-sing-14299990 (Accessed: 12 May 2023).

Chang, H.H., Chen, S.W., Tseng, T.H., Hsu, C.H., & Lo, H.Y. (2019). Market segmentation and competitive analysis of inbound tourists: a case study of Singapore. *Journal of Destination Marketing & Management, 28*, 100–112. Doi: https://doi.org/10.1016/j.jdmm.2018.11.002.

STB (2021). *Singapore Tourism Board launches inaugural MICE virtual show* [Online]. Available at: www.stb.gov.sg/content/stb/en/media-centre/media-releases/Singapore-Tourism-Board-launches-inaugural-MICE-virtual-show.html (Accessed: 27 May 2023).

STB & Visa (2020). *Impact of COVID-19 on tourism in Singapore and the road to recovery and transformation* [Online]. Available at: www.stb.gov.sg/content/dam/stb/documents/mediareleases/Impact%20of%20Covid-19%20on%20tourism%20in%20Singapore%20and%20the%20road%20to%20recovery%20and%20transformation%20by%20STB%20and%20Visa.pdf (Accessed: 30 May 2023).

10 Best World International overcoming regulatory challenges in the direct selling industry

Dimitrios N. Koufopoulos
Director of the Online Global MBA Programs, Visiting Professor Queen Mary University, Honorary Research Fellow at Birkbeck University, United Kingdom

Best World International is a Singapore-based direct-selling company that specialises in the distribution of health and wellness products, such as skin care, nutritional supplements, and personal care products. The company has faced several regulatory challenges in the direct selling industry, which is subject to strict rules and regulations in various markets. However, the company has managed to succeed through a range of strategies, such as strong corporate governance, product innovation and differentiation, reputation management, and stakeholder engagement.

The company has encountered a number of challenges and dilemmas as they are briefly discussed.

Regulatory compliance: The direct selling industry is heavily regulated, with strict regulations governing sales practices and product claims. Best World International has had to ensure compliance with these regulations while still promoting its products and growing its business. For example, the company had to comply with the Multi-Level Marketing and Pyramid Selling (Prohibition) Act in Singapore, which prohibits unfair and deceptive practices in direct selling (Euromonitor International, 2020). The company also had to adapt its online strategy to different markets, such as using direct selling in China, reselling in Taiwan, and agency selling in Singapore, depending on local regulations and consumer preferences (Zhang et al., 2020).

Reputation management: The direct selling industry has faced criticism and scepticism from consumers, regulators, and the media. Best World International has had to manage its reputation and build trust with stakeholders to overcome this scepticism and gain acceptance. For instance, the company had to deal with allegations of falsifying sales records and inflating earnings in China, which led to a drop in its share price and a probe by the Singapore Exchange (Tan, 2019). The company also had to enhance customer satisfaction and loyalty by providing high-quality products and services, as well as reducing switching costs for customers who want to change their direct selling companies (Lee et al., 2001).

Global expansion: Best World International has expanded its business to multiple markets around the world, each with its own regulatory frameworks

DOI: 10.4324/9781032660547-100

and cultural nuances. The company has had to navigate these differences while still maintaining compliance and a consistent brand message. For example, the company had to segment its global market based on different customer characteristics and preferences, such as age, income, lifestyle, and motivation for direct selling. The company also had to tailor its marketing mix and product offerings to suit different market segments and create value for customers (Chang et al., 2019).

In response to those challenging issues and strategic challenges the company responded as follows.

Strong corporate governance: Best World International has implemented strong corporate governance practices to ensure compliance with regulations and build trust with stakeholders, such as customers, distributors, regulators, and investors. This includes establishing an independent board of directors that oversees the company's strategic direction and performance and implementing stringent internal controls that monitor the company's financial reporting and risk management. The company has also adopted the Code of Ethics and Conduct for Direct Selling Association of Singapore (DSAS) members, which sets high standards for ethical conduct and consumer protection, such as honesty, integrity, transparency, and fairness (Best World International, 2020).

Product innovation and differentiation: Best World International has focused on product innovation and differentiation to stand out in the competitive direct selling industry, which offers a variety of health and wellness products. The company has introduced new product lines that cater to different customer needs and preferences, and collaborated with research institutions to develop unique formulations and delivery systems that enhance product efficacy and quality. For example, the company launched its DR's Secret range of premium skincare products, which uses nanotechnology to deliver active ingredients into the skin, resulting in improved skin health and appearance (Best World International, 2020).

Reputation management and stakeholder engagement: Best World International has engaged with stakeholders through transparent communication and education initiatives to build trust and credibility. The company has also implemented rigorous quality control measures to ensure that its products meet the highest standards. For example, the company established a Consumer Advisory Panel, which consists of independent experts who provide advice on product safety and efficacy. The company also conducts regular training sessions for its distributors to educate them on product knowledge and ethical sales practices (Best World International, 2020).

Overall, Best World International has successfully overcome the regulatory challenges in the direct selling industry through strong corporate governance, product innovation and differentiation, reputation management, and stakeholder engagement. These strategies have helped the company to build a strong brand and expand its business globally while still maintaining compliance and a focus on quality and transparency.

References

Best World International (2020). *Annual report 2019* [Online]. Available at: www.bestworld.com.sg/wp-content/uploads/2020/04/BWI-Annual-Report-2019.pdf (Accessed: 5 June 2023).

Chang, Y.-C., Chou, P.-F., Tseng, C.-H., & Chang, C.-H. (2019). The impact of market segmentation on customer satisfaction for the direct selling industry in an emerging market. *Journal of Business Research, 101*, 819–831. https://doi.org/10.1016/j.jbusres.2019.07.036

Euromonitor International (2020). *Direct selling in Singapore* [Online]. Available at: www.euromonitor.com/direct-selling-in-singapore/report (Accessed: 5 June 2023). https://doi.org/10.1016/j.jbusres.2019.07.036

Lee, J., Lee, J., & Feick, L. (2001). The impact of switching costs on the customer satisfaction-loyalty link: mobile phone service in France. *Journal of Services Marketing, 15*(1), 35–48. https://doi.org/10.1108/08876040110381463

Tan, C.W. (2019). *Best World shares plunge after short seller report, The Business Times* [Online]. Available at: www.businesstimes.com.sg/companies-markets/best-world-shares-plunge-after-short-seller-report (Accessed: 5 June 2023).

Zhang, X., Zhang, Z., Wang, Y., Tan, K.H., Goh, M., Chua, G.A.K., Lim, J.S.C., Liang, L., Lim, E.P., & Zhuang, Y. (2020). Direct selling, reselling or agency selling? Manufacturer's online channel choice. *Journal of Interactive Marketing, 51*, 65–80. https://doi.org/10.1080/10864415.2020.1715530

11 TOYOGO overcoming increasing competitions, societal expectations shift, and rising cost

Cheryl Yu

Interim Director of International Partnerships, London College of Fashion, University of the Arts London, United Kingdom

TOYOGO is a leading plastic products manufacturer based in Singapore that has been in the business for over 30 years. The company produces a wide range of plastic products, such as containers, crates, baskets, and bins, for various industries and applications. However, the company has not had an easy journey to success. The company has faced several challenges over the years, such as increasing competition, societal expectations shift, and rising costs, which have threatened its survival and growth. However, the company has not given up. The company has managed to overcome these challenges and succeed through various strategies, such as product innovation, process optimisation, and diversification. This case will examine some of these challenges and strategies in detail, and how they have helped the company to achieve its goals and vision.

Challenges

Increasing competition: The plastic products industry is highly competitive, with many established players competing for market share and customer loyalty. TOYOGO has had to differentiate itself from competitors and offer unique value propositions to clients that create value and satisfaction. For example, the company has focused on providing customised solutions and high-quality products that meet the specific needs of different industries, such as food and beverage, healthcare, and education, by understanding their requirements and preferences (TOYOGO, 2020).

Societal expectations shift: With growing concern about sustainability and the environment, consumers and businesses are increasingly demanding eco-friendly products (García-García et al., 2021). TOYOGO has had to adapt its product offerings and manufacturing processes to meet these expectations. For example, the company has launched eco-friendly products made from recycled materials, such as its Eco-Box series, which reduces plastic waste and carbon footprint (TOYOGO, 2020). The company has also participated in industry initiatives to reduce single-use plastic packaging and items, such as the Plastic Action (PACT) programme by WWF-Singapore (WWF-Singapore, 2020).

DOI: 10.4324/9781032660547-101

Rising cost: The cost of raw materials, labour, and other inputs has been rising, which can impact the profitability of manufacturing companies like TOYOGO. The company has had to find ways to manage costs while maintaining quality and customer service. For example, the company has optimised its manufacturing processes to improve efficiency and reduce costs. The company has implemented lean manufacturing techniques, automated processes, and other efficiency measures to increase productivity and reduce waste (TOYOGO, 2020).

Successes

Product innovation: TOYOGO has been innovative in developing new products and solutions to meet the evolving needs of clients and offer unique value propositions. The company has launched eco-friendly products made from recycled materials, which reduce plastic waste and carbon footprint, as well as new designs and features that enhance functionality and convenience. For example, the company launched its Smart Box series, which uses smart technology to monitor temperature, humidity, and motion inside the box, allowing users to track and control the storage conditions of their items (Boucher et al., 2020).

Process optimisation: TOYOGO has optimised its manufacturing processes to improve efficiency and reduce costs while maintaining quality and customer service. The company has implemented lean manufacturing techniques, automated processes, and other efficiency measures to increase productivity and reduce waste, as well as to ensure the consistency and reliability of its products. For example, the company adopted a closed-loop water system that recycles water used in the production process, saving water and energy costs, as well as reducing environmental impact (Kitayama, 2022).

Diversification: TOYOGO has diversified its product offerings to reduce its reliance on any single product or market, and to capture new growth opportunities. The company has expanded into new markets and product categories, such as storage solutions and home organisation products, which cater to the growing demand for space optimisation and convenience. The company has also explored new applications for its products in various sectors, such as agriculture, construction, and logistics, which require durable and versatile plastic products (Palich et al., 2000).

In conclusion, TOYOGO has overcome various challenges in the plastic products industry by innovating its products, optimising its processes, and diversifying its products and markets. These strategies have helped the company to differentiate itself from competitors, improve efficiency and reduce costs, and position itself for long-term growth in a rapidly changing industry. The company has also reduced its environmental impact and promoted eco-friendly products, contributing to the sustainability and circular economy goals. The company's success story is an inspiration and a lesson for other manufacturing companies.

References

Boucher, J., Friot, D., Carmichael, A., Brooks, A.L., Ryan, P.G., Wilcox, C., & Jambeck, J. (2020). Plastic pollution solutions: emerging technologies to prevent and collect marine plastic pollution. *Environment International, 136*, 105494. https://doi.org/10.1016/j.envint.2020.105494

García-García, G., Martínez-Ruiz, P., Jiménez, A., Martínez-García, C., Martínez-García, R., García-Haro, S., García-Haro, J., García-Haro, F.J., García-Haro, E., & García-Haro, M.J. (2021). Plastics in the context of the circular economy and sustainable development goals: a review of current status and future perspectives. *Journal of Cleaner Production, 314*, 128237. https://doi.org/10.1016/j.jclepro.2021.128237

Kitayama, S. (2022). Process parameters optimization in plastic injection molding using metamodel-based optimization: a comprehensive review. *The International Journal of Advanced Manufacturing Technology, 121*, 7117–7145. https://doi.org/10.1007/s00170-022-09858-x

Palich, L.E., Cardinal, L.B., & Miller, C.C. (2000). Curvilinearity in the diversification-performance linkage: an examination of over three decades of research. *Strategic Management Journal, 21*(2), 155–174. https://doi.org/10.1002/(SICI)1097-0266(200002)21:2<155::AID-SMJ82>3.0.CO;2-2

TOYOGO (2020). *About us* [Online]. Available at: www.toyogogroup.com/about-us/ (Accessed: 29 June 2023).

WWF-Singapore (2020). *Over 12 million pieces of single-use plastic packaging and items saved with industry initiative: WWF-Singapore* [Online]. Available at: www.wwf.sg/over-12-million-pieces-of-single-use-plastic-packaging-and-items-saved-with-industry-initiative%e2%80%8b-wwf-singapore/ (Accessed: 29 June 2023).

12 Carousell expanding in new markets outside of Singapore

Saikat Gochhait

Assistant Professor, Symbiosis International University, India

Imagine a platform where any individual can buy and sell anything, from clothes and books to cars and properties, with just a few taps on his/her phone. That is Carousell, the leading online marketplace in Singapore that has grown rapidly since its launch in 2012. But Carousell's ambition is not limited to its home market. The company has ventured into several new markets across Asia and beyond, facing various challenges and opportunities along the way. How did Carousell overcome the cultural, legal, and competitive hurdles in each new market? What strategies did Carousell use to adapt its platform, form partnerships, and build communities? This case will explore some of the examples of Carousell's expansion journey and its key success factors.

Challenges

Cultural differences: Each market has its unique cultural differences, which can impact the way people use and interact with online marketplaces. Carousell has had to adapt its platform and services to meet the specific needs and preferences of users in each new market. For instance, Carousell has found that users in Indonesia prefer to chat before making a purchase, while users in Hong Kong prefer to meet up in person (Mik, 2019). Therefore, Carousell has enabled features such as instant messaging and location-based search to cater to these preferences.

Legal and regulatory challenges: Regulations around online marketplaces and e-commerce can vary greatly between countries, and Carousell has had to navigate these regulations to ensure compliance and avoid legal issues. For example, Carousell has had to deal with different tax regimes, consumer protection laws, data privacy laws, and intellectual property rights across its markets (Lung, 2020). Carousell has also had to comply with local content moderation policies and remove prohibited items such as drugs, weapons, and counterfeit goods from its platform (Carousell, 2021).

Competition: The online marketplace space is highly competitive, with many established players competing for market share. Carousell has had to differentiate itself from competitors and offer unique value propositions to

DOI: 10.4324/9781032660547-102

users in each new market. For example, Carousell has faced competition from Shopee, Tokopedia, Lazada, and Bukalapak in Southeast Asia, as well as eBay, Facebook Marketplace, and Gumtree in other regions (Yap, 2021). Carousell has tried to stand out from its competitors by focusing on user experience, community building, social responsibility, and niche segments such as property, automobile, and luxury goods (Chan, 2021).

Successes

Strategic partnerships: Carousell has formed strategic partnerships with local companies and organisations to help it expand into new markets. For example, the company partnered with the Indonesian conglomerate Salim Group to enter the Indonesian market in 2017. The partnership gave Carousell access to Salim Group's resources, network, and expertise in the local market (Chua et al., 2019). Carousell also acquired control of Laku6, a leading electronics e-commerce platform in Indonesia, in 2022 to bolster its expansion of electronics e-commerce in Greater Southeast Asia (Carousell, 2022).

Product localisation: Carousell has localised its platform and services to meet the needs of users in each new market. For example, the company added support for local languages, currencies, and payment methods to make it easier for users to buy and sell on the platform. Carousell also leveraged artificial intelligence (AI) to provide personalised recommendations, price suggestions, and image recognition features to enhance user experience. Additionally, Carousell adapted its platform design and layout to suit the preferences of users in different markets. For example, Carousell used a grid layout for its app in Singapore and a list layout for its app in Hong Kong (Burgos, 2021).

Community building: Carousell has focused on building a strong community of users in each new market to drive growth and engagement. The company has implemented various community-building initiatives, such as user meetups, social media campaigns, online forums, user feedback sessions, and charity drives (Lung, 2020). These initiatives have helped Carousell to establish a presence in each new market, foster trust and loyalty among users, create word-of-mouth referrals, and promote social causes.

Carousell has shown that expanding into new markets is not an easy feat, but a rewarding one. By forming strategic partnerships, localising its platform and services, and building a strong community of users, Carousell has been able to overcome the challenges and seize the opportunities in each new market. These strategies have not only helped Carousell to differentiate itself from competitors but also to meet the specific needs of users in each new market, creating value and trust for both buyers and sellers. Carousell's expansion journey is not over yet. The company is constantly innovating and adapting to the changing needs and preferences of its users, as well as the evolving trends and technologies in the online marketplace industry. Carousell's vision is to make secondhand the first choice for everyone, and it is well on its way to achieving that goal.

References

Burgos, J. (2021). *Online marketplace Carousell becomes Singapore's newest unicorn after raising $100 million.* Forbes [Online]. Available at: www.forbes.com/sites/jon athanburgos/2021/09/15/online-marketplace-carousell-becomes-singapores-new est-unicorn-after-raising-100-million/ (Accessed: 27 May 2023).

Carousell (2021). *Prohibited items policy* [Online]. Available at: https://support.carous ell.com/hc/en-us/articles/115011889707-Prohibited-Items-Policy (Accessed: 27 May 2023).

Carousell (2022). *Carousell Group acquires control of Laku6 to bolster expansion of electronics recommerce in Greater Southeast Asia* [Online]. Available at: https://press. carousell.com/2022/07/26/carousell-group-acquires-control-of-laku6-to-bols ter-expansion-of-electronics-recommerce-in-greater-southeast-asia/ (Accessed: 27 May 2023).

Chan, E. (2021). *Carousell needs to scale up quickly in property, auto verticals as it mulls exit strategy.* The Business Times [Online]. Available at: www.businesstimes.com. sg/startups-tech/startups/carousell-needs-scale-quickly-property-auto-verticals-it-mulls-exit-strategy (Accessed: 27 May 2023).

Chua, A., Lim, W., Tan, C., & Wong, M. (2019) Carousell: the future of online classifieds. *Asian Journal of Business Cases, 12*(1), 1–19. https://doi.org/10.1177/0218927518818258

Lung, T. (2020). *How Carousell, one of the largest secondhand marketplaces in South East Asia, is handling the pandemic.* Forbes [Online]. Available at: www.forbes.com/sites/tiffanylung/2020/07/28/asians-embrace-second-hand-sales-on-marketpl ace-carousell-during-coronavirus/ (Accessed: 27 May 2023).

Mik, E. (2019). Legal and regulatory challenges to facilitating e-commerce in the ASEAN. In: Hsieh, P.L. and Mercurio, B. (eds.) *ASEAN Law in the New Regional Economic Order: Global Trends and Shifting Paradigms.* Cambridge: Cambridge University Press, pp. 342–370. https://doi.org/10.1017/9781108563208.018

Yap, C.W. (2021). *Carousell bets on second-hand car marketplace to boost revenue.* Bloomberg [Online]. Available at: www.bloomberg.com/news/articles/2021-04-07/carousell-bets-on-second-hand-car-marketplace-to-boost-revenue (Accessed: 27 May 2023).

13 Singapore Press Holdings' response to declining print media revenue

Nishad Nawaz

Associate Professor, Kingdom University, Kingdom of Bahrain

Singapore Press Holdings (SPH) has faced significant challenges in response to declining print media revenue, which has been a trend across the media industry globally.

SPH faced the challenge of adapting to the changing media landscape and declining print revenue (Aruba, n.d.). To address this, they heavily invested in digital transformation, expanding their online presence and creating innovative digital products (Tan, 2021). Initiatives targeted younger audiences and aimed to boost digital revenue. The government provided funding and incentives to support SPH's digital media transformation, fostering innovation and outreach. However, the constraints of being a listed company made it difficult for SPH to sustain its media business while meeting shareholder expectations. As a result, SPH chose to delist its media business and become a company limited by guarantee (CLG), prioritising quality journalism as a public good, unaffected by commercial pressures (Khaw, 2021).

SPH encountered the need to expand its revenue streams amidst the decline of print media (*Singapore Business Review*, 2016). To address this, the company diversified into sectors such as property, healthcare, and education while also expanding its digital media offerings (Chew, 2016; Yahoo Finance, 2016). These strategic moves contributed to SPH's growth and resilience. Additionally, SPH opted to divest non-essential assets and concentrate on its core operations. However, the challenges of managing costs and new ventures during the pandemic arose. Consequently, SPH underwent a restructuring process, transforming its media business into a non-profit entity to serve the public interest without financial pressures.

SPH confronted the challenge of managing costs amidst declining revenue. To tackle this, the company implemented cost optimisation measures, including operational streamlining, workforce reduction, and contract renegotiation with suppliers and partners (Chew, 2016). These initiatives aimed to enhance efficiency, agility, and profitability in a competitive and uncertain environment. SPH embraced a comprehensive approach to cost optimisation, employing a framework that prioritised investments based on value and impact (Gartner, n.d.). Leveraging data analytics and technology, SPH identified and eliminated

DOI: 10.4324/9781032660547-103

waste, rationalised services, and optimised processes (KPMG Canada, 2021). However, striking a balance between cost optimisation, growth opportunities, and innovation posed challenges for SPH. Consequently, the company sought external funding and partnerships to support its media business and facilitate digital transformation (Chew, 2016).

SPH fostered innovation and experimentation to thrive in the evolving media landscape. They established an innovation lab, encouraging idea generation and product development. Collaborations with startups and organisations further fuelled innovation (*The Straits Times*, 2019). The lab involved SPH staff and students from Singapore Polytechnic, utilising design thinking to identify user needs and propose interior design solutions. Additionally, SPH hosted Tech Day to showcase innovations and gather insights from industry experts on digital transformation and disruption (*The Straits Times*, 2019). SPH invested in cutting-edge technologies like AI, blockchain, and cloud computing, elevating their products and services to create additional customer value.

Through these efforts, SPH has successfully adapted to the challenges of declining print media revenue and established a strong digital presence. The company has diversified its revenue streams and expanded its business into new areas, while also optimising costs and fostering a culture of innovation. As a result, SPH is well-positioned to navigate the rapidly changing media landscape and continue to grow its business in the years ahead.

References

Aruba (n.d.). *SPH embarks on digital transformation journey that delivers on seamless connectivity, security and differentiated user experiences* [Online]. Available at: www.arubanetworks.com/sea/resources/case-studies/sph/ (Accessed: 7 May 2023).

Chew, H.M. (2016). *My paper and the new paper to merge; SPH to cut staff by up to 10 per cent over 2 years through series of measures* [Online]. Available at: www.straitstimes.com/business/my-paper-and-the-new-paper-to-merge-sph-to-cut-staff-by-up-to-10-per-cent-over-2-years (Accessed: 7 May 2023).

Gartner (n.d.). *Cost optimization guide* [Online]. Available at: www.gartner.com/en/insights/cost-optimization (Accessed: 7 May 2023).

Khaw, B.W. (2021). *Transforming SPH Media for the digital era* [Online]. Available at: www.straitstimes.com/opinion/transforming-sph-media-for-the-digital-era (Accessed: 7 May 2023).

KPMG Canada (2021). Cost optimization strategies and actions [Online]. Available at: https://kpmg.com/ca/en/home/insights/2021/06/cost-optimization-strategies-and-actions.html (Accessed: 7 May 2023).

Singapore Business Review (2016). *Why SPH needs to diversify revenue streams* [Online]. Available at: https://sbr.com.sg/commercial-property/news/why-sph-needs-diversify-revenue-streams (Accessed: 7 May 2023).

Tan, J. (2021). *Hiving off SPH's media business will help accelerate its digital transformation efforts: Analysts* [Online]. Available at: www.straitstimes.com/singapore/hiving-off-sphs-media-business-will-help-accelerate-its-digital-transformation-efforts (Accessed: 7 May 2023).

The Straits Times (2019). *Inaugural SPH Tech Day hosts industry players and experts, showcases latest innovations* [Online]. Available at: www.straitstimes.com/tech/industry-players-and-experts-speak-at-inaugural-sph-tech-day (Accessed: 7 May 2023).

Yahoo Finance (2016). *Why SPH needs to diversify revenue streams* [Online]. Available at: https://sg.finance.yahoo.com/news/why-sph-needs-diversify-revenue-044300 930.html (Accessed: 7 May 2023).

14 SATS' expansion into airport management and catering services

Hala Mansour

Associate Professor, University of Northampton, United Kingdom

SATS is a company that specialises in providing food solutions and gateway services for various industries, such as aviation, hospitality, healthcare, and retail. The company has a history of innovation and excellence in delivering quality products and services to its customers. However, when SATS decided to venture into new markets of airport management and catering services, it faced significant challenges in terms of competition, regulation, customer expectations, and operational efficiency. How did SATS overcome these challenges and achieve success in its expansion strategy?

Complying with the aviation industry's regulations and standards was a major challenge for SATS. The CAAS, which regulates civil aviation safety and security in Singapore, has set various rules and guidelines for aviation service providers (Civil Aviation Authority of Singapore, 2023). SATS tackled this challenge by training its employees and fostering a culture of safety and compliance. Its Safety Compliance Manual states that SATS strives to "provide a safe and healthy working environment for all employees, contractors, customers and visitors" and to "comply with all applicable legal and other requirements" (SATS Ltd., 2019). This way, SATS not only satisfies the regulators but also boosts its image and edge in the aviation industry.

SATS is a leading food solution and gateway services provider that uses cutting-edge technology and innovation to serve various industries, such as aviation, hospitality, healthcare, and retail (SATS Ltd., 2023a). To expand into airport management and catering services, SATS invested in state-of-the-art facilities and technology, such as automated warehouses, temperature-controlled storage, and advanced tracking systems. For instance, SATS runs two large airline catering centres with up to 120,000 meals a day, using state-of-the-art food technologies and an in-house panel of award-winning SATS Culinary Consultants (SCC) (SATS Ltd., 2023b). SATS also offers institutional catering services for government agencies and institutions with large-scale events, using innovative food technology and state-of-the-art facilities (SATS Ltd., 2023c). These investments improve SATS's efficiency, quality, and competitiveness.

DOI: 10.4324/9781032660547-104

SATS competes in the highly competitive airport management and catering services market, which is expected to grow at a CAGR of 4.4% from 2021 to 2029 (Fortune Business Insights, 2023). SATS offers high-quality products and services, competitive pricing, and exceptional customer service to its customers in various industries, such as aviation, hospitality, healthcare, and retail (SATS Ltd., 2023d). SATS uses cutting-edge technology and innovation to provide a wide range of in-flight catering services, such as full-service carrier catering, low-cost carrier catering, airport lounge management, private jet catering, and travel retail. SATS has two large airline catering centres with up to 120,000 meals a day, using state-of-the-art food technologies and an in-house panel of award-winning SATS Culinary Consultants (SCC). These strategies give SATS a competitive edge in the global flight catering supply chain (Sundarakani et al., 2018).

SATS formed partnerships and collaborations with other businesses to expand its business. The company partnered with airlines, airports, and other service providers to offer integrated solutions and grow its customer base. For instance, SATS and Mitsui & Co., Ltd. worked together to strengthen the food value chain by diversifying supply sources, developing innovative products and services, and expanding sales and distribution channels (SATS Ltd., 2023e). SATS also teamed up with alternative protein brands and food-tech startups to provide plant-based alternatives to meet the rising demand for sustainable and healthy food options (SBR, 2023). These partnerships and collaborations enable SATS to use its expertise, capabilities, and resources to create value for its customers and stakeholders.

Through these efforts, SATS succeeded in expanding into airport management and catering services and establishing a strong presence in the aviation industry. The company has developed a robust infrastructure and logistics network and a strong reputation for quality and reliability. SATS has also diversified its business into other areas, such as hospitality and healthcare, to broaden its revenue base and drive growth. As a result, SATS is well-positioned to continue to succeed in the highly competitive aviation industry in the years ahead.

References

Civil Aviation Authority of Singapore (2023a.). *Legislation & regulations* [Online]. Available at: www.caas.gov.sg/legislation-regulations (Accessed: 24 April 2023).

Fortune Business Insights (2023). *Airport services market size, share & COVID-19 impact analysis, by airport type (international and domestic), by application (aeronautical services and non-aeronautical services), by infrastructure type (greenfield airport and brownfield airport), and regional forecast* [Online]. Available at: www.fortuneb usinessinsights.com/airport-services-market-102855 (Accessed: 13 April 2023).

SATS Ltd. (2019). *Safety Compliance Manual* [Online]. Available at: www.sats.com. sg/docs/default-source/tender-documents/sats-supplier-safety-compliance-man ual.pdf?sfvrsn=5d4d6837_0 (Accessed: 21 April 2023).

SATS Ltd. (2023a). *Leading provider of food & gateway services* [Online]. Available at: www.sats.com.sg/ (Accessed: 23 April 2023).

SATS Ltd. (2023b). *Aviation catering* [Online]. Available at: www.sats.com.sg/servi ces/details/aviation-catering (Accessed: 13 April 2023).

SATS Ltd. (2023c). *Institutional catering* [Online]. Available at: www.sats.com.sg/ services/details/institutional-catering (Accessed: 13 April 2023).

SATS Ltd. (2023d). *Leading provider of food & gateway services* [Online]. Available at: www.sats.com.sg/ (Accessed: 23 April 2023).

SATS Ltd. (2023e). *SATS and Mitsui sign MOU to collaborate on strengthening food value chain.* [Online]. Available at: www.sats.com.sg/media/latest-news/article/ 2023-04-sats-and-mitsui-sign-mou-to-collaborate-on-strengthening-food-value-chain (Accessed: 13 April 2023).

SBR (2023). *SATS partners with brands, startups for alternative proteins* [Online]. Available at: https://sbr.com.sg/food-beverage/news/sats-partners-brands-start ups-alternative-proteins (Accessed: 21 April 2023).

Sundarakani B., Razzak, H.A., & Manikandan S. (2018) Creating a competitive advantage in the global flight catering supply chain: a case study using SCOR model. *International Journal of Logistics Research and Applications, 21*(2), 121–139.

15 The challenges and opportunities of being a REIT

The Ascott Limited

Katalin Illes

Associate Head of College – External Relations at the University of Westminster, United Kingdom

Ascott Limited is a leading international serviced residence owner-operator and developer with over 100,000 units across more than 180 cities in over 30 countries. As a real estate investment trust (REIT), Ascott's business model is based on owning and managing properties and leasing them out to tenants. While there are many benefits to being a REIT, there are also challenges that Ascott has faced and continues to navigate.

Ascott requires substantial capital to acquire and develop properties. Ascott generates revenue by owning properties that offer lodging services. Acquiring and developing properties entail high costs. Ascott incurred S$1.1 billion of capital expenditure for this purpose in 2022. Maintaining and enhancing properties also involve significant costs. This can adversely affect Ascott's profitability. Lee and Lee (2020) demonstrated that REITs that incur higher maintenance expenses tend to have lower returns on assets and lower dividend payouts. Ascott also faces competition from other lodging REITs in the Asia-Pacific region, which may increase the prices of desirable properties and reduce its bargaining power (Fitch Ratings, 2023).

Another challenge that Ascott faces is the reliance on rental income from tenants. As a REIT, Ascott derives its revenue from leasing properties to tenants, which are exposed to market fluctuations and economic cycles. During periods of economic downturns or market volatility, occupancy rates and rental prices may decline, which may affect the REIT's financial performance. However, being a REIT also offers opportunities for Ascott. One key benefit is the tax advantage. REITs enjoy tax transparency treatment by IRAS (subject to certain conditions) as long as they distribute at least 90% of their taxable income to shareholders as dividends. This enables Ascott to reduce tax expenses and potentially enhance returns for shareholders (MoneySense, 2018).

Ascott can seize another opportunity by diversifying its property portfolio across various locations. As a global operator, Ascott has the advantage of investing in properties situated in different countries and regions. This strategic approach helps to mitigate risks associated with specific markets or property types. As per Ascott's latest annual report, they currently possess 105 properties comprising over 18,000 units in 47 cities across 15 countries as

DOI: 10.4324/9781032660547-105

of 31 December 2022. Furthermore, Ascott has recently secured contracts for 26 new properties encompassing over 4,600 units across 11 countries in January 2023. This expansion not only bolsters their global presence but also marks their entry into the Netherlands market for the first time. Research conducted by Chan et al. (2019) suggests that diversifying property holdings across different locations enhances performance and reduces the volatility of REITs. By capitalising on diverse economic cycles and varying property market conditions across regions, Ascott can optimise its operations and achieve greater stability.

Ascott, in its quest for success as a REIT, has embraced numerous strategies. Among these tactics is a dedicated emphasis on asset optimisation and portfolio management. This involves pinpointing underperforming assets and employing strategies to enhance their financial performance. Moreover, Ascott actively seeks out fresh investment opportunities to expand its portfolio. Another integral strategy involves harnessing the power of technology and innovation to elevate the guest experience and streamline operations. For instance, Ascott has developed user-friendly mobile applications that enable guests to effortlessly make bookings and access various services. Additionally, they have implemented cutting-edge smart building technologies to improve energy efficiency. By leveraging data analytics, Ascott optimises pricing structures and maximises occupancy rates to achieve its business goals (The Ascott Limited, 2022).

In conclusion, while there are challenges to being a REIT, such as high capital expenditures and dependence on rental income, there are also opportunities, such as tax advantages and portfolio diversification. Ascott has successfully navigated these challenges by implementing strategies to optimise its portfolio and leverage technology and innovation to enhance its business operations and guest experience.

References

Chan, K., Hendershott, P., & Sanders, A. (2019). The benefits of international diversification: evidence from Asian REITs. *Journal of Real Estate Finance and Economics, 59*(4), 537–558. https://doi.org/10.1007/s11146-018-9673-8

Fitch Ratings (2023). *Fitch upgrades CapitaLand Ascott REIT to 'BBB' – Outlook Stable* [Online]. Available at: www.fitchratings.com/research/corporate-finance/fitch-upgrades-capitaland-ascott-reit-to-bbb-outlook-stable-17-05-2023 (Accessed: 26 April 2023).

Lee, J., & Lee, C.F. (2020). The impact of maintenance expenses on REIT performance. *Journal of Property Investment & Finance, 38*(5), 435–454. https://doi.org/10.1108/JPIF-01-2020-0004

MoneySense (2018). *Understanding real estate investment trusts (REITs)* [Online]. Available at: www.moneysense.gov.sg/articles/2018/10/understanding-real-estate-investment-trusts-reits (Accessed: 21 April 2023).

The Ascott Limited (2022). *Ascott opens first coliving property in Singapore's research and innovation hub one-north* [Online]. Available at: www.capitaland.com/en/about-capitaland/newsroom/news-releases/international/2022/jan/Ascott_opens_first_coliving_property_lyf_one north_Singapore.html (Accessed: 6 April 2023).

16 Far East Hospitality's challenges and opportunities of being a hospitality provider

Lo Wai Meng Sally

Academic Director, Amity Global Institute, Singapore

Far East Hospitality is a Singapore-based hospitality group that manages a range of hotels, serviced apartments, and residences across Asia. The company was established in 2013 as a merger between the Far East Organization's hospitality division and The Straits Trading Company Limited's hospitality division.

Challenges

Intense competition: Intense competition characterises the hospitality industry, as numerous players strive to capture market share. Far East Hospitality, a key player in the industry, faces fierce competition from well-established multinational hotel chains, local hospitality brands, and home-sharing platforms. In its pursuit to stay competitive, the company manages over 100 properties encompassing nearly 18,000 rooms across 9 countries, owning more than 10 hospitality assets. However, the uncertainty surrounding the duration of pandemic-related restrictions poses a challenge for the company (Far East Orchard, 2021). Moreover, it must address the evolving preferences of travellers who seek personalised and unique experiences (Newport, 2018).

Changing customer preferences: To adapt to changing customer preferences, Far East Hospitality has implemented various strategies. It launched three distinct properties in Sentosa, a renowned tourist destination in Singapore, in 2019, catering to different market segments (Newport, 2018). Furthermore, the company introduced new brands such as A by Adina and Collection by TFE Hotels to provide premium and distinctive lodging options. Leveraging digital platforms and social media, Far East Hospitality engages with customers, enhancing their loyalty and satisfaction (Far East Orchard, 2021).

Human capital management issues: Talent acquisition and retention are significant challenges in the hospitality industry, especially considering the need for skilled and experienced staff. Far East Hospitality faces obstacles in attracting and retaining talented individuals due to low unemployment rates in the market. To overcome this challenge, the company invests in its human capital and fosters a supportive work environment. It implements various

DOI: 10.4324/9781032660547-106

initiatives, including training and development programmes, employee recognition schemes, staff welfare benefits, and career progression opportunities. These efforts aim to attract and retain top talent within the organisation. During the pandemic, Far East Hospitality displayed adaptability by redeploying staff to different roles or projects, providing voluntary leave options, and offering financial assistance to support its workforce (Far East Orchard, 2021).

Success

Diversification: Diversification has been instrumental in Far East Hospitality's success, allowing the company to cater to a wide range of customers with varying preferences and budgets. With 10 unique and complementary brands, such as Oasia, Quincy, Rendezvous, Village, Far East Collection, A by Adina, Adina Hotels, Vibe Hotels, Travelodge Hotels, and Collection by TFE Hotels, the company has established a strong presence in the hospitality industry (Far East Hospitality, n.d.; Far East Organization, n.d.). Moreover, Far East Hospitality owns and manages over 18,000 rooms across 9 countries, offering travellers a comprehensive and diverse selection of accommodations (Far East Hospitality, n.d.; Far East Organization, n.d.).

Innovation: Maintaining a focus on innovation has been crucial for Far East Hospitality to stay ahead of the competition. The company constantly introduces new products and services to enhance the customer experience. Notable innovations include the implementation of mobile check-in and keyless entry systems in select properties. Additionally, Far East Hospitality launched three new properties in Sentosa, a popular tourist destination in Singapore, in 2019, each catering to different market segments. By introducing new brands such as A by Adina and Collection by TFE Hotels, the company continues to offer premium and distinctive lodging options (The Edge Singapore, 2021).

Strategic partnerships: Strategic partnerships have played a vital role in the growth and expansion of Far East Hospitality. Collaborations with industry giants like Expedia and TripAdvisor have allowed the company to extend its reach and provide innovative services to customers (The Edge Singapore, 2021). In 2013, Far East Hospitality established a joint venture with The Straits Trading Company Limited, positioning itself as a regional hospitality owner and operator. The same year, the company formed another joint venture with Australia's Toga Group, resulting in the creation of Toga Far East Hotels (TFE Hotels), a prominent hotel operator across Australia, New Zealand, and Europe (Far East Organization, n.d.).

Focus on sustainability: Emphasising sustainability has been a priority for Far East Hospitality, resulting in various eco-friendly practices implemented throughout its operations. The company has received accolades for its efforts, including the prestigious Green Mark Gold Award from the Building and Construction Authority of Singapore. Far East Hospitality actively reduces energy consumption, water usage, and waste generation while promoting green awareness among staff. Furthermore, the company supports social causes as part of its commitment to sustainability (The Edge Singapore, 2021).

References

Far East Hospitality (n.d.). *About us & our brands* [Online]. Available at: www.fareast hospitality.com/en/Far-East-Hospitality (Accessed: 12 May 2023).

Far East Orchard (2021). *Annual report 2021* [Online]. Available at: www.fareastorch ard.com.sg/downloads/agm2021/FEOR_Annual_Report_2021.pdf (Accessed: 11 May 2023).

Far East Organization (n.d.). *Far East Hospitality* [Online]. Available at: www.fareast. com.sg/en/about-us/business-units/far-east-hospitality (Accessed: 12 May 2023).

Newport, A. (2018). *Q&A with Arthur Kiong – CEO of Far East Hospitality. Travel Daily* [Online]. Available at: www.traveldailymedia.com/443016/ (Accessed: 15 May 2023).

The Edge Singapore (2021). *Far East Hospitality's Arthur Kiong: remaking the hotel industry* [Online]. Available at: www.edgeprop.sg/property-news/far-east-hospital ity%E2%80%99s-arthur-kiong-remaking-hotel-industry (Accessed: 17 May 2023).

Index

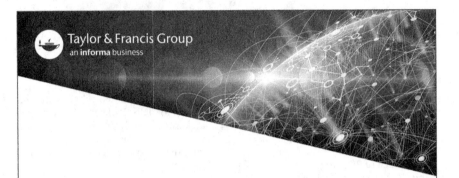

Printed in the United States
by Baker & Taylor Publisher Services